My Girls

My Girls

THE POWER OF FRIENDSHIP IN
A POOR NEIGHBORHOOD

Jasmin Sandelson

UNIVERSITY OF CALIFORNIA PRESS

University of California Press
Oakland, California

© 2023 by Jasmin Sandelson
Library of Congress Cataloging-in-Publication Data

Names: Sandelson, Jasmin A., author.
Title: My girls : the power of friendship in a poor neighborhood /
   Jasmin Aviva Sandelson.
Description: Oakland, California : University of California Press,
   [2023] | Includes bibliographical references and index.
Identifiers: LCCN 2023001528 (print) | LCCN 2023001529 (ebook) |
   ISBN 9780520388888 (cloth) | ISBN 9780520388895 (paperback) |
   ISBN 9780520388901 (ebook)
Subjects: LCSH: Girls--Social aspects—Massachusetts--Boston—21st
century. | Friendship.
Classification: LCC HQ784.F7 S35 2023 (print) | LCC HQ784.F7
   (ebook) | DDC 302.34083--dc23/eng/20230130
LC record available at https://lccn.loc.gov/2023001528
LC ebook record available at https://lccn.loc.gov/2023001529

Manufactured in the United States of America

32 31 30 29 28 27 26 25 24 23
10 9 8 7 6 5 4 3 2 1

To Jenny and Adam, for their love and their permission

In the recognition of loving lies an answer to despair.

AUDRE LORDE, *Zami: A New Spelling of My Name*

Contents

Preface

Aisha rolled down the window and stuck out an arm. Spring wind whipped through her fingers, and she flexed her hand. Aisha managed the music, as Seeta, at the wheel, gazed out at the road. Their best friends, Joanne and Brittani, lounged in the back, and I squeezed in beside them.[1]

Seeta's dad's Dodge sped down residential streets, quiet with Saturday's calm. The song on the radio faded out, replaced by the first beats of a familiar hit. Aisha nudged the dial.

"*Yesss!*" Seeta squealed.

The girls laughed at her excitement, their giggles coursing through the grooves of an inside joke: Seeta was Indian American, the only non-Black girl in the foursome, but the one who was most into rap music.[2]

As A$AP Rocky's anthem throbbed through the speakers, the girls belted lyrics and laughed harder. Aisha, energized, leaned out the passenger-side window. She screamed the explicit chorus while we raced past fine, hedge-fenced houses, as if daring the world to have a problem.

"Be quiet!" Seeta scolded, smiling. "I don't have my license!"

But quiet was not Aisha's forte.

Aisha was seventeen, self-possessed, and magnetic. She could customize unique outfits from Goodwill as expertly as she could filter selfies. And when she spoke, people listened. Heads turned when Aisha strolled down the street; strangers whistled from windows, neighbors hollered *Heys*. She knew everyone in her neighborhood—North Cambridge, Massachusetts, known as "NC"— and everyone knew her.

Still, for all Aisha's confidence, her youth slipped sometimes into view like accidentally exposed skin. She brushed off compliments, saying, "No!"—but the word raised like a question, all hope.

In the car, Aisha danced exuberantly on the spot, movements mimed from videos streamed on YouTube and practiced in her room. Her seatbelt strained to hold her, and her clique whooped her on.

"I swear," Joanne said, clapping her hands through laughter. "Guys can't have fun like girls can!"

"Right?" her friends echoed.

It was March of the girls' senior year. In a few months they would graduate from high school. Then, they hoped, would come college, jobs, and homes of their own. They all imagined leaving the housing project where they had grown up.

With so much soon to change, the girls seized each chance to be together. And this afternoon, levity felt especially welcome. Just three weeks earlier, they had lost a friend in a shooting—the second such tragedy they had faced in nine months. As with other shocks and traumas, the girls had leaned on one another. For years, in fact, they had helped each other out, not just in life's hardest moments but also day to day. Friendships helped the girls navigate tough teenage years while staying on the path they felt led to the futures they yearned for. These friendships are the focus of this book.

I first met most of the young women who appear in these pages at their high school, where I set out to study classroom dynamics. But as I got to know two cliques of girls—joining them at their homes, hangouts, and house parties, and also interacting online—what struck me instead was the versatility of their relationships. Over four years, I saw the girls feed and soothe and hear one another. I saw them together respond to the harms of racism, sexism, poverty, and trauma. I saw the girls meet a full spectrum of one another's needs, including social and emotional necessities that researchers rarely emphasize but that were, to them, vital. Friendships helped the girls in NC cope, thrive, and dream.

Yet social scientists and policy makers often write off as "risky" close ties between young people growing up in poor neighborhoods, like the one where Aisha and her friends lived. Peers, many researchers warn, draw each other toward "deviance" and downward mobility. This stance ignores the competence and care that exist among teenagers. It can also lead to programs and policies that undermine valuable bonds.

This is not, however, a book about young women pulling themselves, or each other, up by their bootstraps. Friendships are not all, or even most, of what young people need to flourish. Still, in person and online, the girls offered one another support that was critical, multifaceted, and, largely, overlooked.

The chapters that follow describe what the girls taught me. In doing so, this book does not compare the NC girls to other teens—to boys, to middle-class girls, or to white girls—because I believe their experiences are important on their own. Nor does it tell the girls' "story"; they have many stories, and they can speak for themselves. Finally, this book does not seek to "humanize" young women who are eminently, and inherently, full of value and life and ambition—like any teenager gazing down her future's open road.[3] Instead, I hope to share what I learned from spending time with these young women—and what I hope researchers and policy makers might learn too—about their needs, their desires, and how they supported their friends when few others would.

Introduction

When Aisha left Uganda for Massachusetts at the age of eleven, she had, she said, "no idea what America was gonna look like." She hoped to find "heaven, with a lot of candy." Instead, Aisha moved with her mom and two older brothers to North Cambridge, or NC, a place she described as "the hood, the modern-day hood."

It was not what Aisha had imagined. But when she enrolled in seventh grade and met Joanne—her "first American friend"—things started looking up. The girls grew close, fast. Like Aisha, Joanne was driven and creative. Also like Aisha, Joanne had come to NC from another country, emigrating from Haiti when she was five. The girls played together after school, dashing through the housing project where their apartments were minutes apart. Years later, as seniors in high school, their friendship was deeper than ever.

Aisha, who had a tense and often painful relationship with her mother, spent as much time as she could with her friends. She rarely felt particularly relaxed at home, where the fridge was mostly empty and where paint flecked from grime-streaked walls. Aisha preferred to pass her hours outside—walking, talking, and hanging out. When a curfew or bad weather kept her in, Aisha headed straight for the computer, a small desktop in the corner of her living room. Cross-legged on a blue desk chair whose cushion had worn down flat, Aisha opened Facebook, Twitter, and Instagram. She shared streams of filtered selfies—all glamour and edge—and watched likes tick in.[1] Dubbed "Miss Social Media" by her best friends, Aisha knew her photos were cool. She had come a long way since the media diet of her childhood back in Kampala: Jean-Claude Van Damme and Rambo. Online, Aisha polished her profiles and caught up with friends until she could head back outdoors.

Joanne, by contrast, spent much of her time at home. Ten family members shared her apartment, which Joanne warmly called a "theme park." Inside, children gleefully shrieked, their small feet thudding on big stairs. In the kitchen, food sizzled in oil, and Kreyòl crackled from a small TV. Two yellow birds in a white cage squawked and pecked at each other's beaks; "they're kissing," Joanne liked to say. Friends and neighbors dropped in through the back door, often joining Joanne's grandma at the table. Outside, commuter rail trains thundered down tracks yards from the house. The trains ran thirty-four times each day, from 6:35 a.m. until twenty minutes after midnight. Visitors sometimes raised their voices to be heard over the din. But Joanne and her family knew to pause at a train's first tremor. Several seconds later, suspended sentences resumed.

Joanne's mother worked in the janitorial department of a neighboring town's hospital. During her mom's shifts, Joanne faithfully watched her four young siblings. She prepared snacks, helped them color, and occasionally threw at-home spelling bees using lists of grade-appropriate words she found using Google.

When she needed a moment alone, Joanne retreated to her bedroom. She had her own room, as did her twenty-year-old brother. Joanne's mom took the third bedroom, with her partner and their baby son. The fourth was for the other five family members: Joanne's grandma and four-year-old sister slept in one bed; her six- and seven-year-old brothers slept in the other; and on a fold-up camp bed in the corner slept a cousin who had moved in after fleeing an abusive uncle.

To relax, Joanne clicked the door closed and lay on her bed, joining the stuffed teddy bears—one from her boyfriend, another from Aisha—propped on her pillows. Around her, pencil drawings were pinned to the walls: self-portraits sketched in art class; copies of a Picasso painting she liked. Tubes of lotion and some bottles of jewel-toned nail polish sat on a dresser, beside a bulk-sized tub of Ibuprofen she kept on hand for her migraines.

In her room, Joanne journaled, messaged friends on her phone, and eased into novels. She also wrote poems. *Writing brings me peace, I can get lost in a page and words for hours,* she once tweeted. Joanne wrote through grief and gratitude. She wrote to indict social inequality and a school system she often felt was failing her peers. Sometimes Joanne performed her poems at slams, joined by Aisha and other friends from school. Sometimes she kept them to herself.

Aisha, Joanne, and all the girls I met had unique personalities and dreams. They had distinct families and life experiences. Yet as young women of color growing up in a poor neighborhood, they faced some similar hardships, including the daily assaults of white supremacy and poverty. These made even more challenging a time of life known to be vulnerable: adolescence. To get by, the girls leaned on their friends.

Peer Effects and Social "Contagion"

The NC girls were not alone in relying on their friends.[2] For teens from all backgrounds, friendships offer vital comfort and understanding.[3] In fact, friendships are so elemental that of all the factors shaping young people's experiences—including schools, neighborhoods, and families[4]—most teens say the most important part of their life is their peer group.[5]

Teens spend countless hours with friends—at and after school and, increasingly, on social media—and they jointly form identities, habits, and norms.[6] Unsurprisingly, friends have a large and measurable impact on one another, an impact social scientists term "peer effects."[7] Peer effects mean that teens tend to match their friends in multiple realms, ranging from academic achievement to moral values and more.

Often, however, researchers studying peer effects focus on something else: what they label "risk behaviors," like drinking alcohol, using drugs, getting pregnant, or committing crimes.[8] Such risk behaviors, researchers argue, are socially transmissible: "social problems are contagious and are spread through peer influence," claims the sociologist Jonathan Crane.[9] Researchers worry that in poor neighborhoods in particular, peer effects transmit beliefs and activities that harm communities and derail teens' trajectories.[10]

Certainly, teens' trajectories are precarious, particularly for young people of color living in poor neighborhoods, like Aisha and her friends. For teens who face more surveillance and punishment than white and middle-class teens, adolescent mistakes can be enormously costly.[11] "Putting one puzzle piece in the wrong place can drastically alter trajector[ies]," explains the sociologist Ranita Ray, "as the formidable constraints of poverty . . . leave no room for minor mistakes."[12]

Yet researchers and policy makers too often frame *friendship* as a threat to young people of color growing up in poverty. As such, some suggest that social isolation can protect teens from peer effects and peer pressure, and help them "get ahead." For instance, writing about the children of immigrants in New York City, the sociologist Philip Kasinitz and colleagues note, "Being heavily 'embedded' in networks . . . among the worst off can be a real disadvantage. In such groups, many of the most successful members describe themselves as 'loners.'"[13]

It is not only academics who take this view. Some parents in poor neighborhoods force or cajole their kids to stay away from others.[14] And some young people themselves shy from peers to avoid "trouble."[15] In Chicago's infamous Henry Horner Homes, for example, the journalist Alex Kotlowitz met a boy who "figured the only way to make it out of Horner was 'to try to make as little friends as possible.'"[16] Similarly, the sociologist Nikki Jones found that young Black women in a poor Philadelphia neighborhood used "relational isolation" to dodge friendships' costs—like the duty to physically defend a friend who was attacked.[17] "By avoiding close friendships," Jones explains, "girls reduce the likelihood of their involvement in a physical conflict."[18]

Peers can, of course, be harmful. But the focus on these harms—and on negative peer effects that spread "social problems" through friendships—tells only a partial story.

Partial Portraits of Friendship

Teens like Aisha, Joanne, and the other girls I got to know are often overlooked in research. Instead, social scientists have written disproportionately about young people labeled "deviant," like gang members, teen parents, drug dealers, "fighters," and "fugitives."[19] This outsized emphasis is problematic; even so-called sympathetic studies—those that show, for instance, how teen parenthood or selling drugs can be rational choices amid few school or work opportunities[20]—risk, especially in the aggregate, entrenching negative stereotypes about poverty.[21] In reality, most young people in poor neighborhoods—like most young people in any neighborhood—are not involved in what researchers label "deviance." Given this, some researchers, including Ranita Ray, have written recently about young people "who, having grown up in marginalized families[,] . . . play by the widely accepted 'rules of the game'—by avoiding drugs, gangs, and parenthood and focusing on education."[22] Still, the stories of teens like the NC girls, who generally "play by the rules,"[23] remain underrepresented.

Along with this overemphasis on "deviance," girls get short shrift in research about poor urban communities.[24] Black and brown boys and men are more exposed than girls and women to harms including police brutality, incarceration, and interpersonal violence. But, as Nikki Jones explains, "girls are not isolated from the social consequences of racial segregation, concentrated poverty, and inner-city violence." Rather, "girls are touched—figuratively, literally, and daily—by violence."[25] Girls face different risks from boys, including domestic violence and "the female fear" of sexual harassment and assault.[26] They also face different demands, including family care.[27]

Yet boys and men dominate the urban ethnography canon, albeit with critical exceptions.[28] "For over a half a century," explains the anthropologist Aimee Meredith Cox, "Black girls have been the absent referent in urban ethnographies[,] . . . which instead have been chiefly invested in explaining the life patterns of poor young and adult Black males."[29] Many studies about women focus on mothers,[30] and the few books that center low-income girls of color often feature fighting and violence.[31] This is for good reason, since these hardships harm girls. Yet the daily lives and friendships of girls like those in NC—who rarely faced social violence—also warrant attention.

A final factor limits what is known about young people like the NC girls: cell phones. Ninety-five percent of American teens, from all racial and socioeconomic backgrounds, have a smartphone,[32] and 89 percent are online "almost constantly" or "several times per day."[33] In NC, the girls used their phones around the clock. On waking up, they scrolled through content posted overnight and shared a "Good Morning" tweet or Snapchat. Before bed, screens beamed as fingers swiped a last refresh. The girls' connection imperative made no concessions for meals, movies, or school, where phones were slipped into pockets, tucked into Ugg boots, or lay cabled into outlets like IVs.

Phones were non-negotiable. Girls unable to afford cell service paired a secondhand phone with Wi-Fi, the hunt for which shaped their social geography. Ideal hangouts, which had free and reliable internet service, were typically sites of consumption, like malls or coffee shops. But other places made the cut too; as Aisha once noted, "Half my church can get Wi-Fi. The left side."[34]

As well as Wi-Fi, phones needed power. Teens monitored their battery percentage, and unease grew as the number fell. Eyes scouted for outlets in classrooms, cafés, or friends' kitchens. Arriving at a local hotel one afternoon for a banquet to mark a cohort's graduation from an after-school program, the girls filed straight to the corner table. They claimed the nearby outlets before taking their seats. One of the organizers approached, warning, "Girls, if you sit there, you won't be able to see the stage or all the videos we have!"

"No, we're good," rang their chorus.

Heavy social media use has costs, some of which this book explores.[35] But social media's impact is more complex than sensationalist headlines warning of cyber-bullying, online predators, alienated young people hiding behind screens, or dopamine-hungry teens "tethered" to their phones.[36] In reality, social media has not replaced adolescent friendships; instead, it mostly involves and deepens friendships that exist "face to face."[37]

Still, cell phones and social media have transformed adolescence. They have also transformed the experience of poverty. Historically, *disconnection* has been a key feature of American urban marginality; many classic ethnographies chart how people survive isolation.[38] But with cell phones the NC girls could access endless connection and information, just like their middle-class peers. In this way, their lives diverged starkly from earlier research on young people living in poor neighborhoods.

New technologies pose important questions about place, poverty, connection, and community. As studies begin to offer answers, many focus on crime, gangs, and violence—understandably, since social media can expose people to injury and arrest.[39] Yet as this book shows, social media can also enable peer support and help teens build what the communications scholar Paul Byron calls "digital cultures of care."[40] On their cell phones, girls passed time, made plans, broke news, shared jokes, processed trauma, and more. The NC girls skillfully used multiple apps and platforms to care for one another and protect their friendships.[41]

Drawing on four years of ethnographic fieldwork, this book centers friendships often missed by research: those between young women of color growing up in a poor neighborhood, girls not involved in what researchers label "deviance" but who used their constant contact—in person and online—to survive adversity and plan for the future. Friends met needs that adults could not or would not meet, including social and emotional needs that were essential to their flourishing.

In the Field

I met Aisha and most of the other girls who appear in this book at their high school. Starting in February 2012, I volunteered once per week in a community service–based elective class, where I got to know some juniors and seniors. Months later, as summer break approached, I told a few teens that I was writing about growing up in Cambridge. I asked if I could spend time with them over the upcoming vacation to learn about their lives.[42]

Through the summer, I spent days and weeks with some of the young women and met their families and friends. That fall, I moved into an apartment across the street from the housing project where all but one of the girls lived with their families. I lived in NC for one year and conducted fieldwork during that time, with follow-ups over the next three years.

Mostly, fieldwork involved "hanging out," after school, on weekends, and during vacations. I joined the girls on their everyday errands and activities, like going to sports practices, movies, or the mall and visiting friends on shift at fast-food restaurants. The girls brought me to birthday parties, cookouts, baby showers, house parties, and graduation celebrations. I also went to a prom, a homecoming game, and two Thanksgivings.

I spent most time with nine girls, six of whom were high school seniors the year I lived in NC. All nine were young women of color, and all were from low-income homes. Eight were the daughters of immigrants—six girls were Haitian American, one was Indian American, one was Ugandan American—and one young woman, born in Cambridge, was African American.[43] I also met and spoke to some of the girls' friends, siblings, and cousins, as well as other teens I met at school or around the neighborhood.

The nine central girls split into two social cliques. Aisha's best friends were Joanne, Brittani, and Seeta. Joanne's older brother, Vincent, had a long-term, on-off romantic relationship with Florence, who was in the other clique, together with Florence's sister, Faith, and their friends Stephanie, Zora, and Rosie (see table 1). Growing up, the nine girls had all been close, and they accounted variably for their eventual estrangement. Some blamed tension between Florence and Vincent; others blamed different sources of drama.

All the girls but Brittani lived in Jefferson Park, a North Cambridge housing project.[44] The low-rise development was bounded at the front by a busy main road and at the back by commuter rail tracks. A bustling convenience store, Foodtown, sat by the entrance to the project. Foodtown had seen better days; gray dirt marred its white paint, and graffiti tagged the public phone outside. It was also, as the girls grumbled, much more expensive than stores farther away. But Foodtown was a local institution. Customers bought basic grocery items as well as lottery tickets, household goods, and beer and wine. Beside a small deli at the rear, a handwritten sign taped to the wall offered "Fried Dough." Next door, customers in the adjoining

TABLE 1. Participant list organized by friendship group, including school grade and ethnic background

Name	School Grade at Start of Research	Ethnic Background	Family Relationships
Aisha	High school junior	Ugandan American	
Joanne	High school junior	Haitian American	
Brittani	High school junior	African American	
Seeta	High school junior	Indian American	
Florence	High school senior	Haitian American	Faith's sister
Faith	High school junior	Haitian American	Florence's sister
Stephanie	High school senior	Haitian American	
Zora	College freshman	Haitian American	
Rosie	High school sophomore	Haitian American	

laundromat talked over the constant mechanical hum, pausing periodically when someone tipped a clatter of glass bottles into the machine that spat out change for empties.

Across the street from Foodtown was a playground and a public pool, where children splashed and laughed through hot summer weekends. Behind that, an alley led to the subway station, the last stop on the line.

A fifteen-minute walk away, a retail park housed stores, including Dunkin' Donuts, Starbucks, and Panera Bread, where girls hung out and sometimes found jobs, as well as Entertainment Cinema, a movie theater staffed in large part by local teens. There was also a Whole Foods Market, whose parking lot was filled with shiny SUVs from nearby suburbs. The girls' parents, however, typically rode two buses to neighboring Somerville for Market Basket's cheaper groceries.

The NC girls had mixed feelings about their neighborhood, whose child poverty rate of over 40 percent was almost three times the city's average.[45]

"It is the hood, man," Aisha said. "You see them dealing. . . . There was always someone getting arrested. There was always a fight somewhere. I remember gunshots. It's the hood." Still, she reflected, "It's not, like, extreme. . . . They recycle, you know what I'm saying?"

Joanne was also ambivalent. "Growing up," she said, "I remember lots of violence. Lots of people passed away. . . . My boyfriend's brother died, and people were dying, and it was real." At the same time, she said, "It really was super happy. We had a really good time riding bikes, playing kickball, people breaking their arm, playing tag, hopping fences. . . . But it was that underlying alertness, I-can't-really-walk-around-by-myself type of situation. You'd hear about people getting jumped, women jumping women, grown folks fighting. It was a lot, but it was still a very beautiful place."

To Joanne, the beauty was aesthetic too. "These are nice-looking projects," she once said. Sure, some metal pipes had rusted green, and some window AC units keened on wedged-in cans of beans. Stern signs over entryways warned, "NO TRESSPASSING OR LOITERING" and "AREA UNDER VIDEO SURVEILLANCE." But besides that and the few units whose occupants the girls judged for loose trash and unkempt exteriors, the projects looked smart. There were groomed privet hedges and grand trees. In certain light, the square windows and gas lantern–style lamps made the block look like the Harvard dorms two miles away. The best light was low summer sun, when plump boughs glowed opal and bricks were flecked with gold.

But passions climbed with the temperatures.

"When the summer would come, it would be hectic," seventeen-year-old Faith said.

Joanne agreed. "Summertime was a dangerous time," she explained. "They always say people get real hot during the summer. Lots of gun violence and gang violence."

Through the summer months, when the streets smelled of dust and blossom, songs sailed from porches and living rooms. The girls and I passed many humid evenings lounging around the picnic tables at the back of the project. Sometimes we strolled to the youth center, where, as the boys played basketball, we listened to music or shot a version of pool.

When winter forced life indoors, the girls and I spent icy New England nights bundled in kitchens and bedrooms, eating hot food from paper plates and trading gossip. Year-round, we passed afternoons huddled around a computer screen or walking the streets when nobody had other plans.

While spending time with the girls, I jotted field notes on my cell phone's notes app, typing and expanding these scribbles back at home.[46] I added to the ethnography with informal, unstructured interviews with some teens more peripheral to the central group. I audio recorded these interviews, along with some interviews I conducted with the main participants toward the end of fieldwork, and added the transcripts to my field notes.

To learn more about the girls' lives, I used their preferred social media apps—at the time, Facebook, Twitter, Instagram, Snapchat, and Vine—to connect with roughly sixty teens I met during fieldwork. In total, I gathered over three thousand screenshots and wrote twelve hundred single-spaced pages of field notes, which I analyzed by reading and rereading to identify themes and patterns.[47]

Positionality and Ethics

Through months and years of spending time with these young women, I was not—as no researcher can be—an objective, impartial witness.[48] Rather, researchers' personal identities guide the questions they ask, the relationships they build, and their interpretations of what they see.[49] My own positionality—as a white, British, cisgender woman roughly five years older than the girls—shaped and limited this research.

Some relative similarities proved helpful. My age, for instance, and being six months out of college when we first met let me superficially blend in with the girls' cliques.[50] This likely made them feel more comfortable inviting me places and also meant that we shared familiarity-building cultural references, like music and TV shows. Our common gender was also, I believe, essential for the girls to feel relaxed enough to want me around.

A helpful *difference* was my British nationality. Like many of the girls, I was also an immigrant, having moved to the United States a year earlier to begin graduate school. Yet rather than embrace this as a shared experience, the young women emphasized the novelty of my foreignness, especially early on. The girls enjoyed British pop culture, from Adele to Harry Potter, and often appreciatively mimicked my accent. Aisha nicknamed me "British Jasmin," and sometimes, when her friends complimented my accent, she smiled and said "Thank you!" on my behalf.

Being foreign also seemed to complicate my whiteness, another key difference between the teens and me. One day at school, Aisha's friend Josiah, a Black senior, asked me, "Do you know Idris Elba?"

"The actor?" I replied.

"Yeah," he said. "I have a question. How is he Black?"

"How do you mean?"

"Like, he's Black," Josiah said. "But he's from England?"

"Black people live in England," I said.

"Oh, for real? Word," he said, nodding.

Occasionally, the young women described how they viewed the interplay between my race and nationality.

"I don't even see you as white. You're English," Joanne told me.

"What are the differences?" I asked.

"Obviously it's kind of the same thing, but it's just like, totally different," she replied. "An American white girl and you—it's two totally different things. You guys talk differently, and like, your thought processes are totally different."[51]

However, I *am* white and therefore had a lifelong form of privilege that the girls did not. Despite trying to be attentive and receptive when girls discussed race and racism, my whiteness precluded a comprehensive grasp of these parts of their lived experience. It also constrained what I noticed, understood, and wrote about. This fact limits this work.

Moreover, positionality involves power. Even if the girls perceived me as different from an "American white girl" and even if this let them speak more candidly with me about race—and I don't know for sure that it did—there remain troubling power dynamics inherent to being a white person crafting narratives about people of color. Given the entwined legacies of social science and racist, colonial exploitation, these dynamics might be even more problematic for a British white person. I considered whether this work might add to the long and harmful history of white people writing about people of color, for "science," curiosity, or amusement.

Ultimately, I have chosen to tell these stories—partial as they must be—not just because I think they are important and can inform social policy to better support young women like Aisha and her friends but also because, as I describe in "A Note on Research and Writing" later in this book, the girls enthusiastically encouraged me to do so. Participants' approval, however, does not neutralize ethnography's power inequities, and I consider these further in that section.

The Power and Potential of Friendship

The girls in NC consistently understood and met one another's basic needs. Basic needs include not only food, housing, and clothing but also other things young people need to thrive, like dignity, agency, and validation. Friends were often best placed to provide these kinds of social and emotional goods. In doing so, they offered care adults could not or would not give and eased some of poverty's hardships.[52]

In contrast to research and tropes that frame peer groups as risky for teens living in poor neighborhoods—a site for the epidemic spread of "social problems"—the chapters that follow show how young women looked out for one another, both day to day and during times of immense strain. Adults—from parents and principals to researchers and policy makers—rarely grasp the insight, compassion, or creativity with which teens support their friends. As a result, they design programs and interventions that fail to nurture—and sometimes even undermine—these patterns of care.

The first of the book's three parts, "Friends and Forms of Care," shows the resources embedded in teens' friendships. Chapter 1 explores how girls got hold of money or made do without it. Although they mostly did not have to worry about shelter or food, their youth intensified other dimensions of poverty, especially threats to their status. By mitigating material hardship, the girls met needs that were much more than financial.

Chapter 2 considers boredom—an underrecognized hardship facing teens who have little money but plenty of time. Girls used connection to pass hours: consuming and producing content, and making or magnifying fun. Ceaseless interaction had drawbacks, however, leaving some of the girls with "time management" skills different from those often rewarded by schools.

Chapter 3 turns to emotional support. Girls empathized with family disputes and proved dependable when adults did not. They affirmed one another in the face of stigma and disrespect. But girls' emotional safety net frayed sometimes into conflict, because their needs in this realm were so critical and so vast.

Chapter 4 spotlights the young women's experiences as they navigated beauty norms, dating, and sex. Generally, the girls were skilled problem solvers. But friends had less power when it came to romance and sexuality than in other domains.

Part 2 shows how the girls responded when their relationships—and the support they channeled—came under threat. Chapter 5 looks at trauma caused by neighborhood violence and the deaths of peers. When catastrophes upended daily life, girls made trauma manageable. They used their social networks, on- and offline, to disseminate, comprehend, and cope with crises. Their coping strategies existed largely out of view of adults and clashed sometimes with teachers' expectations for trauma management.

Chapter 6 reveals how the girls defended old friendships from new differences when some dabbled with what researchers call "risk behaviors," like drinking alcohol and smoking weed. Departing both from popular ideas about peer pressure and from academic studies showing a "contagion" of peer effects, the girls pragmatically protected their relationships by accommodating a degree of difference.

In part 3, chapter 7 turns to the girls' long-standing goal: college. It first chronicles how the young women encouraged one another to apply and enroll. It then follows them to campus, where they struggled with the hardships awaiting low-income, first-generation college students. The girls faced another test too: leaving each other. What would happen when they lost this source of support just as they needed it most?

The conclusion outlines what the young women can teach adults about teens' friendships, needs, skills, and social media use. It notes the limits of peer support, identifies avenues for further research, and suggests pathways to invest in young people harmed by inequality. Next, in "A Note on Research and Writing," I consider the ethics and methods of conducting fieldwork, both in person and online. And finally, I catch up with the young women ten years after they first welcomed me into their classroom.

Aisha and the other NC girls were not uniquely straitlaced, bookish, or sheltered. As they grew up, some experimented, as do many teens, with alcohol and weed. They embraced new freedoms of age. They made mistakes. Still, they were attentive, loving witnesses to one another's lives. They offered support elsewhere in short supply and strove together toward what they hoped would be bright futures.

These young women's experiences challenge the negative light in which researchers and policymakers often cast friendships among teens marginalized by racism and capitalism. Instead, they reveal, in bonds between girls, a deep well of potential and power.

I *Friends and Forms of Care*

1 *Broke*

Getting By

On a March Saturday, the first warm day after a stubborn, snowy winter, Aisha threw a surprise celebration for Joanne's upcoming birthday. Aisha invited her clique to her apartment, where she set the scene before Joanne arrived. With Brittani's help, Aisha selected a Pandora station. Then she laid out the food: chocolate chip cookies and a store-bought cake, chocolate with chocolate frosting.

Aisha set the cake tray on her living room chair, hefting onto the floor two plastic bags stuffed with blankets and clothes. She would have to replace them before her mother returned from her shift at the psychiatric hospital where she worked as a residence counselor. Aisha's mom forbade guests. Any friends Aisha snuck in had to scramble down the back stairs when they heard her mom approach. Some days Aisha got a heads-up when her mother called the landline before leaving work; Aisha's lively chatter dropped to murmured Luganda as her friends stifled laughs at the transformation.

Knuckles rapped on the front door. Joanne walked into the living room, accompanied by Seeta.

"Happy birthday, Joanne!" Aisha yelled. "Look at you, all legal!"

Joanne's brown eyes widened. "It's not my birthday for another two weeks!"

"Duh!" Aisha said. "But we're celebrating today. Were you surprised?"

"Obviously! Look at all this food!" said Joanne, clutching both hands to her chest.

"We need to light these," Aisha said, bending to the six pink and two yellow candles sunk into the cake's thick frosting. The candles framed the words "Happy 18th Birthday Joanne!," iced in white. "But how?"

"I have a lighter," Seeta offered.

"Why do you have a lighter?" Aisha asked.

"Don't judge me," Seeta said, reaching for her purse.

Seeta was a spirited seventeen-year-old, born and raised in NC; her parents emigrated from Kolkata, India, before she was born. When Seeta wasn't with friends, at her job, or caring for her sister's young son, she took to her bedroom and tuned out the world to the beats of J Cole and other rappers.

Aisha took Seeta's lighter, lit the candles, and drew in a deep breath. "Happy Birthday to *youuuuu!*" she sang. Seeta, Brittani, and I joined in. The girls lifted their cell phones to take photos and videos, angling their screens for lighting.

"Hey!" Seeta said. "We should pack all this up and take it like a picnic!" After cold, cooped-up months, the girls cooed approvingly. "I can even pitch in some leftovers from home," Seeta added.

Aisha nodded, heading to her kitchen. "Let me see what I can contribute!" She swung open the refrigerator and scanned the shelves: a plastic container of cooked white rice, a tub of butter, ketchup, bottled water. Aisha slammed the door closed. "Damn, I'm broke," she cringed through a grin.

"We cleaned out her fridge. It's not even her fault!" Joanne said, massaging the moment and her best friend's ego.

All the girls in the clique came from families that often struggled to get by. But times, for Aisha, could be especially lean. She barred friends from her bedroom, where she slept on a bare mattress on the floor. She stored her clothes in garbage bags—everything low to the ground.

Above all, however, Aisha hated not being able to give. "Christmas is my worst," she once told me. Her family didn't trade gifts, and she never had money to reciprocate presents from friends. Each month, Aisha's mom gave her $30 for the bus to school. She also gave her cash for the laundromat next to Foodtown, which was rounded up to a ten if Aisha was lucky. Sometimes, Aisha found that a vociferous testimonial of daughterly love at church on Sunday earned a bill or two. But it never felt like enough.

In Aisha's kitchen, the girls decided to pool what money they had and visit a local Chinese take-out. Seeta and I pulled out fives.[1] Brittani and Joanne pitched in $4, and Aisha had a dollar in change. We trooped downstairs and piled into Seeta's dad's Dodge.

At the restaurant, we unfolded paper menus over a sticky linoleum table. Joanne asked for scallion pancakes; Aisha, crab Rangoon. The rest of the $19 went to egg fried rice, prawn crackers, and a family-sized Sprite.

Waiting for the food, Aisha tapped at her cell. "Do you think I can get Wi-Fi in here?" Then she glanced up from her screen at the people passing by outside. "Is that Daniel?" she said. "Oh, I saw Jontray yesterday. You know Jontray is seeing Tina now?"

"White Tina?" Brittani asked.

"Yeah. She's blonde now."

The girls talked about friends from school until the cashier brought out our brown paper bags. Arms full, we filed back to our ride.

At Danehy Park, the trees were still bare, and the grass rose in stuttered patches through hard brown earth. But the sky was perfectly blue, and beside a small lake glittering in the sun sat empty wooden picnic tables. Wordlessly, the girls chose one. They unpacked the warm, white take-out boxes and Joanne's cake and cookies. They spooned fried rice onto the paper plates Aisha had brought from home and filled red cups with soda. Between bites, the girls shared thoughts, jokes, and stories. They took photos of everything.

A chill stole through the afternoon. Joanne pulled on a cream cardigan; Brittani dug her toes into her shearling-lined moccasins. But the girls were cheery, warmed by the food and the singular ease of each other's company.

Aisha smiled. This celebration was just right.

Teens and Needs

For over a century researchers have explored how relationships—with family members, friends, fictive kin, or strangers—help people in the United States survive poverty.[2] As teenagers, however, the NC girls had a different set of needs from the adults long studied by sociologists. The girls lived in government housing, so stable shelter was not a major worry. Nor did it fall to them to feed or clothe children. Yet such urgencies were not their only basic needs; so too were acceptance and affirmation. As the social scientist Christopher Jencks explains, "Neither morality nor common sense requires human beings to value their health and physical comfort more than their honor, pleasure, or self-respect."[3]

Honor and respect—otherwise called social status—are fundamental needs. This is particularly true for teenagers. Teenagers have few freedoms; rarely do they control their own schedules or whereabouts. "In one realm," however, "their power is supreme," explains the sociologist Murray Milner. This realm "is status power: the power to create their own status systems based on their criteria."[4]

And young people's status systems often hinge on consumption—on wearing the right clothes and having the right possessions.[5] Consumption, in a society that often conflates money with personal worth, is widely seen as a type of empowerment.[6] This path to status can be especially pertinent when other routes are limited. As a result, while teens everywhere care about style and consumer goods, these things—as sociologists like Ranita Ray show—can be more meaningful for young people whose access to opportunity is curbed by poverty and racism.[7]

Along with claiming status, teens use consumption to express their identities and assert that they belong.[8] Young people, explains the sociologist Allison Pugh, generally desire consumer goods not to outdo but to connect with their peers. The goal, Pugh writes, is usually "joining the circle rather than . . . bettering it."[9]

The NC girls were no different. They wanted consumer goods that made them feel worthy and included. They also wanted to join in social activities that cost money: grabbing snacks or coffee after school, buying tickets to the occasional concert.[10] Moreover, money meant freedom, both the grown-up thrill of spending and the very real freedom to ride the train and get around.

Being broke, then, jeopardized the girls' access not just to fun and consumer power, but also to status and inclusion. Their two main solutions to this problem were *getting money*—from jobs, peers, and boys—and *bypassing money,* meeting ostensibly material needs in other ways.

Getting Money

Jobs

Joanne, who described herself as "real smart and super nerdy," worked part-time through the school year as a lab assistant in East Cambridge's technology hub. Some of her friends also worked year-round, staffing grocery store registers or food service counters after school and on weekends. Most, however, worked only through summer breaks, often enrolling in city programs that connected high school students to paid administrative positions.

Joanne felt challenged and valuable at her job, where she won respect from older colleagues. She also liked snapping selfies in her lab coat and goggles during the odd slow moment. The role, she said, did have drawbacks, like how her contract barred her from running track. Joanne thought she could have managed both obligations. Still, the money was useful.

"I paid for my own stuff since I was fourteen," Joanne explained. Somewhat unusually among her friends, Joanne and her older brother, Vincent, had helped their mom with money from the start of high school. "I help pay the phone bill . . . [and] for kids' field trips. We paid for [my brother] Jonas's saxophone lessons for a semester," she said. There wasn't as much left over as she would have liked, but Joanne stretched the fun: "I . . . go shopping and try on twenty thousand clothes and pose and take pictures and then buy one shirt."

Joanne and the other girls all praised work and self-sufficiency. They also shared information about job opportunities, discussing what and who they knew when spots opened at a catering company, the toy store, or the new Panera. One summer, a man posted flyers throughout the housing project recruiting teens to sell cooking knives door-to-door in the suburbs. The girls were tempted by $18 per hour plus commission. Florence even went to interview. But Stephanie warned her off. They decided that the gig with "knives guy" was "sketchy," too good to be true. Together, the girls appraised their options and helped identify more promising prospects.

The Peer Group

The girls all leaned on their friends to get by, but perhaps no one did so more than Aisha. Growing up, Aisha had eyed her classmates' shoes and cell phones. "I always felt like I had less," she recalled.

"Things that cool kids were doing or having, I didn't have. I didn't wear Jordans. I didn't have the brand."

As a child, Aisha thought she deserved to have less. Conflict with her mother—who, unimpressed by indulgent parenting, described herself as "not very good at pampering"—wounded Aisha's self-esteem.

"My mom made me believe I was this evil person," she said. So when Aisha's friends had more—and cooler—things than she did, it made sense. "My mentality was like, 'I'm bad. I'll never amount to anything.' That's what I was instilled by my mom."

Over the years, however, Aisha had invested in those around her. She knew how to draw people close or hold them back. She could make people useful and make them want to be. For a few months, Seeta paid for Aisha's cell phone. Other friends gave her food. Aisha ate slowly, cutting and chewing with focus. But being unable to return the favor embarrassed her; before a party she threw when her mom left town, Aisha taped shut her empty fridge, mumbling, "So n***as didn't drink my juice."[11]

Close friends helped meet Aisha's needs, but so too did classmates and acquaintances.

"Let's go to Pinkberry and get samples," she suggested when I met her after school one day. In the frozen yogurt store, girls sometimes filled up on complementary flavor samples. But that day, as we walked in, Aisha found a classmate, Kayla, staffing the register.

"You work today?" Aisha asked Kayla.

"Yeah! Wait for those guys to leave," Kayla whispered back.

As Kayla rang up an older couple, Aisha pressed her hands to the glass and peered at the toppings. She liked the strawberries best. Once the door swished closed behind the couple, Kayla poured out a full sized fro-yo and slid the cup, free of charge, into Aisha's hands.

"No way! Thank you, honey. You are the best!"

Kayla was one of many peers keen to please.[12] In part, Aisha's popularity stemmed from her vitality; she was charming and funny. But she also used the *affordances* of social media—the unique, usable features—to boost her status.[13] For instance, the fact that apps tallied and displayed the many likes Aisha's selfies received meant that her posts both quantified and enhanced her popularity. You couldn't argue with math.

Aisha also used social media to thank peers who helped her out, tweeting things like, *Shout out to Kayla for hooking it uppp with #Pinkberryyy* and *Peterson buying me Chinese food ? My n***a doe*. Aisha's popularity gave these "shout-outs" value.[14] And, by instantly "repaying" gifts with her expressions of thanks, she avoided any kind of debt to classmates with whom she had, often, somewhat "disposable" ties.[15] Aisha's real loyalty and generosity were reserved for her best friends.

When Aisha and the other girls found material support from peers, what they gained was more than economic; it was dignity and inclusion too. Aisha was moved when her friends looked out for her. It was not just cell service or frozen yogurt. It was care.

Boys

The boys the NC girls knew and hung out with—brothers, cousins, friends, and boyfriends—were, on average, a few years older and had more access to money. Their age and gender let them take jobs girls avoided, like driving for Uber or working security night shifts at a local community college. Some boys also launched their own business ventures, including Joanne's brother Vincent, who used his National Guard experience to sell $5 personal training sessions. The most prominent NC entrepreneur, however, was Ty, who sold clothes online; shirts and caps splashed with his logo dotted the neighborhood. Ty also threw parties for local teens, renting bars or hotel rooms and booking friends with DJ skills and social media buzz to bump up numbers. Girls always paid half price.

Boys' money trickled down to girls through social or romantic relationships. Eighteen-year-old Florence favored this dynamic. Florence, with a big heart, generous curves, and curls that haloed her face, was quick to intimacy with friends and boys alike. She shared anything she had: a carton of juice grabbed from her mom's fridge, a spritz of her new drugstore perfume. And if she wanted something, she asked for it, like the Friday we went bowling to celebrate her sister's birthday.

A group of us met outside Foodtown and walked the mile to the alley. When we arrived, some girls chose to sit out the game; there wasn't just the lane to pay for, you also had to rent shoes. Instead they took photos and cheered from the sidelines. After bowling, we all headed to the attached café, where we split into two tables for dinner. I joined Florence and her best friend, Stephanie.

Florence and Stephanie had the type of friendship where they could communicate just with glances. At dinner, they sat in contented calm. They both scrolled Instagram, tilting their screens to share content between bites from our family basket of French fries and chicken wings.

Florence narrated as she swiped: "I got twenty-four likes on this selfie. . . . This Ghanaian guy is obsessed with me! He likes all my pictures, but I never met him. . . . Mmm these couture gowns, I love fashion!"

Suddenly, Florence looked up and saw a man she recognized sliding smoothed green bills into the vending machine. She stood, strode over, and returned, moments later, waving a five.

"He gave me money, so this is our dinner," Florence said, slapping the note down by the napkins.

"How'd you do that?" I said, laughing.

Stephanie jumped in: "You gotta know a lotta people, know the right ones who have money, treat them nicely, and then it's all about timing. You see 'em 'bout to pull some money out, they can't lie and say they don't have money when they're right there with it!"[16]

Florence nodded. "I was like, 'Hey wassup, you have money?' And he's all like, 'How much you need?' And I'm like, 'Oh, you can just give me five dollars.'"

We laughed at the turn of phrase.

"I know!" Florence said. "It's like reverse psychology!" She continued, "You need to do the right amount though. The right amount or nothing."

Florence used social expectations to get money, which—that evening and frequently—was a shared resource in the girls' cliques.[17] Yet while girls pooled cash, it rarely changed hands so directly between them. More often, boys gave girls money, especially when romance was involved.[18]

Florence loved romance. Dating offered an escape, imaginatively if not literally, from a home where she frequently felt trapped and frustrated. Florence lived in the Jefferson Park housing project with her parents, her sister, Faith, and her young cousin, Charity—a seven-year-old girl with learning disabilities sent from Haiti to NC for better care. Florence's father worked long shifts at a dry cleaner an hour away. Her mother spent afternoons in the kitchen, often peeling vegetables into a silver bowl and speaking with family on a phone propped on her shoulder.

One day, after setting Charity on the plastic-covered living room couch with a bowl of cereal and her favorite cartoons, Florence sat with me on the steps outside her apartment. We were joined by her sister, Faith, and the other three girls in their clique: Stephanie, Zora, and Rosalie.

"Aquariuses are so moody," Stephanie said, noting Florence's frown.

"Shut up," Florence replied.

"You're like, bipolar," Faith jumped in.

"No, I am not," Florence said. "I'm just fucking depressed in this house!"

Florence's parents wanted her in, but she wanted out. They wanted demure, but Florence, all hustle and hope, favored looking and feeling good. Florence's growing need for independence led to more and more conflict.

Boys, however, liked Florence. They liked her kindness, her silhouette, and the way she walked like she knew they were watching. And Florence liked boys. As she searched for a partner worthy of her ample love, spending was one yardstick to measure intentions: open wallet, open heart. "If you feel like he doesn't really care," she explained, "make him spend his money."[19]

Boys often spent money on a girl they liked and on her friends. In this, Florence spied opportunity. One afternoon, she watched Faith inspect her own splayed hands.

"I need someone to take me to get a mani-pedi," Faith said.

"Have Richard do it," Florence said, referring to a guy she had been texting for a few weeks.

"He would do that?" Faith asked.

"I'll tell him to do it for you," Florence said, seemingly cheered both by the thought of treating her sister and by the idea that Richard would show he was serious.

But resources did not always flow freely between boys and friends, like when Florence tried to borrow money from Zora's boyfriend, Junior. One evening, as Florence strolled through NC with her clique and me, Junior drove up beside us and stopped his car in the middle of the street to say hi. As Zora kissed her boyfriend through his open window, Florence slid into the empty passenger seat.

Rosie, sixteen and the baby of the group, followed Florence into the car, hopping into the backseat. Faith stayed on the sidewalk and folded her arms. She had never much liked Junior, who, as Florence explained, had served time for dealing and was part of what the girls disparagingly called "that life."

Junior, in the driver's seat, pulled a wad of notes from his jeans. He peeled off a few and passed them out the window to his girlfriend.

"Thank you, baby," Zora said.

"Can I get some?" Rosie asked Junior, grinning.

Junior folded five twenties, turned back to face Rosie, and held out the cash.

Rosie's jaw dropped. She snatched the money and leaped out of the car, thanking Junior.

Junior then reached up and pinged the flimsy strap of Zora's short, khaki romper.

"You should cover this up," he said.

"No, it's fine," Zora replied, half-smiling, as she rejoined Faith, Rosie, and me on the sidewalk.

Finally, alone with Junior, Florence asked to borrow $150. She knew he could get the cash, and since Zora was one of her best friends, she assumed he would come through. But Junior hedged. Instead Florence later turned to a close male friend and admirer for the money.

When leveraging unreciprocated romantic interest to get things she wanted, Florence set boundaries for her comfort. "These guys wanna pay," she shrugged. "If they're like, 'Can we go grab something to eat?' I'll go, but after that I'm going home, like deuces. Movies, I wouldn't do that. No intimate typa setting things."

But other girls felt warier about getting money or gifts from boys. Aisha, for example, got "scared" when boys asked her out. "I always feel like when they take you places, they think you owe them stuff," she explained. Once, when Aisha did accept a boy's movie invitation, she tried to offset his gift of the tickets. "You *know* I don't buy snacks," she told me. "But I was like, 'I'm getting us a popcorn, large!'" Unlike with friends, when a quick Twitter shout-out might free her from debt, Aisha, alone with a boy, made a purchase of her own to reset the balance between spending and obligation.

Through familial, social, or romantic relationships, boys' money often flowed to girls and into their cliques. The NC girls navigated complex relationships not only to meet their own needs but also to provide for their friends. Sometimes these relationships tied to romance. Sometimes they didn't. Girls could exploit this ambiguity, but at times it left them feeling vulnerable.

Getting By without Money

Something to Do

Brittani, seventeen, was shy around strangers but playful with friends. She lived down the street from the Jefferson Park project that housed her friends, in a Section 8 apartment with her mother. Brittani, an only child, was close to her mom, who had also grown up in Cambridge. As a kid, Brittani knew that her mom felt guilty about not having money to give her. But some of Brittany's friends had it worse. "Aisha didn't really always have money," she told me. The girls had learned to make do: "There was always something to do that didn't involve money."

The NC girls industriously found ways to have fun without spending. To this end, cell phones and social media proved invaluable. Along with the girls' constant and engaging communication, phones held memes and viral videos to watch together and re-create. Online, there were also movies, TV shows, and songs to pirate or enjoy in exchange for a few ads on streaming sites.[20]

Still, home's demands and distractions could disrupt movies streamed in bedrooms. For real escape, the girls went to Entertainment Cinema, a dated theater in a strip mall half a mile from the project. At Entertainment Cinema, speakers alternately boomed and cut out. Sneakers gummed on sticky carpets. Rosie complained, "It be smelling in there. It be smelling like pee." But week by week, the girls happily hiked over, managing a steep shortcut down the side of a four-lane parkway. The shortcut—a path through trees and trash—had long ago been trampled by other teens walking the same way. Girls knew the route so well that even in the dark they dodged loose stones and a length of metal pipe that jutted from the soil.

The theater's enduring appeal owed largely to its staff: mostly local high school students who ushered in friends for free. Aisha showed me how it worked one Friday night, steering us straight past the counter to a classmate tearing tickets.

"Hey, Marshall," Aisha said.

"What's up, Aisha?"

"Which screen is *Haunted House?*"

"Screen four," he said. "Take the elevator so my manager doesn't see."

Aisha hugged Marshall, and we scuttled on back.

Entertainment Cinema was also parent approved, so even curfewed girls could often wrangle extra hours. Sometimes adults needed coaxing, like the time Florence "rescued" her best friend, Stephanie.

Stephanie was a thoughtful, funny, eighteen-year-old, who lived in the Jefferson Park project with her mom and stepfather. Stephanie's mother was strict. Growing up, Stephanie had been forbidden to play outside. Florence, who lived nearby, remembered a strange girl peering out from her living room. "She was locked down," Florence recalled. "We would see her looking at us out the window and be making fun of her." But soon Florence felt sad for the girl stuck indoors. One day, she explained, "we was like, 'Just come down!'" and Stephanie risked it. It turned out that Stephanie's mom knew Florence's dad, so she let Stephanie keep playing. "From there on," Florence said, smiling warmly, "it's like history."

But a decade later, Stephanie's mom still had firm rules. She preferred Stephanie home on weekends, and Stephanie, whose older sister had been kicked out, typically didn't protest.

So when Florence wanted to see a movie with her best friend one Friday night, she asked Stephanie's mother herself. I walked with Florence into the apartment.

"Hey sexy!" Florence beamed at Stephanie's mom, who was sitting on a chair in the living room.

Stephanie's mom smiled, skeptical.

"We wanna take Stephanie to the movies," Florence said.

Stephanie's mom shook her head and swatted the air.

"Please," Florence asked. "We'll bring her back to the door. Right here!"

Stephanie's mom hesitated, and Florence sensed an opening. "The movie finishes at ten, and we'll come straight," she said. "Please!"

With a slight nod, Stephanie's mom sent her daughter scampering to grab her coat.

Minutes later, the girls giggled along the main road and down the shortcut.

In the theater, we marched up to a young white man taking tickets. As we approached, he closed the scuffed paperback he was reading and smiled. Florence smiled back. The man raised his eyebrows expectantly.

"Oh," Florence chuckled. "We want to see *Red Dawn.*"

"Okay. Your uh, your tickets?" he asked, making a tearing gesture.

Florence's smile fell. As she fumbled for a face-saving answer, the ticket man rubbed his beard and leaned close, whispering, "Or, um, who sent you?"

"Oh!" Florence said, cheeks dimpling once more. "We're with Damba." Her cousin was not on shift, but he worked at Entertainment Cinema too.

"That's cool!" The man said, beckoning us through. "Just say Dam' sent you, and you're cool."

Friends offered free access to fun. Those employed at movie theaters helped girls keep up with new releases. Those staffing cafés sometimes comped treats or let girls occupy tables saved for paying customers. In turn, girls performed peer-enabled consumption by uploading photos of movie screens or selfies at restaurants, winning social status from classmates.

Getting Around

The Jefferson Park project was minutes from a subway station—the final stop on a line that crossed Cambridge and Boston. But girls couldn't always pay the fare or even afford the discounted subway pass the transit authority offered to high school students. So they spent a lot of time on foot, traipsing through sweaty summers and icy winters, and waiting for buses, which were slower but cost less.

Faith disliked walking enough to prioritize buying a subway pass; this choice meant a free ride for friends who bundled behind her through the barriers. When nobody present had a pass, however, the girls used other tricks to ride for free. The first time I rode the subway with Stephanie, I reached for my wallet as we entered the station. Stephanie pushed my hand back down.

"Oh, we're not paying," she told me. "Welcome to America!" Stephanie dangled her purse through the barriers, activating the sensors that detect exiting passengers. The screens swung open, and we strolled through.

At times, however, guards were on duty, meaning girls could not trick the sensors or rush through open gates with friends (or, as they sometimes did, as a last resort, with strangers). When guards patrolled stations, girls usually, grudgingly, paid. But not everyone could.

When Aisha had no train fare, she made a virtue from necessity, bragging about her choice not to travel. For some weeks, Aisha shrugged off flirty texts from a boy she had met at church. "He lives in Boston," she explained. "You know I would never travel to a boy's house . . . I don't care if you're sitting next to God. I ain't taking that train to nowhere."

Sometimes Aisha's friends helped her out. One evening, she and I entered Harvard Square station with a classmate whose Dunkin' Donuts shift had just wrapped. Aisha, spotting a guard, followed her friend to the ticket machine. As Aisha slid a crumpled dollar bill from the pocket of her denim shorts, her friend pulled a Ziplock of change from his backpack.

"Can you believe he gets to take that whole thing home?" Aisha said, nodding at the dumped-out contents of the tip jar.

Aisha's friend dug out his own fare, fishing for silver among the copper. Then he passed Aisha the bag to make up hers.

"You're the greatest guy *ever*," Aisha told him.

If Aisha was really in a pinch, she could improvise. She described to me how she got to school some days: "I literally beg people on the bus. You start pretending, 'Oh my God. I don't have any coins.' You're tapping," she said, miming patting her pockets. "Strangers are like, 'Girl, I'll just pay for it. It's just a dollar.'" She grinned. "I should win an Oscar."

Aisha used her talents one Thursday night after a poetry slam downtown. Aisha, Joanne, Seeta, and I walked through soft spring drizzle from the slam to the subway station. Expecting unstaffed barriers after 10 p.m., the girls bounced down the stairs to the trains. But the sight of a woman in an MBTA uniform stopped them.

"Shit," Joanne whispered to the group. "Can I borrow a dollar?" But nobody had cash. "I don't even have my ATM card," Joanne said. Nor did anyone else. Joanne felt a migraine coming on, and the leg cramp she got when she went too long without eating.

In the old purse I had brought out, I found an expired foreign debit card.

Aisha smiled.

"Give it to me," Aisha told me. She passed her own ticket, which she had saved for, to Joanne, who frowned in confusion. "Come!" Aisha instructed, and we followed.

Aisha approached the guard, holding out the old debit card. In a thick and affected Ugandan accent, she mumbled, "I'm so sorry but I just arrived in this country. My card won't work on the machines . . . I'm so sorry."

We stood, barely breathing.

"Okay," the guard said, opening the gate to let Aisha through. The rest of us used tickets, with Joanne swiping the one Aisha had slipped her.

The girls trooped to the back of the platform, then cracked up laughing. Aisha stomped on the spot as she announced, in her regular voice, "You ain't never come up with nothing 'til you're broke!"

Aisha was glad to help Joanne, and her skills got everybody home that night.[21]

·   ·   ·

In the fall of her senior year, Aisha decided to run for Homecoming Queen. Her friends supported her candidacy with tweets and Facebook posts and helped her bake campaign cookies to hand out at school.

A homecoming dance would follow the game at which the king and queen would be crowned. Aisha needed a dress.

One Saturday, I met Aisha in Central Square to head to the mall. I complimented her new braids; she had just seen Esther, a talented friend who never overcharged.

"No, it's ugly," Aisha said, deflecting praise, as she often did.

Aisha was joined by her cousin, Afiya, who was visiting from Uganda. Afiya clutched a crisp hundred-dollar bill, from a friend in Kampala who had requested an American dress for an upcoming wedding.

At the mall, the three of us breezed through stores. Aisha, discerning, wove through aisles and dodged displays, squinting as she judged dresses' fabric and fit.

"I like this a lot," she said, pulling one from the rack. Then she peered closer, inspecting the seams. "Actually, it looks cheap." Aisha replaced the dress and scrutinized several others, before finally finding one that made her smile.

"Look at this!" Aisha said, holding it against herself admiringly. Then she flipped the price tag in her fingers.

Aisha pursed her lips and rehung the dress on the rail. As she walked on, she held onto the hem with one hand. After a few steps, Aisha let go and sat on the floor under a row of hanging skirts. She propped her head on her bent knees.

"I'm bored of shopping," Aisha said. "Let's go now." She stood and made for the exit. As Afiya and I rushed to keep up, Aisha turned back to face us. "With that hundred, she could buy us all a dress," Aisha said. Afiya said nothing.

On the bus home, Aisha decided to return to the consignment store she had visited earlier and buy a dress she had tried on there: pink, satin, and just short enough.

"But I don't have enough money," she said. "I only have eleven dollars, so I need eight more."

"So you're not gonna get it?" Afiya asked.

Aisha chewed her lip. "I mean, can't I borrow some or something?"

"It's not my money, Aisha. I can't do that."

"I mean, it's not like I'm not gonna pay you," Aisha said.

"I know, Aisha, but it's not mine!"

Aisha, whose peers usually helped her out, thought fast: "I can pay you back next week from laundry money," she said. "My mom's gonna give me ten dollars for the laundromat. If I give you money from that, is it okay?"

"Um, yeah."

A week later, the pink satin dress lay ready, draped gently over the garbage bags on Aisha's bedroom floor. First, though, was the game.

On a bitter October evening, Joanne and I shivered on metal bleachers. Aisha crouched, trembling, by Joanne's feet.

"It's cold isn't it!" I offered.

"I'm scared," Aisha murmured, almost apologetic.

"Don't be scared," Joanne lulled, rubbing Aisha's back the way she soothed her siblings. Around us, hundreds of students laughed and talked.

At halftime, the MC called the candidates for Homecoming Queen down to the field one by one. Kiara, a friend of Aisha's, hugged her fellow cheerleaders and tightened her pink hair ribbon before sashaying down. Rae, in bright red lipstick, joined Kiara. Finally, Aisha's name boomed through the speakers. Aisha stood and exhaled hard, as if to force out the jitters making her hands shake. Heads turned, and Aisha flashed a smile. She climbed nimbly down the bleachers and marched over the field like it was a fashion runway, pausing every few steps to drive up the drama. The cheering crowd grew louder and louder.

The three candidates nodded civilly at one another. As class-mates roared in anticipation, Joanne fidgeted while staring straight at Aisha.

"The winner . . .," called the MC, "of Hooomecoming Queeeeen, is . . .!" She paused. "*Aishaaaa!*" she yelled into the mic.

Joanne sprung to her feet.

Aisha broke into a wide grin and graciously hugged Kiara and Rae.

"Yeah, Aisha! Woooooh!" Joanne yelled, stamping and clapping.

On the field, black and silver helium balloons were released into the cloudless dark. Aisha accepted a bouquet of flowers and ducked at the knees to receive her plastic crown. She waved out at the bleach-ers. Among those smiling back were friends and classmates—people who had shared their belongings, who had fed her when her fridge was empty, and who had, for years, made her feel loved.

What Money Means

Money is loaded with meanings. It guides how people see themselves and others. It shapes what we think of as moral or good. As economic sociologists like Viviana Zelizer have shown, money transforms—and is itself transformed by—our values and relationships.[22] Because of the meanings embedded in money, poverty's harms are not only financial; they are also social and emotional. Poverty, as bell hooks explains, can be "a mark of shame, a sign that one is not worthy or chosen."[23]

The NC girls creatively tried to solve some of the problems caused by being broke. They supplemented paid work with cash and goods from friends and acquaintances. They leaned on boys, whose money was shared in their cliques. They also determinedly found ways to have fun and get around without spending.

By helping one another get by, the girls met mutual financial needs. But they also offered emotional resources that motivate people as much as—or more than—money.[24] They made one another feel valued, a key developmental need for adolescents.[25] In doing so, they helped alleviate the status-related harms of poverty, harms that their age amplified.

Parents could rarely spare cash, and, perhaps as importantly, they could not confer social status. Friends, however, offered both. When Aisha received a free frozen yogurt, she felt included. When Florence bought her friends dinner with money from a guy she knew, she felt valuable. Flows of material support confirmed belonging; sharing really was caring.[26] The girls helped one another feel like they had enough and also feel like they were enough.

2 *Bored*

Time Management

After school one Friday, Florence gathered her clique, hoping to make plans. On the steps outside her apartment, she sat with her sister, Faith, as well as Zora, Rosie, and me. The day was stifling; we bunched our dresses beneath us, between our thighs and the scalding stone.

Waiting for Stephanie to arrive, the girls fanned their faces and looked out at the project's bustle. Kids sped by on micro scooters. Older folks on benches squinted into the afternoon. Haitian kompa drifted from one nearby window; hip-hop from another.

Nearby, a car pulled into the project.

"Who's that?" Rosie asked. As the girls sat around, they often noted comings and goings.

"It's Frankie," Faith said.

"Oh, yeah," Rosie said. "He has the 2012? I thought his car was older."

Faith shook her head.

A few feet away, Rosie's brother, Leon, threw a ball with a young neighbor.

"Come on, little man!" Leon encouraged the boy.

The kid thrust out his hands to catch, but Leon's arms went suddenly slack. He was distracted by Stephanie, approaching in a long jersey dress that clung. The girls saw Leon gawk and busted out laughing.

"I'm done! Look at Leon!" Faith cracked.

The girls mocked Leon's build. "You're like one of them Ethiopian kids," Faith said. "All skin and bones!"

"I been in the weight room!" Leon protested, grinning and flexing a bicep, before taking his ball buddy elsewhere.

Stephanie joined the girls on the steps. With her clique all together, Florence shared her summer goals: hopefully get a job at the youth center, work with a cousin "on fashion," and travel, maybe to Miami, or perhaps Jamaica.

That afternoon, however, plans felt elusive. It was too hot to sit out much longer, but there was no privacy inside. Not everyone had money for food, and some were under eighteen, too young for the club party they had heard about in Boston that night.

Gradually, boredom slowed the girls' talk. Hoping a change of scene might lift spirits, Florence roused us to our feet. With no destination in mind, we shuffled down the main road, where a confetti of sun-browned blossoms littered the gutter. The girls chatted to one another and to neighbors we passed. But as sweat rolled down our backs, the street soon lost its appeal.

We walked past a pizzeria, and Faith swung open the door.

"Is it air-conditioned?" Faith asked aloud. Feeling the answer on her skin, she quickly turned back. The two men behind the counter catcalled as she left.

The only other nearby business was a laundromat. Zora opened the glass door to a rush of cool air, and we trooped in eagerly for some relief.

"Man, that feels good!" said Faith, enjoying the chill.

The girls settled on benches, ignoring glances from customers folding clothes.

"I needa get some money," Zora said, perching on an empty dryer.

"See, that's why I need a sugar daddy!" Florence said, her full cheeks dimpling.

"Yeah, I need a sugar daddy!" concurred Rosie.

"Okay, girl, no! You're like, twelve," Zora said. Zora, the oldest of the group at nineteen, was protective of Rosie, the youngest at sixteen.

Rosie bowed her head and smiled.

An employee approached us. "Are you guys waiting for something?" she asked.

"We're waiting for some*one*," Zora improvised, flashing a gracious fake grin.

"I, uh, don't know if you can stay," the woman mumbled. "I might get in trouble."

"We'll be quiet," Florence offered.

The woman walked away. Moments later, she returned, stiff-backed. "Customers only." She declared.

We filed back outside.

The struggle to find something to do was not new for the NC girls. Their age, their curfews or family obligations, and even the weather curtailed their social lives. And, as Black and brown teens, they faced racism and hostility, which, combined with their limited disposable income, restricted their access to public or commercial places, from cafés to malls.[1] The girls often had time to fill or kill.

Time, Tedium, and Inequality

Social time is not the same as *scientific* or clock time.[2] An hour might always be an hour, but time can rush by, or it can drag; minutes laughing with friends pass differently from those spent waiting for the bus in midwinter or anticipating test results.[3] "Our experience of time," notes the sociologist Michael Flaherty, "reflects desire as well as circumstances."[4] This means that time alone in a quiet room might feel restorative if what we want is to relax; otherwise, it might feel dreary.[5]

For the NC girls, hours often unspooled tediously.

One Saturday night, Seeta and I joined Joanne in her kitchen. Outside, a thick mist hung over the darkness. The two yellow canaries shrieked in the corner, flapping their wings and chomping on their coop's wire bars.

"Can't you make the birds shut up?" Seeta asked.

Joanne shrugged. She was used to fading out noise. "I've learned how to zone out and read a book in the middle of the party," she once explained. "It's life skill when you live in the middle of this family."

But the din got to Seeta, who sighed as Joanne's kid siblings ran around, doing star-jumps and reading aloud from a "Knock Knock" joke book. Nobody asked, "Who's there?"

Joanne suggested dessert. She split a chocolate brownie into three paper bowls, heaping each with the vanilla ice cream we had bought earlier from Foodtown.

"I hate buying food from here. It's a rip-off," Seeta had grumbled, in line with customers hauling six packs. But the next nearest store was fifteen minutes away, and it was raining.

We ate with plastic spoons. The gloom felt close, along with the weight of a weekend squandered.

Seeta pushed her empty bowl away and pressed the heels of her hands into her temples. She suggested we go upstairs, where Joanne's brother Vincent was chilling in his room with two friends. Seeta hoped the boys might have plans.

Seeta flopped on Vincent's bed, readjusting her weight as she sank into the spots where the mattress sagged. Joanne lagged by the door, frowning at the boys' bong.

"Why you being awkward?" asked one of Vincent's friends.

"I don't wanna breathe that," Joanne cut back.

Joanne and Seeta peered expectantly at the boys. But they had no plans either. Vincent started a movie he had downloaded to his laptop, but the tinny sound wouldn't travel.

"This is not entertaining," Seeta sighed. Beside her, Vincent's friend shot strip club patrons in *Grand Theft Auto* on a small TV above the dresser.

A train thundered by. Seeta looked out the window. Then she turned to Joanne. Then she gazed at the ceiling.

Boredom, which can make people feel depressed and disempowered,[6] was one of the girls' chief complaints. Generally, young people are more susceptible than adults to boredom.[7] And young people from low-income homes—whose hours, typically, are less structured than their middle-class peers'—often bear more of boredom's burdens.[8]

This inequality surfaced in class sometimes at the city's single public high school, Cambridge Rindge and Latin School (CRLS), which all the girls attended. At CRLS, which had good funding, a strong teacher-pupil ratio, and a recently renovated building,[9] 45 percent of the eighteen hundred students were from families with incomes low enough to qualify for free or reduced-price lunches.[10]

On the first day after Spring Break, Faith and Stephanie arrived at CHANGE, their community service–based elective. Each week in CHANGE, one student led "check-in"—an ice-breaker activity to start class. This morning, it was Faith's turn to lead. Other students planned games or taught songs from camps they had attended, but that wasn't Faith's style. Faith was calmer and more sedate than most of her classmates.

Faith, seated opposite me in the chair circle, crossed her Uggs. For check-in, she said, the class should go around and say what they did over break. Some students perked up at the instruction; others slouched down. Some needed coaxing, like Darrell, a seventeen-year-old African American boy who lived in NC. Darrell, with a lean build, long eyelashes, and a smile that girls returned, often whispered through circle time, or hummed, or tapped his chair leg with his sneaker. When his turn came, he pulled his hoodie up over his mouth.

"How was your vacation?" nudged the teacher, Ms. Flores.

"Boring," he said, looking at his lap.

"That's it?" she pressed.

"Yup."

"Why was it boring?"

"'Cause," Darrell said. "It just was."

Ms. Flores paused. "Mkay." She looked to the next chair.

"I went to Vermont," said Melanie, a middle-class white girl. "I stayed on my cousin's sheep farm. It was really awesome."[11]

Lillian, a middle-class white girl with dyed red hair, went next. "I planned out my whole summer. I really hope it all works out! Oh, I got into college too!" The class clapped.

In addition to experiencing more boredom, certain teens are more likely to be punished for how they spend their free time. All teens get bored and seek thrills; as the sociologist Mary Pattillo-McCoy notes, "Adolescence is color-blind in its demands for excitement and its propensities to test boundaries."[12] But testing boundaries more often leads to discipline, suspension, and even arrest for Black and brown teens and young people from low-income families, compared to similarly acting white and middle-class peers.[13] Boredom, then, was not just a subjective discomfort for the NC girls, but one that left them vulnerable to surveillance and harm.

After school ended at 2.30 p.m., some girls headed to jobs or to Workforce, a youth program run by Cambridge Housing Authority. Many had chores or baby-sitting obligations. Still, nine or ten hours often loomed between the last bell and bedtime. While some of their middle-class peers fought for downtime between scheduled extracurriculars, the NC girls had to find things to do.[14] They practiced time management: not learning how to plan, prioritize, or delegate, but rather making time pass.

The girls found social solutions to boredom. Although some psychologists describe self-entertainment as a skill for individuals to cultivate alone,[15] the girls used their connections to fill time and disrupt tedium. Social media helped them do "time work," defined by Flaherty as "interpersonal effort directed toward provoking or preventing various temporal experiences."[16] Together the girls created excitement and made moments memorable.

Social Media: Passing and Playing with Time

Connection Online

The slowest and most stubborn hours were those spent alone.[17] Jobs, weather, "trap" parents, and family duties separated teens from their friends. Yet when the girls were apart, cell phones kept them connected, both to each other and to hundreds of friends and followers.

The girls used several social media apps, and their conversations crossed multiple platforms. For example, Aisha could send Joanne a Snapchat to respond to her Instagram post, which Joanne might answer with a text message.[18] Along with these continuous conversations, social media offered further paths to connection. One was an interaction "trade," like that posted on Facebook one afternoon by Aisha's friend, Ariana: *LMS* [like my status] *for a confession and a <3.* Seventy-nine people liked Ariana's status, and, as promised, Ariana visited the likers' profiles, commented a heart—<3—on one of their photos, and sent them a private message.

The girls also posted personalized responses to trending Twitter hashtags like *#15factsaboutme, #waystoruinarelationship, #dontwifeherif,* and *#tweetyourshoesize* and joined digital practices that spanned platforms. On Thursdays, for example, the girls could participate in *#throwbackthursday* by uploading an old photo from their phones, sometimes stitched digitally into a collage with a new photo for comparison using a free app. On *#MCM,* Mancrush Monday, some posted photos of boyfriends or celebrities they liked; and for *#WCW,* Womancrush Wednesday, the girls shared platonic but appreciative photos of famous women or their friends. One Wednesday, Zora posted a photo of Florence wearing a monochrome outfit and stylish black hat, captioned, *Meet my WCW but that's erryday though. Shawty bad like a bag of money.*

Such digital practices brought the girls a type of "collective effervescence," defined by Émile Durkheim as the energy, excitement, and community membership that people feel when part of a group with a shared focus.[19] Memes and hashtags made the girls feel part of something, even when physically alone. Collective effervescence could stretch over space but not over too much time, as viral trends mostly flared up fast and then fizzled.

An Audience of Peers

Online, the girls cataloged their days.[20] As Aisha once explained, "I Snapchat, like, my life." The girls shared photos of food, described the length of a shower, posted outfits for church, and tweeted things like:

Why does my sister always have to come in my room wtf go away
I can't find my hair tie but it's probably under all my clothes on my bed

I'm hungry but not enough to go get food lol
My nails have really grown so much
I gotta be in a certain mood for certain cereal
I wanna put makeup on but idk which colors to pick Lol

Such updates helped the girls feel seen and connected. Moreover, they battled boredom thanks to an always available audience of peers. This audience had two key features: *publicity* and *reciprocity*.

All social networks were public; some, like Facebook and Snapchat, only to approved contacts, and others, like Twitter, to anybody on the platform.[21] Publicity made solitary acts social and turned thoughts into expressions. This made tweeting more engaging than journaling.

Reciprocity obliged teens to view and interact with one another's posts. Aisha, for example, studied her friends' faces for recognition when telling a story referencing something she had posted about. "You didn't see my tweet?" she would chide if she didn't see nods and smiles. But mostly, her friends did see her tweets—and her Snapchats, Instagram pictures, and Facebook posts—just as she saw and interacted with theirs. Keeping up could demand hours each day or impose pressure to be constantly attentive.[22] But the imperative also meant nobody could feel too lonely or bored.

With a peer audience, each post offered two distinct moments of engagement. The first, expressive, moment, was the act of sharing. This might be a quick tweet. Or it might be more consuming. Choosing photos, writing captions, and mulling emojis could draw the girls into a state of "flow." Flow, the mental state of focus and enjoyment that arises from complete immersion in an activity, can help people lose track of time.[23]

A second, interactive, moment of engagement ensued when friends liked, retweeted, or commented on posts. The girls in turn responded to this engagement, extending social media's fun. Faith, for instance, live tweeted while watching her TV shows alone and replied to comments she received. She also sent Snapchats during evenings baby-sitting her niece and nephew, posts that became conversations when her friends engaged.

The publicity of social media and teens' norms of reciprocity meant that the girls disrupted boredom both while posting and again in their resultant interactions.

Passing Time Together

The girls used social media to pass time when they were together too. They pored jointly over peers' posts and feeds. They "twatched"[24] and scrutinized relationships: who posted what; who liked, followed, or unfollowed whom. They used their "idioms of practice"—norms formed when "groups of friends . . . develop together their own ways of using media to communicate with each other"[25]—to decode information and gossip infused in posts.

Drama was pervasive. "You can't put anything as a status," a senior once explained to me. "Like, it could be about pie, and people would still fight about it."[26]

The sociologists dana boyd and Alice Marwick define drama as "performative, interpersonal conflict that takes place in front of an active, engaged audience, often on social media."[27] For many teens, boyd notes, "inciting drama is a source of entertainment [and] a practice to relieve boredom."[28] Mostly, the NC girls observed drama instead of inciting it. But even watching online gossip and conflict could momentarily beat back boredom.

Social media also helped the girls get creative. When Vine—the app with looping, seven-second videos—was popular, the girls took inspiration. As Brittani explained, "We'll watch a Vine and then we'll talk about it, and we'll try to replay it by acting it out and just laugh about it for hours."

Along with consuming and producing content in one another's company, the girls often scrolled individually through their own social media feeds while, for instance, lounging together in a bedroom or an IHOP booth. To classical theorists of interaction like Erving

Goffman, this kind of "external preoccupation"—giving one's "main concern to something that is unconnected with what is being talked about at the time and even unconnected with the other persons present"—would indicate a problem.[29] But among the girls, the freedom to use their phones and chat with absent others was a sign of closeness. This "distance" was in fact intimacy.

Sometimes, while scrolling their own feeds, the girls turned their screens to the group, sharing content. Goffman argued that in a healthy conversation, "[messages] not part of the officially accredited flow are modulated so as not to interfere seriously with the accredited messages."[30] But when the girls gathered, this choppy flow of attention was engaging. It was another way in which social media helped disrupt tedium.

The Life Course of a Photo

After school one day, Aisha flipped open my laptop.

"We should take photos!" she said, clicking on the Photo Booth app. Aisha took dozens of selfies, trying out each filter; her favorite was the big eye effect. Then she scrolled through the images, quickly deleting most before editing her favorites and sharing them to Facebook.

"This is what we used to do, back in the day, you know," she said.

"What is?" I asked.

"We would go to the Apple store in the mall, me and Brittani, and take photos. Literally that's all we would do."

Taking photos, alone or in groups, was fun and free—an activity that, like teens everywhere, the girls enjoyed.

The time-passing power of photos was especially clear one June evening as I waited with Florence, Faith, Zora, and Rosie for a party to begin. It was one of Ty's; he had rented a bar in NC, but the DJ was running late. Earlier, a friend had given us a ride from the project to the venue. As we pulled into the empty car park—among abandoned lots, an automotive junkyard, and beat-up buildings—Rosie grimaced at the eerie quiet. Still, the girls hopped hopefully from the car.

They peered through the bar's glass doors and watched the staff set up. Other cars packed with teens crawled by; most, seeing the barren venue, sped straight off. After a while, Florence and her friends leaned wearily against the doors.

Ty spotted the girls through the window and came outside.

Zora was sour. "What is going on?" she said, snapping her fingers.

"Don't snap your fingers at me," he said, low but firm. "Y'all ain't even supposed to be here," he added, pointedly glancing at those under eighteen.

"Okay, I'm sorry," Zora said, softening. "You want a hug? Okay, come here."

Ty hugged Zora, then returned to the bar to wait for the DJ.

Among the girls, energy dipped and the mood dragged. Zora, suddenly upbeat, said to her friends, "I guess there's nothing to do but take pictures!"

Zora didn't mean a quick selfie. Instead she entertained the group for several minutes. First she chose a photographer, handing her phone to Florence. Then she skipped into the parking lot, selected a backdrop, and posed, angling her elbow and tilting her chin.

"Ready!" Zora called, through a smile.

Florence took photos with and without a flash. Zora's friends shouted ideas for how she should pose. She tried new stances and facial expressions: hands on hips, laughing, pouting.

"Alright girl," Florence said, returning Zora's phone. Zora scrolled through the pictures. She chose a favorite and cropped the image, before sliding her finger left to right on the screen to adjust the light and color. She swiped through emojis for the perfect caption and uploaded the photo. Her friends refreshed their feeds and liked the picture, commenting words and emojis. As more likes arrived, Zora clicked through to some likers' profiles, scrolling through their own recent posts and maybe liking one back. Later, once the party finally began, Zora continued to check on the photo's progress.

Zora used social media's publicity and reciprocity to entertain herself and her friends. The shared focus raised everyone's spirits and stopped the evening from deflating. Taking the photo—posing, reviewing, selecting, editing, and uploading—was just the first step; interaction with the post prolonged the engagement.

Making and Magnifying Moments

The girls used social media not just to fill empty time but to stretch "full" time too, harnessing their audience to make the most of fun.

One Friday evening in November, Stephanie cooked pasta for Faith, Rosie, and me. Rosie and Faith swiped at their phones, and Faith commented aloud on the Halloween costumes of celebrities she followed: "Did you see Kevin Hart and his girlfriend? Oh God, Kim Kardashian thinks she's cute."

Outside, ice laced the windows.

After we ate, Stephanie sighed, bored. "We need to go out!" she said.

Faith, comfortable indoors with heat, food, and Wi-Fi, balked. "Where you tryna go? It's cold!"

"I don't even care!" Stephanie said. "Let's go walk around!"

"Let's go downtown!" Rosie suggested.

Faith was outnumbered. We zipped into puffy coats and strode into the moonless dark. Midway down the unlit shortcut from the back of the project to the main road, a car drove past us and braked sharply, just ahead. The girls froze and grabbed out at each other.

"Oh my God, I'm mad scared," Faith whispered.

"Pretend to call your mom!" Stephanie said. Faith fumbled for her phone, fingers slowed by the chill.

"What's good!" the driver, a male friend, yelled from the window. The girls laughed with the release of tension and crowded his car.

The driver and the girls talked about prospective plans.

"Where you going?" Faith asked.

"I don't know yet. I'm a find something."

"Can you bring us?"

"I don't know where I'm going!"

After the driver went on his way, having gently ignored Faith's request for a ride around the neighborhood, we continued to the subway station, tricked the barriers, and boarded a train.

We got off at Harvard Square and began to wander, hands plunged in pockets. Buzzed groups of students ambled to bars and restaurants.

"I didn't know there was a hotel right there," Rosie said, as we turned onto a concrete plaza where, outside an inviting lobby, string lights glinted around trees' bare branches. "We should go in to get warm."

Faith shook her head. "They'll be like, 'We don't want you.'"

"Yeah, you probably have to like, check in, and stuff," Stephanie seconded.

Rosie shrugged. White teens in formalwear romped around the plaza, taking a break from a function inside. Faith, Rosie, and Stephanie dared each other to ask one of the teens about the event.

"I'll go, but I'm scared," Rosie said. She timidly approached a girl with a pearl choker and pale legs blotched from the cold.

"Excuse me, what's going on in there?" Rosie asked.

The girl looked Rosie up and down. "There's a bar mitzvah," she said, without eye contact. She turned on her kitten heels and rejoined her friends.

"Oh, okay thanks," Rosie mumbled to the girl's back.

"She probably thought we was gonna try and crash it," Faith consoled Rosie as she returned to the group.

We gave up on Harvard and returned to the subway, riding a few more stops to Downtown Crossing. But late on a Friday night, even the busy commercial neighborhood was silent. Without the hoped-for stir, the girls again became subdued as we walked with no destination.

Faith had been happy at home. "Where we going?" she demanded, pointing at the dark distance. "There ain't nothing up there!"

Stephanie shrugged. We shuffled wordlessly through the shuttered business district, dragging our feet down a dirty alley.

Then we stumbled onto a bustling street, with buildings high and close. Amid the glow of two theaters and a sumptuous Macy's Christmas window display, couples and groups wove around us. The street thrilled with life.

"It's like New York here!" Faith marveled, gazing up at the sparkling night.

"Word," Stephanie agreed.

The girls reached for their phones and took photos. The neon and opulence offered entertainment, if not in the conventional way.

When Stephanie's mom called and told her to get home, we headed back to the subway. The girls walked in silence, this time because they were focused on posting photos and statuses to Twitter, Instagram, and Facebook.

Stephanie tweeted, *Fun filled night w/ @Faith, @Jasmin, @Rosie Lovin the crew!*

Faith, earlier vocal in her complaints, tweeted, *best night with these girls >>>>>,* and Rosie replied, *WORDDDD lol.*

Liking, retweeting, and commenting on each other's posts, the girls transformed a dull Friday night spent pacing the streets into an adventure, shared with peers.[31] The gaze of their audience—whether real or imagined—let the girls create, portray, and, crucially, *experience* fun. Social media helped make a moment of real emotional involvement.

Another night, this time during summer break, I joined Florence and her clique in the playground across from the project. Rosie and Stephanie swung on the swings, and the rest of us discussed plans around a picnic table.

"You tryna go somewhere tonight?" Faith asked me.

"Sure," I said. "What is there?"

"My friend's mom works for MIT. I think there's an MIT party," Faith said.

Zora shook her head; nobody knew details.

Faith offered another suggestion: "There's a hotel party in Waltham." Some boys they knew had rented a room. Usually parties were more reliable than age-restricted bars. But transport could be a problem[32]. So too could fees charged for entry, or gatekeeping peers.

"Would we have to pay for that, though?" Zora asked.

"No, but you know the girls will be aggy as fuck," Florence said. "We only know the boys, and the girls will be like, 'You can't come in.' You know what girls are like."

In the end, we stayed at the picnic tables until after midnight when two more friends, Natasha and Marie, arrived. Natasha had a car, and Zora convinced her to drive us all to the late-night liquor store in Central Square.

Behind the wheel, Natasha grimaced as the six of us—Zora, Florence, Faith, Stephanie, Rosie, and I—piled into the back; one girl on each seat, another on each lap.

"Is this gonna work?" Natasha asked, turning to face us.

"We're gonna get stopped, n***a," Marie said, sitting shotgun beside her.

"What if we see police?" Natasha asked.

But there were no other plans. Florence and Faith—determined to go somewhere, anywhere—swore it would be fine, and Natasha turned the key. The red car groaned and grumbled out of the parking lot. Its metal undercarriage snagged on the speed bumps that Natasha took at five miles an hour.

Out on the main road, Marie hooked her music up to the speakers. Chatter grew loud as we drove, as the girls shared gossip and discussed which bottles to buy.

When we pulled up to Central Square minutes later, the liquor store had just closed. The girls shrugged; at least they had left NC. Natasha ferried us back to the playground, stopping for ten dollars' worth of gas from a dingy station near Fresh Pond. The two men pumping the night shift saw eight girls in a car and chuckled.

We returned to the picnic table, where I watched the Snapchats Faith had posted during our drive. The videos—raucous talk, loud music, and streetlights' rhythmic strobe—were captioned *Turn upppp*. They showed a fun Saturday night. This was not a digital deception; it *was* a fun Saturday night. Witnesses made the experience more meaningful. The audience changed what had happened, and helped *make* a moment.[33]

Social media could also *magnify* moments. The girls used their audience to build up to exciting events, posting, for instance, daily countdowns to birthdays. They also posted during and after experiences to stretch their life spans.

One Thursday, for example, Aisha tweeted her excitement en route to IHOP with her cousin and me. As we ate, she posted selfies clutching syrup bottles and uploaded photos of her cousin's whipped cream–topped hot chocolate. She shared more on our way home. Rather than diminish the experience, Aisha's uploads let her exploit what was, for her, a rare treat. She had ordered two pancakes for $3.20—an option unlisted on the menu that she dubbed "the Aisha special"—and paid with coins, scrambling to retrieve three pennies that fell from the counter. But with social media and her peer audience, Aisha magnified the meal. Her focus on the fun far outlasted our stay at the restaurant, helping her disrupt boredom for as long as possible.

Alone Together?

Boredom taunted the NC girls. But as a social problem it sometimes had social solutions. Alone and together, they consumed and produced content online. A peer audience—formed by social media's publicity and norms of reciprocity—made solitary time communal and helped the girls make or magnify moments of fun.

Connection disrupts tedium. When people focus on the same thing and sense one another's involvement, they join an energizing "interaction ritual," explains the sociologist Randall Collins.[34] However, to Collins, physical co-presence is essential. Since online encounters "lack the flow of interaction in real time," he argues, they are unlikely to create emotional energy.[35]

Yet online interactions did create emotional energy.[36] A sense of shared attention generated togetherness and excitement, even when the girls were apart. Memes and hashtags fostered an animating intimacy, whether themes were somber or banal; even tweets beginning *That face you make when* . . . or *That feeling when* . . . drew on and reaffirmed connection with others. Despite lacking the full intensity of face-to-face fun, social media helped the girls beat back boredom.

The NC girls still got bored, of course. For all their creativity and collaboration, they would have benefited from more public space, resources, and opportunities. And while social media could be distracting and exciting, its thrills could feel fleeting.

Moreover, young people's time use informs their long-term trajectories. As the sociologist Annette Lareau reveals, middle-class children typically manage schedules filled by parents, while children from low-income homes face more leisure hours, as did the NC girls. This difference exposes young people from poorer families to more boredom. It can also, crucially, rob them of the sense of entitlement honed, Lareau found, by organized activities and lead, instead, to a sense of constraint.[37]

Relatedly, wealthier classmates' extracurriculars not only gleamed on résumés and college admissions essays. They also prepared middle-class youth for the time pressures to come at college and beyond; while affluent classmates still fervently socialized online, they also practiced multitasking. The NC girls were left less practiced in time management or, at least, in what time management typically means in colleges and workplaces.[38]

Nonetheless, the girls imaginatively entertained each other without turning to the "risk behaviors" on which research about teens in poor neighborhoods often dwells. Leaning on friends and peers, the girls pierced monotony with spikes of thrill and fun. In doing so, they eased an underrecognized but significant teenage hardship.

3 Emotional Support and Breakdown

One Saturday afternoon, Aisha visited the East Cambridge mall. She checked out some stores near the entrance, before heading to her favorites, which were up on the second floor. As she rode the escalator, Aisha leaned languidly on the handrail, two steps in front of a uniformed police officer.

The officer leveled his badge, then suddenly poked Aisha between the shoulders. She turned around, eyes wide.

"Officer Jacks! No *wayyy*," Aisha squealed, coming to face him. "How are you? I saw a cop and I was like, 'Don't turn around, don't turn around!' but it's you!"

At the top of the escalator, Aisha and Officer Jacks talked for a minute or two before Jacks went on his way.

"That made my whole day," Aisha told me as we walked toward Charlotte Russe. "He is daddy, that man. Isn't he daddy?"[1]

Jacks, a tall Black officer in his late thirties, patrolled near CRLS. He was friendly with many students and knew some by name. But Aisha's familiarity went deeper.

"My mom used to call the police on me all the time," she explained. "If I was half an hour late when I went out, she called the cops. Once I wasn't even out—I was sleeping in my bed!—and she didn't check, and she called the cops. That's why you see me so friendly with the cops."

Aisha laughed, cavalier. But her face fell as she imagined addressing her mother: "What's the police going to do? It's not like they were going to beat me more than you were going to."

The topic of her mother was one of the few chinks in Aisha's armor. Once, she compared her childhood to "a cult," because of the harsh discipline she had suffered for being a "normal five-year-old." Aisha remembered her mother threatening, "I'm going to sign the papers to send you away. You're a bad child."

In one recent fight, Aisha had been reprimanded for sweeping the floor too slowly. "If you're taking your time like that, get out of my house!" Aisha recalled her mom shouting. Aisha told me, "I grabbed my purse and a book, and walked out."

Aisha crashed for a restless night with Brittani, who let Aisha process her emotions. Getting kicked out, Aisha said, was "mentally disturbing." She then spent a week with an aunt, keeping in constant touch with her friends, before returning home.

Teens everywhere grapple with fraught feelings. Many turn to their friends to cope with family conflict, insecurities, and more. The NC girls faced further emotional injuries, in the form of racism, poverty, and exclusion. Such social marginalization can be brutally harmful; the stress of ongoing stigmatization can damage well-being even more than discrete, traumatic life events.[2]

The young women acknowledged, validated, and worked to mitigate a range of emotional harms they encountered in day-to-day life.[3] They formed what the psychologists Kathleen Call and Jeylan Mortimer call an "arena of comfort": a "safe haven" among friends.[4] "If a person has an experience that is harmful or threatening to the self-image in one context," Call and Mortimer explain, "the injury can be soothed, or compensated for, in another domain through . . . strong, positive relationships."[5]

The NC girls did exactly this; they met strain with comfort. They empathized with family fights, providing stability when things felt chaotic. They also made each other feel worthy, amid stigma and surveillance at school and elsewhere. But resilience was draining. When the girls' balance of emotional care was upset—when someone failed to properly give or take support—conflict often followed.

Home, Conflict, and Instability

For many of the girls, family life was shaped by the jobs their parents worked, jobs that often involved unconventional hours. Stephanie's mom worked the graveyard shift at a sportswear factory. Zora's dad rose at 2:30 a.m. to get his cab on the road. Florence and Faith's mother worked evenings at a candy factory sixteen miles away. "When I . . . come home from school," Faith explained, "she's already on her way to work." She usually returned "about midnight," once her daughters were asleep.

Researchers and policy makers suggest that involved parenting can protect young people growing up in poverty from the negative effects of "neighborhood disadvantage."[6] But the 1996 welfare reform act curbed the time many low-income parents had to spend with their children. With the stated aim of reducing welfare dependency, the bill mandated work requirements, forcing many parents to accept low-wage jobs outside the home. These jobs, which often entail unpredictable or unconventional hours, limit parents' free time after school and on weekends.[7]

Brittani wished for more quality time with her mom, with whom she, among the girls, was unusually close. "She only came to like, what, two of my games?" Brittani said. When her mom couldn't make her varsity volleyball matches, her friends, Brittani explained, "came and cheered me on." Aisha whooped and clapped from the bleachers, howling at the coach to take Brittani off the bench.

Along with cutting family time, mandates that parents work outside the home change family dynamics in other ways too. Older children, for example, often experience what researchers call "adultification": they are tasked with adult responsibilities, including caring for younger siblings.[8]

In NC, many girls looked after young relatives with deft skill and sometimes great joy. Florence, for instance, expertly handled her brother's baby son and daughter, changing diapers and wiping tears. Each morning, Joanne left home at 6:50 to take her little brothers to school, moving, she said, "at a lightning pace" to catch her own 7:10 bus to CRLS. After school, Joanne explained, "I took them to their recitals and their little school concerts . . . to doctors' appointments." Joanne adored her siblings, but the obligation was taxing. "I was a mom, I was a provider," she said. "I had to grow up really, really fast."

Friends empathized with each other's caretaking commitments. They also offered emotional support when other challenges came up at home.

Conflict

Florence and Faith lived with their parents. Both girls, Faith said, called their father "by his name, instead of 'father' or 'daddy.'" Faith added, "Me and my dad, we're not close." She was closer to their mother, a bond Florence did not share.

"We don't have conversations like, 'How was your day in school?'" Florence said of her mom. "I wouldn't mind talking to her about what's going on in my life, it just never happens."

Florence resented her parents' traditional expectations, including curfews and clothing rules never imposed on her brother.[9] When tension escalated into conflict, harsh words hurt Florence. Still, she tried to understand their perspective. "Haitian parents, it's not really their fault," she reasoned. "They say all this stuff, but they don't know psychology. They don't know sociology. They don't know how it affects kids."

Parenting under any circumstances is difficult. Yet the immense strain of raising children amid financial scarcity can tax family relationships. Studies find that neighborhood poverty negatively affects maternal warmth and leads to more punitive parenting.[10] Although some research suggests that strict parenting can protect young people in poor neighborhoods, harsh discipline can also hamper children's development.[11]

Girls vented about conflict at home to their friends, both in person and online. Seeta, who often felt misunderstood by her parents, sometimes tweeted cathartically after arguments, knowing her friends would see what she shared. One evening, for instance, she tweeted:

> Despite all the change.. This is why me and my dad will never be cool.. Ever.
> My kids will never deal with this.
> My mind is scarred. for life..[12]

Simply expressing hurt could be a relief.[13] But friends also offered support by interacting, like when Faith replied to Seeta's tweets about a different fight:

SEETA: *I hate going to my parents for comfort when I'm upset or physically hurt. They yell at me for being upset or hurt. WTF?*
FAITH: *@Seeta Your Okay Girl?!!*
SEETA: *@Faith Im trying to be.*
FAITH: *@Seeta Damn Well I Hope You Feel Better*
SEETA: *@Faith thank you .. You didn't see or hear nothing right!?*
FAITH: *@Seeta Noo Just Based Off Your Tweets Lol*
SEETA: *@Faith THANK GOD. shit is always so embarrassing*

Faith comforted Seeta, who in turn consistently replied to her friends' mentions of family tension. When Joanne tweeted, *I don't depend on you because you're always an unreliable parent to me,* Seeta replied, *@Joanne we come from the STRUGGLE.* Joanne answered, *@Seeta Ain't that the truth!*

Since adults were rarely on Twitter, such tweets were aimed only at peers. Friends either responded directly or reached out with a private message or call.

For Aisha, care from friends felt transformative. Growing up, she had felt like the "bad child" that her mother said she was. But friendships changed how she saw herself.

"You attract what you are," Aisha reflected. "I attracted Joanne, and Joanne's not a bad person. I attracted Brittani, and Brittani's not a bad person." Aisha's friends made her feel worthy.

Instability

In NC, Aisha lived with her mother and the younger of her two older brothers. But back in Uganda, she had loved the bustle of her big extended family. Aisha had especially looked up to her Aunt Grace, often seeking her out after school instead of playing with her brothers.

Eventually, however, Grace moved out. She went, Aisha recalled, to live with a sister who was sick and needed care. The sister died not long after, from a disease people whispered about, a disease Grace contracted too after being raped by her late sister's husband. Four years later, Aisha explained, Grace died of AIDS.

Devastated, Aisha prayed for God to bring Grace back.

"I know you resurrect," Aisha remembered pleading, hands clasped.

The grief sullied her faith. "That girl served," Aisha said. "Every part of her was God. For her to die like that, to go through what she went through . . . I was like, 'There's no God who'd do anything like that.'"

The grief also, over the long term, shaped how Aisha formed relationships. After school one day, Aisha sat cross-legged on the desk chair in the corner of her living room and said, "Just now, my friend was telling me, 'You literally cut off anyone, without thinking twice.' But that's just me. I just know everyone's gonna leave."

"What do you mean?" I asked.

"I feel like the reason why I am how I am, why I don't get emotionally attached, is because when my aunt died, she was the one I really cared about, I really loved," she said.

But Aisha's best friends had earned her trust. For years, they had come through and helped out, and she knew she could count on them. "Obviously I really cherish Joanne, Seeta, and Brittani," Aisha continued, "'cause they've actually been there and shown me. But *bye!* anyone else!"

Aisha relied on her best friends, and they relied on her. But beyond that inner circle, Aisha was unattached, and proud. "I am the best at cutting people out," she said.

Other girls echoed this narrative, bragging, online and in person, about their power to "drop" all but a few close friends.[14] Many attributed this independence to people who were unreliable or who had left or died.[15] Feeling agitated one afternoon, Joanne tweeted:

> I can count on one hand the number of people who I trust
> You can only get slapped in the face so many times before
>   #LessonLearned

Joanne's tweets referenced and reinforced a discourse of distrust, as did Seeta's retweet of a post that read, *I push people away: Mainly because I'm scared I'm going to get hurt . . . and most importantly because I know their going to leave sooner or later anyway.*

The girls' best friends, however, were exempt from cynicism. Failing to acknowledge this could get girls called out, like when Zora challenged Rosie on Twitter:

ROSIE: *Can't ever count on anyone or anything*
ZORA: *Ummm excuse me!?!?*
ROSIE: *@Zora lol whatttt?*
ZORA: *@Rosie I took some offense to that one baby girl.*
ROSIE: *@Zora my bad girl . . . All love <3 <3*

Zora's tweets also reaffirmed her reliability.

The girls bore witness to one another's lives. They shared with each other their problems, hopes, and fears. Their mutual vulnerability fostered a sturdy intimacy that proved mostly stable when families felt chaotic, or worse.

Stigma and Surveillance

CRLS had a racially diverse student body: 38 percent were white, 32 percent were Black or African American, and 30 percent identified as members of other racial or ethnic minority groups.[16] The school, whose motto was, "Opportunity, Diversity, Respect," was committed, outwardly, to ideals of inclusion. Yet the girls perceived a gap between these stated goals and their own daily experiences.[17]

One morning in CHANGE, the student leading check-in told each member of the class to summarize their past week using one word.

"My week was fail," sighed a white senior with brown hair. Classmates giggled.

"Wait, did you say *jail?*" another white student called out. Giggles became throaty laughs at the suggestion.

Amid the gasping and thigh-slapping, Deja, a quiet African American senior who lived in NC, turned to the girl on her right.

"I went to a jail," Deja mumbled, hands in the lap of her gray flannel sweatpants. Because of hyperpolicing and the mass incarceration of people of color in low-income neighborhoods, Deja—like many Black teens—knew people affected by the criminal legal system.

"Was it scary?" replied Ariana, a Latinx senior with kohl-lined brown eyes.

"It was," Deja nodded. "Mad scary."

Ariana waited.

"He was hurting himself," Deja said quietly.

As the room's laughter tapered off, the two girls hushed. "I gotta go visit my brother," Ariana said, before the pair looked up for the next student's word. Rather than being welcomed or shared in the main class discussion, the girls' experiences were marginalized.

Along with racialized othering by peers, girls protested the insensitivity of certain teachers, even those they saw as well intentioned. Aisha, for instance, explained how a white teacher's overtures only exacerbated the discomfort she already felt as the only Black student in her AP US history class.

"He was always singling me out," Aisha explained. "It was for all these opportunities. You know, good things. But it still made me mad, 'cause I did not want all that extra attention." Aisha resented the disparate treatment based on her Blackness.

Girls also observed racism in school discipline practices, dress code enforcement, and academic tracking.[18] "They always say you can do whatever you want," Joanne said, of CRLS. "But when it comes to academic things, there's a clear divide in terms of who's taking what classes, and how many kids of color are in the technical school programs. It's really noticeable. . . . In the [advanced] classes it's no Black people. They would all be put in the chorus class. So, it's like, 'Oh, I can only sing?'"

Joanne knew the harm of low expectations. She shared some of her experiences with me one afternoon, after we discussed George Zimmerman's acquittal for the murder of Trayvon Martin.

"I have two negatives against me," Joanne said. "I'm Black and I'm female. . . . People are surprised when I'm intelligent. Culturally, there's just so much associated with being a woman. They don't expect much from you in the first place, and then on top of that, being Black. They don't expect too much from you."

Still, Joanne reflected, "I'm not a person that needs to be pushed that much." But she worried about others: "When you see people who don't have anyone to push them, and they let themselves get dragged into the system that's not working for them, it's really sad."

Joanne never forgot her middle school science teacher, who had told her mostly Black class, "You're just gonna be bums on the street." She wished the teacher had tried to understand her peers: "He had no patience for students who were obviously lashing out in anger because they weren't being treated fairly. He would just go off on them."

Joanne wanted students built up, not torn down. She understood personally what research has shown: low confidence can limit young people's academic success.[19] "How can you motivate yourself without confidence?" she said. "If you don't have confidence, you're not gonna raise your hand because you think you're dumb."

To support young people, Joanne dreamed of founding a non-profit. Her organization, she said, would use "creative means to get students reengaged in school." She had a clear plan to get there. First, she would study psychology in college—maybe child psychology, given all she had learned raising her siblings. Then she would enroll in graduate school; Columbia topped her list. Joanne was determined to encourage other teens, especially those who, she felt, had been undermined or excluded at school.

Outside of school, Joanne and her friends faced further exclusion, including stereotyping and surveillance in public places like stores.[20] One evening, as Vincent drove us to the movie theater, Joanne described a visit to CVS earlier that day.

"The second we walked in, this [employee] literally started following us," Joanne told her brother and me. "Seeta needed tampons. There was a camera right there anyway. Like, we're not stealing tampons!"

"It *is* a recession!" Vincent joked.

"No," Joanne said, firm. "That's so stereotyping. That's like racial profiling. It was wrong." She thought for a moment, then went on: "It would be one thing if we looked like the hobos outside. We looked very nice, mind you. All sophisticated. Not wearing sweatpants or anything."[21]

"What did y'all say?" Vincent asked.

"Nothing! He's following us around, pretending to be fixing up the tampons right next to us. He's like, 'Do you need some assistance?'"

"You should have been like, 'Yes, which type is best?'" Vincent said, chuckling. Joanne did not laugh.

Young people know how they are perceived.[22] For the NC girls, racist and classist stereotypes clashed with how they saw themselves: as striving, successful young women. Such disparities are harmful. When our self-beliefs are affirmed by others, we experience positive feelings like pride; but when they are undermined, we experience anger, shame, and guilt.[23] Moreover, stereotyping and microaggressions do not only cause negative emotions. They can also damage physical and mental health.[24] And they can affect long-term trajectories if teens internalize degrading messages or seek to fix wounded pride by lashing out.[25]

The NC girls together processed stigma and marginalization. To do so, they often drew on their common experiences, which adults did not always share. For instance, when Joanne's migraines began, her doctor prescribed breathing exercises and wrote a therapy referral. Joanne liked her therapist, a white woman; none of her friends had access to such formal emotional support, and Joanne was grateful. But she found that she could not always speak plainly, especially about race and racism.

"I walk around here," Joanne told me, at a picnic table in the project, "and see a bunch of people who look like me. But I go outta here, I don't see Black people. But you can't really say much, even to my therapist. She's white, and she was like, 'I don't want you to feel you can't say things to me about race.' But it's like, I don't want to offend with my thought process. . . . Like, some people hate white people. I don't even hate white people, I just wish they would understand."

Joanne sometimes censored herself around her therapist, sensing what sociologists call "feeling rules": tacit norms that limit what people can comfortably express in a given situation.[26] Feeling rules, when they stifle people's actual feelings, can exacerbate painful emotions.[27]

With her friends, by contrast, Joanne could be candid. The girls shared their feelings, including those—like anger and resentment—they could not always air elsewhere. One day, Aisha posted on Facebook about an experience at a subway station. She wrote: *Today when I was going to meet my friends I got racially profiled at the train station . . . I watched the train guy help a lighter skinned man get on the train because he was missing a few cents.. When I approached with a similar reason telling him I had a wrinkly $20 dollar bill that the machine couldn't take and that I was missing a dollar he told me to walk across the city to go to cvs and get change. . . I just had to share with y'all.. #fergusoneverywhere.* Dozens of friends read Aisha's story, and, with their 'like' button, fifty-six people offered something like support.[28]

Sometimes the girls used humor, which can help release feelings of powerlessness provoked by marginalization.[29] One day, after riding the subway, Joanne tweeted, *so this old lady was scared to sit next to me -_- I only jump old ladies Monday-Friday hun. The weekends are my days off.*

The girls also joked together, transforming their shared "outsiderness" into a basis for intimacy. Once, in Seeta's bedroom, Aisha and her clique poked fun at their immigrant parents' faux pas. Aisha began with a skit: an aunt volubly praying in Chuck-E-Cheese. Her friends cackled at her performance.

Then Joanne jumped in: "My mom can never put stuff in the cart in Market Basket. She gotta weigh everything. She finds all the Haitian people by the bell peppers, like, 'Eh eh eh!'"

The girls thrashed and rolled on the mattress. Brittani, whose mother was born and raised in Cambridge, joined in too: she mimed her mom blocking the Market Basket aisle with her cart. The girls laughed and laughed.

When the giggles ebbed, they lounged on Seeta's bed and sighed.

Along with empathy and humor, the girls resisted stigmatization by relentlessly affirming each other. In person and online, they communicated love and care almost daily. Posts could be brief, like when Seeta tweeted, *I have never ever had any friends like @Aisha @Joanne they are the realest friends anyone could have!!!!.* Or they could be lavish. One morning, scrolling through her apps, Seeta saw a photo of herself stirring a pot on a burner. Aisha had posted the image with the caption: *This is my friend @Seeta cooking for me !! This is what you call a real friendship . . . This girl has done the most for me !! She cares so much, it's honestly not ok. She's paid for my phone bill and that's not even half of it. I knew her since 8ᵗʰ grade . . . I've cried in front of her!! When I need someone she's literally the first one to leap!! I cannot say or do anything that can truly explain how grateful I am of her AND I JUST WANT TO SAY I LOVE YOU and THANK YOU for being a #friend !! A true mother fucking friend !!!*

Seeta screenshotted Aisha's post, and uploaded it to Twitter, with the caption: *What I woke up to this morning >>>>>>>>>>>>.*

Even if these kinds of posts were—as some social media critics claim—a little performative, girls liked being their focus and basked in their friends' care.

The sociologist Patricia Hill Collins describes the transformative potential of care between women marginalized by racism. "If members of the group on the bottom love one another and affirm one another's worth," she writes, "then the entire system that assigns that group to the bottom becomes suspect."[30] When the girls built each other up, they challenged everyone who put them down.

Emotional Needs and Social Breakdown

Together the girls spun an emotional safety net. Yet this could fray at times beneath their weight of need. Conflict in this realm had two main sources: *nonreciprocity*—a gap between help taken and given—and *nonrecognition*—a perceived lack of understanding of other people's struggles.

Many social relationships hinge on reciprocity. In NC, the expectation to come through for friends was perhaps clearest on social media, where teens followed hundreds of peers. A follow meant respect and validation; unfollowing implied the opposite.

At basketball practice after school one day, Aisha and I sat on the asphalt during halftime. Aisha massaged her calves and chatted to Damien, a classmate warming up for the guys' game on the next court. Their friend, Dani, jogged over, light with the lift of news to break. Dani had a story: another girl, Lakeisha, had unfollowed her on Twitter.

"I was like, 'Hello, bitch!'" Dani said.

Aisha grunted sympathetically.

Damien shook his head. "But she'll fuck *you* up for unfollowing her!" he said. "That's ratchet!"

"Yeah!" Dani said. "She has that thing where it says who unfollowed you on Twitter. I didn't unfollow her 'cause I was scared. She'll tweet at you like, 'Why did you unfollow me, bitch?' I seen her do it to people before!"

Digital nonreciprocity weakened the audience on which teens relied for fun and support. When Aisha asked her friends, "Did you like my status?" she was concerned not only with her tally of likes but also with her access to care.

Other forms of nonreciprocity also caused friction.

Support between friends, most girls agreed, should be mutual, constant, and unremarked on.

"Everyone does something for everyone," Aisha explained, "but it won't be for credit. If I'm your friend, you shouldn't be keeping tabs." When someone sought something—even praise—in exchange for this kind of care, others bristled.

When, for instance, Joanne went through a difficult few months, some of the girls in her clique found themselves arguing with each other. In particular, Aisha was unimpressed by Seeta's repeated references to how they had helped Joanne.

"Seeta brings it up every day!" Aisha protested to me. Seeta, she thought, was acting transactionally rather than reciprocally.[31]

But around the same time, Seeta was also struggling.

Aisha empathized to an extent. "Seeta's a kid herself, but she spends her entire life trying to raise her sister's kid," Aisha told me. "Her sister bullies her into doing it so she can go roll up."

Yet Aisha grew irritated when Seeta struggled not only to give support but also to accept it. Rejecting care was another type of nonreciprocity, one that robbed girls of the self-esteem they got to feel as loving, loyal friends.

"I guess we're not of a purpose," Aisha said, bitter, as Seeta withdrew.

To try and reset the emotional balance, Aisha and Joanne met up with Seeta.[32]

"It's not fair that you think we're not your number one support system, because we are," Joanne told Seeta.

Seeta started crying, and Aisha and Joanne moved to comfort her.

But Seeta exclaimed, "You don't understand!"

Suddenly, Aisha was angry.

The NC girls, who often found themselves put down and shut out, relied on their friends for recognition—to feel seen, valued, and understood. Nonrecognition, just like nonreciprocity, also caused conflict. This could involve a simple unmet wave,[33] or the more profound refusal to acknowledge others' suffering. Hearing the words, *you don't understand,* Aisha felt that Seeta viewed her own troubles as worse than her friends'.

"Oh, okay!" Aisha told me later, sarcasm thick. "I guess we've never gone through that! You can't tell me that for me and Joanne it's been an easy ride. . . . Maybe we're dying too! Don't make it seem like our lives are perfect. We're all broken."

Aisha wanted to help her friend but needed her difficulties recognized too.

·   •   ·

In their senior year, Joanne and Aisha joined a school poetry team and signed up for a citywide slam. For weeks they practiced individual pieces along with a group poem they had written together in Google Docs.

When the May Saturday arrived, Joanne's stepfather, Ralph, drove us partway to the Boston venue. Joanne rode up front with Ralph, and as we cruised down Rindge Avenue, she scrolled through the poems on her phone. She silently read through each one, her hoop earrings and newly done hair bobbing along. Then she turned to Aisha and me in the backseat.

"If we get through to the semifinals, we'll have to go back tomorrow!" she said excitedly.

"What is it, a beauty contest?" asked Ralph, gazing at the road.

Joanne was not close to Ralph, who spent evenings watching TV behind his closed bedroom door, leaving Joanne to entertain his kids through their mom's shifts at the hospital.

"What? Beauty? No. It's a poetry contest," Joanne said, scowling slightly.

"Oh. Poetry," he muttered.

At the slam, the girls and their teammates pulled on specially printed T-shirts passed out by the organizers. Then they chose seats, stuffed their backpacks under their chairs, and waited for their turn on stage.

"I can't wait to Instagram all this," Aisha said, peering around, phone in hand. Posters of black question marks hung on white walls.

Up front, poets performed at a row of microphones. The girls clapped eagerly for each team.

When their turn came, Aisha and Joanne walked to the stage with their teammates, hand in hand.

After everyone had performed, the girls fidgeted in their seats awaiting the results. Ultimately, although the judges praised their presence and lyricism, they didn't make the semifinals. But there was no time to dwell. Aisha and Joanne dashed straight to the bathroom, holding their bags. Prom was in an hour.

"Those poems were intense," Joanne said beside the sinks, as I zipped up her dress, a strapless aquamarine gown that cinched at her waist and pooled glamorously around her feet.

"That's because everyone's been abused or something like that," Aisha said.

"Yeah," said Joanne.

Aisha dug through her makeup bag. Joanne watched Aisha draw on eyeliner, then studied her own reflection. Joanne didn't know much about makeup. But today was special.

"Can you do eyeshadow for me?" Joanne asked Aisha.

Aisha gently held her best friend's jaw as she daubed. Then she went to change in a toilet cubicle, returning in a floor-length, blue and gold dress her aunt had made. Sequins glinted along the asymmetric neckline. Aisha tried to pin the strap in place like she had practiced earlier, but the pin kept warping against the thick cloth. Aisha flustered. They were running out of time.

"Oh well, I guess I can't wear it!" Aisha snapped.

"Of course, you're gonna wear it!" Joanne replied, in the calm, firm voice she used with her siblings. "You didn't get this bomb-ass dress to not wear it!"

Aisha sighed and passed Joanne the sewing kit. She took small sips of breath as Joanne stitched.

"All good," Joanne said gently.

The girls stood side by side in the front of the mirror. Ready to go, they looked at themselves, beaming.

Dignity under Threat

Emotions lie at the heart of social life. They drive love, work, war, and more.[34] Positive feelings, like dignity and validation, are basic human needs[35]—needs that teenagers, in particular, fervently seek. Yet white supremacy and unfettered capitalism deny many low-income young people of color access to these key components of well-being.[36]

Emotional injuries can cause long-term harm. Some teens internalize negative messages about their value and potential, and curb their own ambitions to defend against feelings of failure.[37] Other studies show young people—usually young men[38]—using force to repair damaged pride.[39] Among young adults working in East Harlem's crack trade, for instance, the anthropologist Phillipe Bourgois found a "street culture of resistance," one that emerged from "a personal search for dignity and a rejection of racism and subjugation" but that ultimately came to trap participants in "lifestyles of violence, substance abuse, and internalized rage."[40]

Many studies about young people's responses to stigma and marginality have shortcomings, however. Researchers who describe youth "subcultures" or "adaptations" to poverty often assume a notion of "mainstream" society from which these teens supposedly deviate. But this image of "mainstream" America—invariably white and middle class—is a myth, not an empirical reality, and can further propagate tropes about race and poverty.[41]

Still, researchers are right to stress the emotional costs of marginality, costs rarely centered in discussions about inequality. Although poverty is an economic relationship, material and emotional well-being are deeply entwined.[42] Growing up in a poor neighborhood often entails financial deprivation. But it can also entail feeling put down, kept out, and undermined. Stiffening before suspicious store clerks or being demeaned at school could, for the NC girls, feel as grim as an empty fridge.

When the girls shored up their friends' emotional welfare—when they empathized with family conflict, proved dependable, resisted stigmatization, and insisted on one another's value—they offered care no less vital than cash. Empathy, advice, sanctuary, and affirmation were among the deepest needs friends could meet.

4 *Bodies, Boyfriends, and Sex*

As children, the girls had kept pace with their brothers, running around outside. But as they became young women, thin limbs slowed and softened; hips took on heft.

Maturity meant new opportunities, relationships, and desires. It also meant new challenges. These included beauty norms that undermined the girls' confidence; romantic partnerships that were confusing, hurtful, or burdensome; and sexual expectations that exposed them to stigma or harm.

The NC girls were skilled problem solvers. But friends' power was often more limited in the realms of dating and sexuality than in others.

Bodies: Self-Esteem and Insecurity

Some of the girls welcomed physical changes. The baby of the group, Rosie, whose nickname was "Yung Twig," felt triumphant as her body finally filled out. One night, Zora took photos of Rosie, who had switched her usual jeans and North Face hoodie for a short black dress. Rosie swiped, smiling, through the images.

"I am feeling myself!" Rosie said. "I look hella thick!"

Most of her friends, however, felt less sure of themselves.

The girls spent hours each day on image-centered social media apps. They uploaded photos of snacks they saw as healthy—like granola bars and tea-based soft drinks—with captions like *#summerbody* or *#antioxidants*. They posted when they went for a run or worked out at home, like when Seeta tweeted, *Just did 50 sit-ups.* Online, they also scrutinized celebrities, Instagram stars, and "Video Vixens," often comparing their own bodies unfavorably.

Along with the insecurity prompted by social media, many of the girls heard disparaging comments from family members.

"My mom tells me I'm ugly every two seconds," Aisha once said, seemingly placid. While Aisha had learned to handle these barbs, other girls were more ambivalent in the face of messages about their bodies.

"My aunt is telling me I have to lose weight," Florence told me. "I dunno. You know, I love my curves. I really do." Still, she sometimes wound Saran Wrap around her stomach and took long walks on hot days to try to sweat off some pounds.

Joanne disliked comments about her figure, even those she knew were intended kindly. One Sunday, as we walked through the project's parking lot, Joanne ran into a former neighbor.

"You're so beautiful, look at you!" the neighbor said, drawing Joanne into a hug. She grasped Joanne by the shoulders and stepped back, scanning her petite, voluptuous frame. "Look how thick you got!" exclaimed the neighbor.

"Thank you," Joanne said gingerly.

After we walked away, Joanne explained that while she knew the neighbor meant well, her words still stung.

"It's like saying, 'Oh you've put on so much weight,'" she said. "I'm like, 'Well I haven't seen you for ten years, so . . .'"

Joanne had long wrestled with body image, worrying she was curvier than her friends. "I just don't look like everyone else," she said. And dating didn't help: "Boys want the big girls in secret and the skinny ones in public."

Joanne's friends tried to reassure her, insisting, as she told me, "You're just like everyone else!" Still Joanne faced a discomfort many of the girls knew: the sense that their appearance was not good enough.

Many of the NC girls and their friends resented the racist and colorist beauty norms that prized their white and willowy schoolmates.[1] In CHANGE one morning, Yanelis, a Latinx senior with light brown skin, showed me on a class computer the images returned by a Google search for "beauty." Headshots of white women, mostly blonde, covered the screen. Only on page 5 of the search results did she see a Black woman. In response, Yanelis wanted to run a workshop at school to help broaden notions of beauty.

Yet while the girls critiqued racist beauty ideals intellectually, the norms remained hurtful. Aisha shared her feelings one afternoon in her living room. "I know how it feels to feel like you're not pretty enough," she told me, her voice thick with emotion. "I've been Black my whole entire life. I've been Black, dark-skinned, and you literally have to learn to love yourself over and over again."

bell hooks considers "standards of beauty as enactments of trauma" for women of color.[2] But researchers, hooks notes, long ignored "the issue of self-esteem and the prolonged psychological trauma inflicted by shaming about skin color and the body." Instead, many male scholars studied issues they saw as "hard," like employment discrimination and criminalization.[3] But, much like discrimination, "holding oneself in perpetually low esteem is a structurally induced condition," explains Brittney Cooper, professor of women's and gender studies and Africana studies.[4] And perpetually low self-esteem can be agonizing. It can also take a long-term toll, leaving girls at higher risk of harms ranging from eating disorders to partnering with abusive men.[5]

In this context, the girls affirmed one another's beauty. They praised each other's looks and clothes. They were tactile, often hugging and appreciatively running hands over arms, backs, and hair. They also bolstered one another online. Although social media could certainly make girls doubt themselves, apps offered validation too. When Ariana posted, *I hate that I have a nice body but an ugly face,* her girlfriends quickly replied with comments like, *your face is so beautiful!* and *WHO LIED AND TOLD U U HAVE AN UGLY FACE??? BECAUSE I SEE A BEAUTIFUL BODY AND A GORGEOUS FACE!!!*

These affirmations added to the small lifts of self-esteem the girls gave their friends by consistently liking and commenting on each other's photos.[6]

Boyfriends: Hurt, Burden, and Danger

In high school a few of the girls started dating. Relationships with young men—none of the girls discussed or openly acted on romantic interest in women or people of different genders[7]—could provide independence, pleasure, comfort, and security.

But dating was not always straightforward. Relationships could be confusing or painful. They could also expose girls to burdensome care work and even, occasionally, danger. Moreover, friends often had little power to solve these problems.

Mediated Intimacy

Social media shaped the girls' romantic experiences at every stage.[8] Many relationships began when teens liked or commented on someone's photos. This act planted seeds of interest that, nurtured through more private conversations by text or direct message, could bloom into intimacy.

But online communication was often more ambiguous than face-to-face interaction. This ambiguity sometimes perplexed girls trying to transition from "talking to" a boy to being "his girl." A boy's delayed response to a message might signify disinterest. But he might also just be busy. Moreover, certain online gestures could be either romantic or platonic, raising endless questions: Why *didn't he like my profile picture? Why does that girl comment on all his photos?*

Yet the NC girls also deployed ambiguity, especially in the form of the "sub." Short for "subliminal," a sub aimed to send a specific message without directly addressing its recipient.[9] Joanne, for instance, once let a boy know she was annoyed at his slow response by posting as her Facebook status, *That little thing on FB that tells you someone has seen your message. Mmhmm* . . . Subs' plausible deniability limited teens' exposure. Still, online ambiguity could make dating confusing, especially at the start.

Once relationships formed, the role of social media morphed. Online behavior could test trust, and "creeping" could uncover betrayals.

Faith, unlike her sister, Florence, had no interest in boys through most of high school. Faith was staid and self-contained, and she knew what she liked: TV and Twitter, preferably in comfy clothes with good snacks on hand. Faith didn't consider herself fancy or know how to flirt, but when a friend she knew in childhood, Micky, swung back through NC, she felt flattered when he put moves on her.[10] When Micky asked Faith to be his girlfriend, she said no. But then he asked again, and again, and eventually she was wooed. After a while, Faith agreed to take things further; having known Micky for so long, he seemed like the right guy for her first time.

Throughout their relationship, Faith and Micky never became Facebook friends. But she did follow him on Instagram, where she saw a photo of him looking fine in formalwear. The picture, he told her, was from his cousin's wedding.

In class days later, Faith received a call from Rosie. Faith couldn't answer. Rosie called again, then texted, *"You need to see this!"*

Rosie had added Micky on Facebook and found him tagged in a wedding photo. Faith had already seen the picture of Mickey in his suit. But Rosie had clicked through to the profiles of other people tagged and found more photos. One showed Micky in a car with the bride. Suspicious, Rosie looked for the bride's Instagram page and uncovered a shocking picture: Micky crouching by her swollen stomach, lips pressed to the bump.

Confronting Micky with Rosie's discovery, Faith felt not only betrayed by his deception but also humiliated by its online traces. "You put all our business out there!" she said, before she dumped him.

After breakups like Faith's, social media could make it hard to move on. One night, Seeta sat with Joanne and me shortly after ending things with her boyfriend, Malachi. Seeta thumbed her screen, pouting. Joanne knew what that face meant.

"Stop twatching him!" Joanne told her friend.

"I can't stop," Seeta said, scrolling through Malachi's tweets.

"Well, don't comment," Joanne offered.

"I'm not commenting. I'm just watching," Seeta insisted.

"But it's making you sad."

Joanne wanted to limit Seeta's contact with Malachi but couldn't divert the stream of online information. The girls' near-constant social media use made avoiding someone almost impossible.[11]

Love and Heartbreak

Romance meant a lot to Florence. Growing up feeling distant from her mother, she had first sought warmth from older women. Back in Haiti, she'd called an aunt "Mom." After moving to NC, Florence bonded with her mother's close friend, a woman, she said, who "called me her daughter, and I called her my mom." Later Florence explained, "I was cool with Zora's mom, and Vincent's mom. You can see the pattern."

As a teen, Florence found approval and comfort from boys.

Vincent, Joanne's older brother, was the first.[12] Florence was in eighth grade and Vincent was a high school junior when they became a couple. They broke up a few months later, but it was not a clean split. Lingering feelings made it hard to keep apart; even after ending their relationship, Florence recalled, they were "still messing around."

One day after school, Vincent's friend Bryan approached Florence. Bryan, Rosie's oldest brother, was a few years older, and Florence had always looked up to him.

"You suck dick," Bryan chided.

"What are you talking about?" Florence said.

"The street talks," he smirked.

Seething and humiliated, Florence swore she was done with Vincent. But before too long, the couple reunited. Then they broke up again.

Years later, as Florence finished high school, she still struggled to move on. She cared deeply for Vincent. And although their on-off relationship had cost Florence her friendship with Joanne, Vincent's sister, she was still close to his mom and grandma. Vincent's grandma still said she thought Florence would bear her first great-grandchild.

Besides, Vincent could be thoughtful, sharing his hookah or giving Florence rides. Other times, though, Florence found him seedy, like when she told him, "I have a sore throat," and he replied, all innuendo, "You know what cures it?"

Florence wrote poetry to clear her head, words that throbbed with heat. Each time they reunited, Florence thought things might be different. But they never were.

Concerned about Florence, Zora at one point tried a bribe. If, Zora offered, Florence kept away from Vincent for a whole summer, she would buy her some new Uggs. Florence eagerly accepted the terms. In the end, however, she did not make good.

With her love and passion still unchanneled, Florence turned next to Robenson, another NC boy in Vincent's group of friends. Right away Florence felt comfortable with Robenson, even confiding in him that Vincent had once given her chlamydia. She was embarrassed, but Robenson reassured her, "Vincent would sleep with anything."

Florence thought Robenson was "a man." He knew her curfew. He drove her home, even watching from his car to see her through the door. When their relationship turned physical, Robenson treated them to a hotel room for the night. "He paid more to get executive," Florence gushed. "He's not cheap. Whenever he has money, he'll spend it on me. It was so fun. We got Henny [Hennessy]. I gave him a massage. I gave him a manicure."

Yet as Florence became invested, Robenson worried about Vincent's reaction to their relationship. He asked her to keep things on the "DL." But Florence didn't want to hide. "I was like, 'Oh now you're interested in your friendship?'" Things soon ended.

Florence felt dejected. To make things worse, Vincent was chasing a new girl, Abigail, who had olive skin and long, brown hair. "Black guys," Florence said, "always want white girls or Hispanic girls 'cause of the hair and the fashion. . . . She's nasty." "There's nothing to be jealous of," she scoffed.

Florence subbed her ex and his new girl. She posted a Snapchat selfie wearing a purple shirt whose neckline plunged beneath the bottom of the shot. In the image, she pushed the rim of a green beer bottle into her tongue, which poked through parted lips. Her caption was a Beyoncé lyric: *Lol I'm fresher then U! I kno u care.*

But Florence was more hurt than she let on. And she certainly did not think Vincent would bring Abigail to Thanksgiving. Each year, Vincent and Joanne's mom, Carole, threw one of the biggest Thanksgiving parties in NC. And each year, even after breaking up with Vincent, Florence stopped by out of politeness to Carole and the family.

That Thanksgiving afternoon, Vincent and Joanne's apartment filled. The kitchen table, draped with a maroon paper tablecloth, held large foil platters. Fried collard greens, rice and beans, mac and cheese, stuffing, candied yams, potato salad, and mashed potatoes crowded the bird at the center. The turkey, garnished with celery and parsley Joanne and I had chopped that morning, sat between two bottles of low-alcohol wine drinks.

After Carole's toast—"Thanksgiving is a time to love," she said, while guests raised their cell phones to take photos—Joanne fed the kids, heaping portions onto red paper plates. Adults served themselves before finding a wall or surface to lean against.

Suddenly the front door banged open. Florence strode in, wearing a long black skirt and white tank. She was trailed by Faith, Zora, Stephanie, and Rosie. Heads turned to the girls, who arrived tipsy and a little rowdy.

The previous year, Florence had come alone. She had stayed until Zora, at her own house, had called to let Florence know about tweets posted from the party:

SEETA: *When people I don't like show up some place I'm having fun* <<
  shrugs
JOANNE: *'Nougghhh said*
SEETA: *lol this bitch* <<<

Alerted to the subs shared about her, Florence, hurt, had promptly left.

This year, hoping to avoid a repeat embarrassment, Florence brought along her whole clique. As the girls hugged and greeted friends and neighbors, Vincent stole a glance at his ex.

Moments later the front door opened again. A pale young woman with product-drenched brown curls walked in. Her sequined white pantsuit glittered in the lamplight.

"Oh shit," Zora said, leaning to me. "That's Abigail."

To make her way to Vincent, Abigail had to slide past Florence and her friends in the entryway. The girls did not reset their sneers.

Florence, displeased, marched into the icy night. She shot some Ciroc and came back steeled. As her friends filled plates in the kitchen, Florence dragged Stephanie into the living room, where they started dancing together to the music.

A crowd gradually formed around them. "Go, go!" guests goaded.

After a couple of songs, Stephanie left for a glass of water. Florence, swept up by the music and the Ciroc, danced alone, running her hands over her body. Sexually explicit lyrics boomed through the dim room as Florence dropped to all fours, her hips vigorously pumping and outpacing the song's beat.

When Stephanie returned from the kitchen with the other girls, they saw Florence straddling an older man on a chair and grinding into his lap. Zora took a step toward her friend, but Joanne and Vincent's mother, Carole, who had barged through the crowd, beat her to it. Carole glowered behind Florence. Amused anticipation rippled through the spectators. Zora was powerless now.

Perhaps perceiving the stares or the quiet, Florence turned and saw Carole, fuming. Florence clambered sheepishly off the man. Then she laughed; there was nothing else to do. This was not the evening she had hoped for. Mad and sad that Vincent still got to her, Florence let her friends take her home.

Friends could not overcome romance's power. Nor could they stop relationships from ending or shield each other from humiliation. They could only pick up the pieces.

Joanne described how to act when a friend's ex got a new girl: "You have to be like, 'She *ugggly.*' Even though she be like a supermodel coming down the runway! You gotta be like, 'She ain't all that!'" Friends helped in any small ways they could.

Boyfriends and Burdens

Breakups were often painful, but even stable, committed relationships could tax the girls. Joanne, for instance, worked tirelessly for her loved ones. Along with caring for her four young siblings and any visiting cousins, Joanne looked after her boyfriend, Rico.

"Rico's been through a lot," Aisha explained to me. "Adoption and foster homes. Joanne really supports him. She's the reason he's not out there shooting people or killing people. She can't break up with him."

Aisha saw how Joanne helped Rico, who was a little older than the girls. But, over time, Aisha also saw her best friend become drained.

Joanne, as she often did, wrote a poem to process her feelings.

He wants a girl who can keep quiet
Intellect will not be in her dialect
'Cause if she tries to utter sophistication
she suddenly is suspect

His bullshit reeks of late nights
On the back porch
trying to catch glimpses
of Daddy as he walks through the front door
He's never walked through the front door

So now he's hollowed out
hollowing you out
so he can find space to hide
in the burrows of your skin

He's never lain his head on a woman's chest
'Cause his Mama's head was always bent
Her sorrow taking up all the space where
He should have learned what it means
To forget your demons
Just breathe in her healing.

You love him, but you're not the hero in his tragedy
Your supporting role
Is code name for his bottom bitch
Stitch your hands together behind
Your back everytime you want to touch him
He's not your responsibility

He won't be the answer to lonely nights that want you to hold on to your
  virginity
Broken beings are a danger to your innocence because there is always a
  consequence

When he rolls away from you at night instead of holding your hand
And loneliness becomes lonelier than ever
You wanna fix him and make him better
But will never make the little boy who's still waiting for Daddy to show
  up and waiting for Mama to sober up
Realize how much you wanna be his wife to cherish and hold
Till death do you part
But you need to live before you die
And your interactions were simply meant as a quick greeting before
  goodbye.[13]

In Joanne's senior year, Rico moved away from NC. Joanne, left behind, felt low on his list of priorities. After a while, to everyone's surprise, Joanne ended the relationship.

"It was too much work," she explained. "Even when he was here [visiting], he'd hang with his boys. It was causing me a migraine."

But Rico's influence lingered. When another guy, Andrew, tried to "bag" Joanne, she felt surveilled by the NC boys.[14]

"It's hard living around here," Joanne said. "Everybody knew me as his girl. The other day, I'm talking to Andrew, and a couple of Rico's friends were just staring at me."

The boys had called out to Joanne, "Mrs. Garcia," using Rico's last name.

"I'm my own individual human being," Joanne insisted.

Joanne and Andrew kept talking. She liked that he attended a private university, not the community college where most of the NC guys were enrolled part-time. While Rico smoked with his boys, Andrew practiced his guitar. "And he plays the piano and the clarinet," Joanne gushed. He also spoke French and Spanish—"The languages," Joanne said, "that I consider the languages of love."

The two spoke every day through his college summer break. Andrew called Joanne his girlfriend and promised that once he returned to campus for the fall semester, he would rent a car and drive back to NC for visits.

"He's making plans for the future," Joanne beamed. "Usually, it's the girl that'll do that."

But when Andrew did return to college, their calls dwindled. Doubt crept in. Joanne feared Andrew had "freaked out" after they had been intimate for the first time.

"He got scared after," she told me. "He was being bombarded with really strong emotions. I was like, 'Well, act on your emotions! Don't get scared.'"

The relationship stalled, and Joanne felt burned. Still, she took Andrew's calls when he was "stressed out" at college. "I'm tryna help him keep calm and stuff, while still being mad at him," she said. "I am helping him get his goals in order and just take it one day at a time."

Unlike the girls' friendships, which were largely reciprocal, power asymmetries and gender dynamics could unbalance romantic relationships. This sometimes left girls burdened with care work while their own desires went unfulfilled.[15]

Romance and Danger

On rare occasions, romantic relationships exposed girls to forms of danger they usually assiduously avoided.

Zora's boyfriend, Junior, was an NC "OG," Florence told me. And Zora—who seemed polished even in sweatpants—had poise and grace that matched his clout. Junior had waited a long time to pursue Zora, who was six years younger. When, eventually, they did start dating, Zora's family was livid. They believed Junior had been involved with the killing of Zora's stepbrother, Sparks. Relatives shunned her. Some of her friends disapproved too, given Junior's ties to what they called "that life." But they didn't cut Zora off, or threaten to. Instead, they stood by, ready to offer help if it was sought.

One night, in a park near the project, Florence and Stephanie discussed Zora and Junior, as well as their own views on risk in relationships. At a picnic table lit dimly by distant streetlights, Florence unpicked a cigar to make a weed rollie.

"Junior gave me these," Florence said, nudging the cigar tin.

Stephanie, who had never smoked, watched Florence crumble weed chunks between her thumb and forefinger. "I'm not that fond of Junior," Stephanie said. "So many times Zora's gotten really sad over how he'd keep her waiting. And all the other stuff."

"But at the same time," Florence said, "she knows what she got herself into." Florence had a new boyfriend, Darius, who dealt too.

"Yeah," Stephanie said. "But you also have to make adjustments. Meet her in the middle."

"Junior definitely tries to," Florence said. "He has so much like, you don't understand how much money he be getting and shit, and plays."

"Is he just selling a lot of weed?" Stephanie asked.

"No. He sells everything."

"Everything?" Stephanie asked.

"Yeah."

Stephanie paused. "No offense to Zora, like if she loves him. But I just wouldn't feel comfortable being with a guy who sells a bunch of shit."

Florence sealed her joint. "I know," she said. "Like, that's how I feel about Darius."

"'Cause a lot of those guys get caught up, you know?" Stephanie said.

"The thing about Darius that I like is that he doesn't just do *that*. He actually has a job too. He's a drug dealer, but he also has an office job at MIT. I like that."

"Yeah, that's good," Stephanie said. "There's a lot of guys like, 'I'm just gonna sell.' And then they don't have a day job."

Florence raised a lighter to her joint.

"Does Junior pack though?" Stephanie asked, inquiring whether Zora's boyfriend carried a gun.

"Mmhmm," Florence said affirmatively.

"Pssssh," Stephanie said.

"That's the thing I get scared of with Darius," Florence said. "If it's in the car, if we get stopped by the police and it's four o' clock in the morning . . . I just don't wanna be in the car with you if you're packing."

The girls did not all agree about acceptable risks in romantic relationships. Stephanie worried when Zora and Florence chose to date boys with access to drugs and weapons. But she did not push her friends to stop seeing them. Boys had a power she lacked, one that might win in an ultimatum. Unable to shield Florence from the secondhand danger girls occasionally faced from their relationships with boys, Stephanie simply offered her thoughts and let Florence share her own.[16]

Sex: Stigma and Abuse

Sex is a normal, healthy part of adolescent development, one that can offer connection, agency, and pleasure.[17] Despite this, and even though most high school seniors are sexually active,[18] young people's sexuality is often framed as "out-of-control, dangerous, and immoral."[19]

Teenagers' sex lives are not equally judged and punished, however. Rather gender, race, and class affect how adults—including policy makers, researchers, and teachers—respond to adolescent sexuality.[20] Girls, for instance, are rarely taught about sexual desire and pleasure. Instead of helping them "explore what feels good and bad, desirable and undesirable," notes the psychologist Michelle Fine, sex education curricula typically treat girls merely as potential victims of male sexuality.[21] In addition, historically racist tropes mean that Black girls' sexuality is often pathologized.[22] As a result of these intersecting inequalities, sexuality can be fraught for many young women of color.

Like many teens, the NC girls had limited access to information about sexual development.

"Sex ed was lame," Joanne said of CRLS's curriculum.[23]

A senior girl concurred: "I only got one class. All I remember is the teacher being like, 'Here is Mr. Woody!' and bringing out this wooden dick and a condom!"

Still this was more than girls learned at home. Most cringed at the thought of discussing sex with their parents. With just a hint of irony, Joanne said she would continue to insist to Carole that she was a virgin, "even if I birth a baby."

Some of the girls talked to their friends about sex. But they struggled to advise each other, given their limited knowledge, the variety in their experiences, and the fact that sex—unlike many other aspects of the girls' lives—took place privately.

Aisha recalled a tricky conversation after a friend, Tia, first had sex.

"Tia was like, 'Yeah, it was good,'" Aisha related. "But then she was like, 'I feel so weird, I don't know what to do.' There was never a process to internalize what just happened." Aisha, who had never had sex, did not know how to support Tia.[24]

Friends could not always help the girls process these new feelings. Nor could they disrupt the stigma and power disparities that sometimes shaped their sexual encounters.

Stigma

One afternoon, I hung out with Aisha and her friends Jenna and Kiara in Jenna's bedroom. Jenna's cousin, Dani, suddenly burst through the door.

"I wanna tell you guys about how Kat got chlamydia," Dani announced.

Jenna and Kiara squealed and clapped.

"So," Dani began, "Kat smashed Xavier. Xavier smashed Dee. Dee smashed AJ. AJ smashed Makayla. Makayla—"

"Makayla smashed *everybody*," Kiara jumped in, drawing laughs. "How did you find out about this?"

"My friend Sydney went with Kat to get tested," Dani said.

"So, Sydney's big ass was like, 'Guess what, Kat has chlamydia?' Loud bitch!" Kiara said.

Although Kiara criticized Sydney for sharing Kat's information, gossip spread rapidly through the girls' broader peer group. Teens often told salacious stories as they hung out, rode the train together, or waited for their game at basketball practice.

"*Tina sucked my brother's dick. In my house! I was like, 'Do you want a toothbrush?'*"

"*Ashley wanted to sleep with JJ, so she started grinding up on him. But she had her period, so JJ smashed Shawna.*"

"*Did y'all know that Orlena got blinded by cum?*"

Such stories exposed girls, though rarely boys, to ridicule.[25]

Students discussed these gendered double standards in CHANGE one day.

"Guys are *meant to*, like it's the way we were made," said a senior boy.

"Yeah," said another boy. "In society, when a male has a lot of partners, it's like, he's the man! But when a female has a lot of partners, it's like, she's a ho."

"But why do you *think* that?" asked a senior girl.

"I don't know," the second boy replied with a shrug.

The girls could critique but not change these double standards.

Moreover, while the specter of shame shaped girls' sex lives, sex appeal was valuable; "sexy" selfies got many likes.[26] Some girls skillfully walked the line between sexy and sexual.[27] Aisha, for instance, shared photos that captured her beauty, figure, and style, but she never had boyfriends and rarely went on dates. She was also vocal about her abstinence, which she attributed, variably, to the loss of her aunt Grace, to her "morals," or to a $300 bet with Joanne's brother Vincent that she would graduate from CRLS a virgin. Aisha posted tweets like *Virginity .. Is a thing you don't toy with .. IDC IDC ..*[28] and *#HonestHour I have never had sex (a proud virgin)*. Still Aisha appreciated boys' interest and occasionally sought it with a suggestive tweet like, *I think I'm sexually frustrated.. Make out scenes in shows and shit turn me on .. #thedilemma*.

Aisha grasped the expectations surrounding female sexuality, but not everyone could so capably navigate the stigma that peers could impose.

Pressure and Abuse

Young women from all backgrounds encounter sexual violence. The *#MeToo* movement and the term "rape culture" testify to the pervasiveness of sexual harassment and assault. Yet the rate of sexual victimization for Black girls and young women is among the highest for any group nationwide.[29] As Hill Collins explains, "Many Black girls live in environments that are hazardous due to the social, political, and economic location invoked by marginality."[30]

Several of the NC girls encountered unwanted sexual attention. In Jenna's room, Dani followed her story about Kat's diagnosis with a story of her own, about a college classmate who dropped by her dorm room night after night. Most evenings, Dani explained, the classmate just used her kettle to cook ramen noodles.

"But one day," she told us, "he climbs in my bed. I ask what he's doing. He says he's cold. I'm like, 'Okay, but when your three-minute noodles are done, you are out.' Suddenly his hand is in my pants, and I'm grabbing his arm like, *woah*. And he's all like, 'Let me smash.' And I'm like, 'No!' And he's like, 'Let me smash.' And I was like, 'No, I'm a virgin, and damn, your noodles are done.'"

Dani used her virginity to justify refusing sex. Without an excuse, it could be hard to say no. One night after Florence and Robenson split up, she sat out at a picnic table in the project. Malik, an older NC boy, approached Florence and invited her to come smoke and drink in his car. She accepted his offer.

"I was really freaking high," Florence recalled. "We had like three, four blunts, and I'm getting drunk off Remy straight." Florence welcomed the distraction from her breakup, but Malik had other plans. "He's like, 'Let's do something.' And I'm like, 'What do I look like? I'm not gonna fuck you in your car.'"

But Malik was prepared. "I can get a hotel," she recalled him saying, as he turned the key. "Don't bullshit me."

"I was like, 'Oh shit, I can't back out,'" Florence described. So she didn't. "I was like, 'Fuck it, whatever.' It wasn't that great for me."

It was not only peers who made the NC girls feel objectified, harassed, or pressured. Walking through the project on the way home one evening, Aisha glanced at a group of men sitting on a low wall, then yanked my arm to speed us up.

"I hate walking through here," she whispered. "This is where the creeps hang out. All the men, just looking."

Another day, I walked with Florence and her cousin through the project. Under a fiery June sun, the girls, in short shorts and strappy shirts, talked happily. Then we passed Ralph, Joanne and Vincent's stepfather, leaning against the back stairs to his apartment.

"Ohhh! Where's your boyfriends?" he called out, silencing the girls.

In private, Florence and her friends called Ralph "a pedo perv." But Florence and her cousin said nothing as he leered.[31]

Florence was especially tense under his stare. Back when she was dating Vincent, Ralph started doing things that made her uncomfortable. At first Florence tried to brush it off. "There's always those Haitian older creepy guys who would just stare at younger girls or whatever," she reasoned.

But Ralph became increasingly lewd. At home or during rides to school, "he'd just tell me all this stupid stuff about him and his sex life," she recalled.

Then, Florence explained, he started asking about his stepdaughter, Joanne, and her boyfriend Rico: *Are they having sex?* He also asked about Florence's relationship with Vincent: *Are you having sex with other guys?*

Eventually Ralph went further. "He would try to kiss me," she said. "He tried to touch me." Florence didn't know what to do. She felt obliged to greet him when visiting the house—"I didn't want to be disrespectful," she said—so she took one of the kids along. "I had to bring Evens or Jonas to go and say hi and then try and get outta there as fast as I can."

Florence considered her options and decided to tell Vincent about Ralph.

"You probably liked it," Vincent joked in response.

"I was like, 'go fuck yourself,'" Florence said.

Somehow Carole learned what was happening and invited Florence over to discuss the situation.

"She was like, 'I'm just sad you didn't come to me about this,'" Florence remembered. She found herself apologizing.

Carole then asked Florence exactly what Ralph had done. As Florence answered, Ralph appeared, surprising her.

"Suddenly he's there, denying everything!" Florence recalled. Florence made to leave but not before Carole offered her solution: in the future Florence should stay downstairs when she visited instead of going upstairs, where the bedrooms were.

Florence turned, finally, to her friends. She talked with Joanne and with Joanne's cousin who, as Florence explained, had "a similar experience from before."

Florence's friends couldn't keep her from harm. But they could listen when she needed to be heard.

· · ·

Darius, who worked at MIT and also dealt drugs, charmed Florence with sweet texts, free weed, and talk of the future.

"He's always talking about plans," she said, grinning.

Florence invited Darius to a neighborhood cookout, and he texted back, "I'm gonna come through, show me and you together."

But Darius didn't show. He stopped answering texts, and she never saw him again. After Darius came Johnson, a personal trainer. To impress him, Florence Googled the names of Boston's sports teams and shared Snapchats saying *Go Patriots!* After that relationship fizzled, there was Richard, fourteen years Florence's senior at thirty-two. Richard was engaged to the mother of his five-year-old, but Florence questioned his commitment.

"He's been engaged for six years," she told me, frowning. "I been doing my research on Google like, 'How long is too long to be engaged?'"

Then she met Samuel—driven, caring, and, like Florence, originally from Haiti. "He's just turned twenty-six," she explained, after they started texting. "And he speaks four languages 'cause he's been traveling, and he wants to do linguistics, so he's gonna start going to school soon."

Samuel called Florence on the phone. He asked about her days. She started to picture a future together.

Suddenly Samuel said he was leaving. His visa had expired, and his uncle had found a woman in Texas he could marry for papers. Florence didn't want to lose him. She Googled "marriage license in Massachusetts" on her cell phone.

As Florence considered marrying Samuel, she felt rushed by his uncle. Samuel, though, was less pushy. "He was like, 'You're such an amazing person, but I understand if you don't want to do it,'" she told me. "I was crying . . . He tells me I'm someone he could spend his life with . . . Maybe I'm not like, in love, but my whole heart is in it," Florence reasoned. "I believe in the whole situation. There's so much coincidences and signs which are so good. He has the same birthday as Zora."

One afternoon Florence suggested she and I ride bikes out to Spy Pond in neighboring Arlington. With both tires flat, her bike trundled down the two-mile path. Florence didn't complain.

"After a certain amount of time with someone, how is it supposed to feel?" she asked me, voice trembling, as we sat on a bench by the water.

Back home, Florence prayed for guidance. She couldn't talk to her parents, and, sure her friends would disapprove, she kept her plans secret.

Florence set a date with a justice of the peace she found online. As the day approached, she worried about her future. "I still wanna travel, do the Peace Corps, maybe outreach work in Haiti, teach kids English and stuff like that," she said.

But on a clear and sunny day, the justice officiated the ceremony.

"I didn't want to," Florence told me afterward. "I had second thoughts . . . But it's not really about me in this situation. I'm doing it for him 'cause he has a lot going for him."

It was not the wedding of her dreams, but Florence's hope would live another day.

Walking the Line

As the girls became young women, their bodies changed. So too did the way men looked at them, the way they saw themselves, and the things they desired. Confronting new opportunities and expectations, the girls were disparaged by racist and colorist beauty norms that left some feeling near-constant discomfort. Romantic relationships could be warm and loving, but they could also be painful, or burdensome, or even occasionally expose the girls to danger. And since sexuality was condemned by adults and mocked by peers, shame and stigma were real threats. So were the coercion and abuse that stole girls' autonomy.

In all these realms, friends' power was limited. Friends could not change beauty norms or break romance's spell.[32] Nor could the girls protect each other from hurt or harm. Yet they did what they could, showering compliments and standing, firmly, by their friends. In this respect as in others, they were constant, loving witnesses to one another's lives.

When Joanne first told me about a new guy she was talking to, she shared a couple of details before turning to her best friend and saying, "Aisha, *you* should supply the information. You know better than anyone!" Still the girls walked young womanhood's tightropes largely alone.

· • ·

The chapters in this part have shown how the girls tried to meet one another's needs and support each other through young womanhood's challenges. They have shown friends' successes and limitations as they strove to provide vital care that was elsewhere in short supply. The next part reveals how the girls responded when their friendships—and the resources they provided—came under threat.

2 Friendships under Threat

5   *Technologies of Trauma*

Joanne planned a class talent show when her turn came to lead the CHANGE check-in. She announced her idea weeks in advance, and peers excitedly prepared performances as the date drew near.

On the February Friday, Joanne dragged classroom chairs into spectators' rows, clearing a stage by the whiteboard. Aisha—like Joanne, a junior at the time—volunteered to curate the between-act soundtrack using the class computer.

One of the first students up was Leslie, a senior, whose talent was makeup. Leslie applied to her own face a cat-eye look she had learned online. After finishing with a flare of liquid eyeliner, Leslie curtseyed to the room and returned to her seat.

Aisha, over at the computer, opened YouTube to find a song to play. A senior, Angelina, joined her at the desktop. Aqua's *Barbie Girl* rang out through the speakers, and the two girls began an impromptu dance.

Aisha and Angelina both enjoyed the spotlight. Both were warm, funny, and comfortable being loud—even restoring classroom order on days when chatter grew too noisy.

Aisha sang along with the video: *"You can brush my hair, undress me everywhere!"* Angelina whipped her long, dark hair around, a diamanté belly bar glinting between her jeans and pink shirt. Classmates whooped as the girls danced.

"Thank you, ladies, for that show!" Ms. Flores said, smiling, after a minute. Aisha and Angelina took seats a row ahead of me.

Up next, Josiah, a senior, walked to the stage. "Am I allowed to curse?" he asked.

"This is our space," said Ms. Flores, nodding.

"Alright. So this is a rap that I wrote and recorded myself when I was going through some stuff," Josiah said. He cleared his throat, then began:

> *Real friends turn to strangers, real quick,*
> *Suddenly your heart go numb and you can't feel shit,*
> *But I promise I was old enough to feel*
> *When my Pops got locked and my graduations he missed,*
> *Or when my cousin's Pop got shot; they emptied four clips,*
> *Some reckless kids without no ambition to live, shit,*
> *This life's a movie with no script,*
> *We know the Black guy's gonna die but we don't never know when,*
> *Around here they count their sins more than their blessings,*
> *Rather play with a gun than attend their English lesson.*
> *Just some wild young adolescents, violent minds,*
> *But in their hearts, they're still searching for acceptance . . .*

Josiah closed his rap with a loud "Peace!" and the class jumped up to applaud.

"Yeah!" Aisha yelled, running to embrace Josiah in front of the room.

After a few more performances—Aisha and Angelina both sang; others played musical instruments or danced—Joanne prepared to read her poem, the morning's final act.

"This is called, 'The Story of an Abused Child,'" Joanne said, from the stage. She flipped through a worn paper notebook to find the page.

The room hushed, and Joanne slowly and commandingly read some first-person spoken word, stanzas describing hurt and fear and hiding. After the last line, she closed her book and looked up at her classmates' wide eyes.

"Oh, it's not about me," Joanne giggled, to a boom of relieved laughs.

. . .

Three months later, Angelina hung out with a friend, Vato, on his front porch in mid-Cambridge.[1] Days before her high school graduation, Angelina twisted Vato some braids as their other buddies lounged around beside them. The teens enjoyed the lingering, late spring daylight. Across the street, Little Leaguers fielded balls outside the elementary school. Nobody paid close attention to the black sedan that crawled down Willow Street and disappeared around a corner.

Angelina caught sight of another friend, Bree, approaching. Bree, sixteen and a sophomore at CRLS, had large brown eyes and full lips into which she had pierced a small gold hoop. Bree loved jewelry and removed her pieces only for track and softball, which she did after school, along with an anti-bullying youth leadership program.[2]

Bree was heading home with her sister; she lived just a few houses down from Vato. The girls stopped by the porch to chat with Angelina. As they talked, the black car returned. It braked, suddenly, outside Vato's house, and from a rolled-down window came hollow, unmistakable pops.

The car blazed off.

Most of the bullets—which, people later assumed, were meant for Vato—lodged in walls or doorframes. But Angelina was struck in the abdomen and Bree in the chest. Neighbors rushed to the panic. Bree's sister bolted for home, screaming for her mom.

In emergency surgery, doctors cut out the lead that had shredded Angelina's intestines and fractured her pelvis. She recuperated for a week in intensive care and another on a ward before being sent home with crutches and a colostomy bag.

Bree died on the street, neighbors holding her hand.[3]

In the following days, stuffed animals piled up outside Vato's house, pink and blue on gray concrete.[4] People laid bouquets and tied helium balloons to the front yard's fence. They lit candles, some new with orange price stickers, others grabbed from shelves at home, halfway burned. Most of the candles—dozens first, then over a hundred—were devotionals.

Friends glued printed photos of Bree to poster board squares and wrote messages in Sharpie: "We love you!" and "The good really do die young :("

Aisha wrote, "I Love You Honey You'll always be in our spirits looking over every one. I have so much respect for you! The realest person. R.I.P. My condolences go out to the fam—Aisha."

Aisha also checked up on Seeta. Bree was the younger sister of Seeta's ex-boyfriend, Malachi, and the girls had been close. "I'm here for you," Aisha told Seeta.

Meanwhile, the community grieved. *Senseless . . . random . . . unthinkable . . .* mourned community leaders, teachers, and politicians.

"My heart is just breaking," said the school superintendent.[5]

Theories spread. The neighbor who managed the operation to distribute hundreds of pins bearing Bree's face addressed dozens of mourners days after the shooting.

"Justice will be served," she told a small crowd. "Because we all know, no need for words, we all know what's really good. We know what happened to her. We know why. We know who. We know how."[6]

But justice was not served. As the police rebuked a "pool of silence" in the neighborhood, Bree's friends and family waited.[7] They waited while the candles melted wax thick over the sidewalk. They waited while the balloons wilted and the flowers browned. They kept waiting.

Violence and Trauma in Poor Neighborhoods

Most young people who live in poor neighborhoods have witnessed violence or been its victim.[8] Moreover, these teens also typically have less access than middle-class peers to the types of resources that can prevent trauma's long-term developmental risks, leaving them doubly exposed to anxiety, depression, and post-traumatic stress disorder (PTSD).[9] Girls are especially susceptible; they are four times likelier than boys to develop PTSD and depression after trauma.[10]

For the NC girls, horrific local violence was far from an everyday occurrence. But, as Zora reflected, "even one loss" was too many.

Trauma tarnished local landmarks and streets. "That pizza place, you know, near where Sparks was shot," the girls said of the restaurant close to where Zora's stepbrother had been killed.[11]

And painful memories endured, like when a man in a motorcycle helmet beat Rosie's brother, Bryan, in broad daylight. Stephanie often thought about that day.

"[The man] was choking him, squeezing the life out of him," Stephanie recalled. "Blood was gushing, and we thought he was gonna die right then. Everyone ran outside. Everyone was screaming, 'Get off him!'" Stephanie had felt powerless as the stranger kicked her friend. "Bryan's mom ran out screaming, 'Get off my child!' But he wouldn't get off." The adults were as helpless as she was. That was a hard feeling to forget.

Amid this insecurity, the girls looked out for one another and bonded over shared vulnerability. And when tragedy did hit NC, they cared for those hurt most. But trauma does not merely harm individuals; it can also fray the social fabric and unravel relationships.[12] To support their friends and shield their friendships, the girls made trauma *manageable*. This process had three key parts. First was dissemination: news spread fast, often between teens on social media. Then came comprehension, when they made sense of what had happened. Finally, there was coping, as the girls began to heal.

Trauma management was collaborative among peers. The girls did grieve with family members and attend wakes and funerals. But many of their responses to crises were not shared or supported by adults.

Safety Strategies

The girls were vigilant around NC, noting passing cars and squinting at plates.[13]

"You have to be cautious of what's going to happen," Faith explained. "Whoever comes through in a car, if it looks different to you, like you've never seen it before, you gotta look at it sideways 'cause you never know." Analyzing comings and goings was part of the girls' time-passing daily talk, but it also kept their eyes on the street.[14]

Moreover, the girls remained alert as they themselves came and went. The project's nearest subway station was a half-mile walk away, past a sports field and down an alley fenced on both sides by chain link. During the day, teens strolled fearlessly down the alley. But it was different in the dark.

"You can't catch me at the train station at night," Joanne said.

Some of the girls were bolder walking around after dark. Brittani, for instance, didn't mind the ten-minute walk from the project where her friends lived back to her mom's Section 8 apartment, even though it led down a blemished road.

"There've been shootings on Rindge Ave," Brittani explained. "Two people got shot. One by Foodtown. One got killed." But, she reasoned, she had walked down Rindge for years. "I walk on that street late at night from my friends' houses," she said. "I'm not really worried about it, 'cause I know so many people that I feel like no one's going to hurt me."

Aisha, however, laughed at Brittani's bravery. "Brittani would walk through Dorchester hoods by herself in the middle of the night!" she said, referencing a low-income South Boston neighborhood the girls viewed as dangerous. Aisha herself ran home from the subway station, sneakers smacking brick as her eyes scanned the shadows. "Some nights it's just bad feelings," she explained. "It's scary!"

That was why, after hanging out together, the NC girls checked to see that everyone got safely home. On Twitter, a friend once thanked Aisha for her zeal: *Aisha texted, snapchatted & tweeted me to make sure I got home safe . . . That's my bitch lmfao.*

Sometimes the girls took each other home. "We walk home with each other," Joanne explained. "It [isn't] really that good of an idea to walk by yourself. Creepy people, creepy men." The girls escorted each other even to buildings in the same project and brought along a brother or friend to avoid returning alone.[15]

Along with these practical safety strategies, the girls often traded stories of harm encountered or dodged. One day at school, for example, Elena—a petite Latinx senior with a sharp brown bob—told three friends and me about how in eighth grade a neighborhood boy stabbed her leg "at a kids' party." Elena rubbed the numb spot on her left calf where an inch-long scar curved like a Nike swoosh. In response, Val, a Latinx senior with round cheeks and braces, described the time she thought she might get stabbed. Three men, one with a knife, had chased her into a store, and she had dashed behind the counter and begged the clerk to call the cops. Val's story was not seen as one-upmanship but rather empathy.[16]

The girls bonded over their experiences, which their parents— who grew up in different eras and places—did not share. But the girls understood each other. They were sincere when, parting ways, they said not "Goodbye" but "Be safe."[17]

Yet despite these efforts, crises still occurred. When this happened, friends supported one another as they disseminated, comprehended, and coped with trauma.

Disseminating Trauma

Nine months after the Willow Street shooting, Rosie was in her living room when she heard a knock at the front door.[18] She paused her episode of *Law & Order SVU* and opened the door to three grave-eyed police officers, two men and a woman. Sensing something awful had happened, Rosie turned and ran up the stairs. Moments later, she heard the officers ask her mother whether her eldest son, Bryan, had a tattoo on his chest. Rosie's mom confirmed that he did. The officers then said that Bryan, age twenty, had been found dead.

The news exploded through NC. Rosie called Zora and Faith as soon as the police left. But other close friends found out the same way as most neighborhood teens: online.

Stephanie learned of Bryan's death on Twitter. "I was like, 'I'm 'sposed to be doing my homework, but I'll just check it,'" she recounted. "Rosie was retweeting stuff and people were tweeting stuff, and it was all on my TL.[19] I was like, 'Oh shit. Okay, let me go call Faith,' and be like, 'What the fuck just happened?' Then Faith and me went to the house."[20]

Teens heard tragic news from friends in the same spaces where they shared memes and daily updates. Information spread fast online, particularly on Twitter, where posts could be replied to publicly or retweeted.[21]

The night the police officers visited Rosie's home, teens scrolling their feeds saw tweets like:

R.I.P to one of the coolest dudes I ever met . . . shits crazy—with @Bryan
Real n***a shit r.i.p. to Bryan Forever missed . . .

*Wtf I hate coming on here and finding out someone died..what
    happened to Bryan?*

Right away, friends and neighbors tweeted condolence messages
or posted on Rosie and Leon's Facebook walls. Aisha wrote to Rosie,
My baby :/ PLEASE PLEASE STAY STRONG, and Stephanie wrote,
*I know this is a hard time for you so please don't hesitate to talk to
me because I've been in a similar situation God Bless you and your family, I will keep you in my prayers, R.I.P.*
Such posts helped disseminate news.

Teens also shared information directly with friends. Two days after Bryan's death, I joined Aisha and Joanne in Aisha's living room
after school. Aisha, at her desktop, skipped between Twitter and
Pandora while Joanne, on the couch, scrolled through Snapchat. As
snow fell hard outside, the girls told me how they had learned about
Bryan's death.

Joanne heard from a cousin. "And I was really trying to tell *this*
girl," she said, pointing at Aisha. "I didn't want her to not know. That
happened to Jada [a classmate] when Bree died. Jada just came to
school and saw all these depressed people, and then she spazzed out.
It sucks to not know what's going on."

"Yeah, I literally had no idea," Aisha said.

"I Snapchatted you!" Joanne replied. "I made a tears face and
I was like, 'Bryan died.' That was my caption. You didn't see the
Snapchat I sent you?"

"No," Aisha said. "My iPod died so I didn't see any of this stuff.[22]
When I charged it, I saw everyone saying all this stuff on Instagram.
I texted Seeta, 'cause I thought someone was making a joke about
Bryan's death. She texted back like, 'No, he's gone.'"

The quick spread of news between teens meant that by the time
CRLS—where Bryan was an alum and where his sister Rosie was
enrolled—informed the students, most already knew.

"What happened at school?" I asked Aisha and Joanne.

"Oh, the usual," Joanne said, eyes on her phone.

"The usual?" I asked.

"You know, an announcement, a silence," she shrugged.

School could lag behind peer groups when it came to disseminating or responding to local tragedies. In fact, teachers sometimes learned of crises from teens' posts. CRLS staff first heard about the Willow Street shooting—and that their students Bree and Angelina had been shot—after a teacher's daughter opened social media. Ms. Flores explained to me: "[A colleague] Raelle's daughter was on Twitter. Raelle texted me. I called [the principal], and it went around from there. It just exploded over Twitter and Facebook."[23]

This metaphor—explosion—was common; when a spark of information touched teens' dense brush of connections, news "blew up." What blew up, however, was not always accurate. Among the teens, who rarely relied on official news sources, social and informational worlds largely lined up. This let both fact and fiction circulate in trauma's chaotic aftermath. Shares and likes could easily spread misinformation; many teens, for instance, believed Angelina too had died when the first tweets appeared about Willow Street.

Moreover, even accurate reports could be hurtful. When teens heard Bryan was dead, several people assumed he had been murdered; some remembered the beating in broad daylight, and others knew that he had sold drugs. Rosie, after reading peers' posts, tweeted, *No one even knows what fucking happen, just shut up.* To support her, one friend wrote, *Shits Not Even About That At All So Stop Tryna Act Like N***as Know How Shit Runs,* and Aisha tweeted, *#ripBRYAN. LET'S PLEASE STOP THE RUMORS !!!* Social media's publicity meant that rumors were no longer whispered privately but clear for everyone to read.

Trauma Comprehension

Making Sense

Six weeks after Bryan's death, a pair of bombs detonated near the Boston Marathon's finish line. Two days after that, the NC girls woke to find their city locked down. Overnight police had identified two suspects in the bombing—brothers. Police had shot and killed the older brother, and the younger had fled, prompting both a manhunt and a citywide shelter-in-place ordinance.

This information lapped, in waves, over the girls' social media. Early messages shared news of the ordinance and the transit system's closure. Some teens cheered a day off school; others protested being "jailed" with "dramatic" families.

But Twitter really blew up when CRLS students realized that the grainy photo of the younger brother beamed by news broadcasts—dark curls poking out of a white baseball cap—showed a familiar face: a former classmate.

Social media exploded as teens confirmed that the fugitive suspect, Dzhokhar Tsarnaev, was, indeed, their peer, "Jahar." Some responded with anger, tweeting, for instance, *OMG wtff!!! I could kill this motherfucker my damn self.* Others defended the young man they knew with posts like *Bitch n***as quiet down, we knew Jahar as a friend not a terrorist* and *He is a *suspect* that means innocent until proven guilty.*

As people fought to define the situation,[24] Brittani tweeted, *Social media is just like a town without a sheriff.* Later, she described the morning to me: "Imagine a group of people in a giant room watching the same story on the same TV and talking to each other about it. That day, that's what Twitter was. Everyone had their own opinion, everyone was coming at people for their opinion, and it was informing and at the same time entertaining."

Yet while, as Brittani noted, teens "talked to" each other on Twitter, these collective, contested exchanges—through which teens often made sense of dramatic events—differed from face-to-face conversations. Many rules that govern dialogue did not apply online; there was, for instance, not always turn taking, so people did not have to wait to speak. Nor did tweets need to tie to anything already said.[25] The suspension of these rules meant teens sometimes talked *past* each other.

Teens also talked *over* each other; everyone could post, but some had louder voices.[26] Popular teens typically had bigger audiences, amplifying their words. A second group also had more authority: teens nearest the crisis.

Social Ownership: A Politics of Proximity

Teens drew close to those hit hardest by trauma, including victims' siblings, best friends, and current or former romantic partners. Young people most affected had a form of "social ownership," which meant peers heard and deferred to what they had to say. For instance, reading the first tweets about Willow Street, Faith awaited clarity not from adults or news outlets but from people proximate to those involved. "I didn't believe it until Bree's brother tweeted it," she said.

People with social ownership not only had more credibility. They also received more attention and greater recognition of their suffering. Bree's older brother Malachi gained 168 new Facebook friends in the month after the Willow Street shooting. Peers inundated his wall with messages like:

> *I'm so sorry for your loss, my condolences go out to you and the family,*
> *stay strong.*
> *Soo sorry Malachi. Ur the last person who deserves something like this.*

*You guys were the first I mean FIRST people I met when I moved to
cambridge in 2nd grade. This is horrible. But please keep ur head
up Malachi, your fam is like my fam!*

Some teens, in posting these kinds of messages, used the publicity
of social media to emphasize their own proximity to the tragedy. They
described, for instance, their closeness to Malachi in posts starting,
My family has been friends with your family for years . . . or *Since we became friends in fifth grade . . .* Others shared photos taken with Bree or
liked older such images to make them reappear on friends' feeds.

Such claims of closeness to traumas earned likes and comments.
Tweets like the one Florence shared about "Jahar" during Boston's
lockdown—*I had a crush on a terrorist and sat with him in class.. I wanted
to go to prom with him #scary #sad #confused*—drew engagement.

But claiming too much closeness courted pushback. This could
be gentle, like when Aisha, after the marathon bombing, uploaded a
photomontage of herself with Vincent, who had been called to join
his fellow National Guardsmen at the Copley Square chaos. Aisha's
caption read: *MY PRAYERS GO OUT TO #Vincent on his first time duty
as a SOLIDER. I want him to come home! That's my brother !! However,
I know his out there protecting our city and making sure we are safe #pray-
4Boston.*[27] Joanne, Vincent's sister, tweeted at her best friend to calm
down and go to sleep.

Sometimes, however, teens hit back with snark. During the manhunt, one mocked peers claiming closeness to the suspect: *All these
ppl sayin they knew this person.. do yall feel special or somthin..like idc if
u partied wit him or watever . . . if yall r so close to him then tell us where
ur boy is at!*

Relatedly, teens "going too hard" for victims' siblings or best
friends also met censure. "Did I tell you about the whole thing with
Rosie?" Florence asked me a few days after Bryan's death. "Seeta and
Joanne went up to Rosie at school and gave her a hug!" Florence

paused for reaction; Seeta and Joanne were in a different clique, so she found the hug inappropriate. "I don't know if Rosie hugged back or not, but I doubt it."

Teens were expected to know their place, on- and offline. Leon, Rosie's brother, tweeted, *Bunch of these fuck n***as actin like they was cool with my bro.* In support, one friend tweeted, *I bet the same people saying they were close to Bryan haven't even hit him up for years . . .*, and another wrote, *I'm jus confused as to why some people are doing THE MOST. If you ain't @Leon or @Rosie take a seat!*

Most teens broadcast hard times when they wanted care. Dramatic or traumatic tweets—about hospital visits or deaths in the family—got instant responses.[28] But overclaiming drama was slammed as attention seeking—being "thirsty" for likes. As Leslie, a senior, tweeted during the lockdown, *People tweeting lies about the bombing for retweets are just fucked up.*[29]

Claiming too much proximity could disrupt the credibility and recognition given to those nearest a trauma. In doing so, it could divert peers' care from those who needed it most.

Coping with Trauma

After disseminating and making some sense of traumatic news, teens began to cope with what had happened. They downplayed their exposure to risk, shared scripts for grieving, and helped each other move on.

(Dis)Locating Danger

After traumatic events, people need "a visceral feeling of safety" to "calm down, heal, and grow," explains the psychiatrist Bessel van der Kolk.[30] To feel safe, some teens drew boundaries that located danger elsewhere, in different physical or social worlds.

One day at school, I sat with Josiah, Angelina's friend and class-mate, as he discussed the Willow Street shooting.

"Vato is a bad guy," Josiah said. "He is from Boston. I predicted he'd be dead this year. That's a bad thing to say on someone, but all this karma's gonna catch up with him." Josiah went on: "People are always like, 'Cambridge is not a safe place to live,' and I'm like, 'It *is* a safe place. He's not even from here!'" Although Bree and Angelina were shot in Cambridge, Josiah used Vato's Boston roots to assert his own neighborhood's safety.

Three weeks after the shooting, I visited Angelina at her East Cambridge apartment with Ms. Flores and Angelina's friend, Leti. Angelina, in ripped jeans and a sleeveless leopard-print shirt, was perched on a stool in her living room, straightening her hair. She muted the hip-hop playing from a TV in the corner as we took seats on the sofas.

"How's it coming?" Ms. Flores asked.

"It's hard walking," Angelina said. "You don't realize how much you use your stomach muscles to walk." She could now manage short distances but only with crutches, which left deep welts on her palms.

Her physical therapist visited a few times weekly, Angelina told us, as did a therapist. "He looks like Jim Carey," she said.

"Is he funny like him too?" Ms. Flores asked.

"Not so much," Angelina said.

Ms. Flores asked Angelina if she felt safe, back at home. Angelina was a witness to the shooting, which she called "the incident," and police had stood guard outside her hospital room.

"Like, I do," Angelina said. "I don't really worry too much. I mean, I worry if they think I saw something. My mom worries about that. My mom wants to move outta here, but I don't wanna move out of Cambridge. Boston, that's worse!"

Leti laughed in agreement.

Yet each tragedy compounded teens' sense of local danger, reflected in tweets posted after Bryan's death, like, *Sorry to Cambridge for losing another one. My respect out to Bryan. Nobody's catching a break man* and *Cambridge Is Really Starting To See More RIPs But Less Happy Birthdays.*

So teens drew a second type of boundary to shore up safety. With terms like "that life," the girls located violence in a different *social* world, even when it occurred nearby.[31]

Natty, a senior and a cousin of Florence and Faith, had dated Bryan a couple of years before his death. "He was my first boyfriend," she told me. They had broken up because their four-year age gap meant they were "in different times." Still they had stayed friends and even joked about getting back together.

"Now that's never going to happen," Natty said. She paused and added, "He was in a whole different world."

Other girls spoke similarly. The night after Bryan was killed, Stephanie, exhausted, sank into a chair in my apartment.

"We don't know who Bryan might have had problems with," Stephanie said. "It's sad that he was part of that lifestyle."

"What do you mean?" I asked.

"Like, he just sold stuff to make quick cash and help out," Stephanie said. "I don't know what Leon is doing right now," she said of Rosie's other brother. "Leon is a smart kid who needs to get his shit together. Leon is not about that lifestyle."

Stephanie used the same language discussing Zora's stepbrother, Sparks, who had been killed years earlier. "It was '09 or '10, I think," Stephanie said. Teens often couldn't remember exactly when friends or neighbors had died, recalling instead where and how. "It was right there on Mass Ave. They shot him through the window. They pulled up next to him and just shot through the car, and the bullet went into his head. That whole lifestyle, man."

Another time, Florence echoed Stephanie: "Sparks had been into that whole life for a while. That lifestyle just caught up, and he died."

When young people persistently feel powerless or unsafe, they anxiously anticipate future trauma. This not only prevents them from processing past trauma but also can lead, over time, to PTSD.[32] Dislocating violence—placing it in distant spatial or social worlds—could make teens feel somewhat more secure.

Grieving Online

After learning online that Bryan had died, Stephanie called Faith, and the pair headed to Rosie's apartment. Behind friends and relatives gathered in the living room, they saw Rosie alone in the corner.

"It was the worst I've ever seen her," Stephanie related. "She was sitting there on Twitter. Just sitting there on her computer, slouched down."

The following night, I joined Stephanie when she returned to the apartment. As we arrived, four adults on their way out nodded a somber greeting. Stephanie and I wiped our shoes on the straw mat and passed through the unlocked door.

Inside, family members sat quietly. One elderly man reclined in an armchair; another rested upright, forearm propped on his cane. Rosie approached us, in gray sweats and with her hair wrapped, and Stephanie passed her the cookies and flowers we had brought. Rosie handed them to her mother before hugging Stephanie and me in turn.

"Thank you," Rosie mouthed, leaning on the wall to stay on her feet.

After we left, Stephanie and I sat on a metal bench outside the building.

"It makes you wanna cry, right?" Stephanie said.

Our phones buzzed. Rosie, who had changed her Twitter handle to *RIP BIG BRO* ❤, had tweeted, *thanks again @Jasmin & @Stephanie* ❤

Stephanie replied, *Anytime boo. We love yall so stay up for your bro & your fam. We support you* ❤

Rosie retweeted this reply and mine to her followers.

After a week off school, Rosie trudged to the bus stop one morning at 7:30. On the bus, Rosie took a seat across from me. She crossed her skinny legs at the knee and shook out her headphones, tucking one earbud under each side of the hat pulled down almost over her eyes. As friends and classmates boarded, they greeted her, tentative but upbeat: *Hey Rosie!*

Rosie nodded acknowledgment, then looked away. Her body rocked side to side as she gazed blankly forward. Startled by a classmate's shrieking laugh, she looked up, then slumped down, as if retreating from a world that did not share her pain. The bus teemed with giggles and gossip—once so illicitly pleasurable, now so painfully trivial. At the stop nearest school, students streamed onto the sidewalk, trooping in cheery, boisterous groups. Rosie dragged her feet over the concrete and disappeared through the doors.

Rosie had always been shy. Now, hurting, she grew almost mute. But Rosie poured her feelings onto her Twitter timeline, starting as soon as those grave-eyed cops left her home. She shared hundreds of tweets over the following several days, including,

> *To see my mom like this hurts just like a fucking bitch !!!!!!*
> *Fell in love wit my bros cardigan <3 <3 <3,im sleeping in it*
> *Hurting ten times more right now . . .*
> *My appetite is just the worse*
> *Didn't even get to tell him that I love him like I always do the last time I*
> *saw him.*

Something is holding me back from crying. I gotta be strong for him
   cause he wouldn't want to see me crying like this.
Thanks for all the love everyone. I appreciate it

Silenced in person, Rosie shared intimate sorrow online. She was unfiltered and unguarded, defying critiques that social media posts are a superficial highlight reel.

Rosie's friends read her posts and responded. Digital condolences carried no obligation to respond; teens reached out from a distance to offer but not compel interaction.

Tweeted condolences could, on occasion, be calculated social performances. They might also have replaced sturdier gestures of support. Yet close friends cared for each other this way during their hardest times, and recipients often valued the "love."[33]

Digital Rituals

Trauma can leave people unsure of what to say or how to act. "It was such a 'I don't know what to say' type of moment," Natty said about recognizing Dzhokhar's photo on the day of the lockdown.

Teens shared scripts and rituals for responding to tragedies. Some were physical, like the buttons, hats, and T-shirts they wore, printed with photos of lost peers and dates of their birth or death. There were also cemetery visits on birthdays and anniversaries; teens laid roses in straight lines, brought balloons, and, for young men, left bottled Hennessy.

Certain digital rituals gave grief shape. When there was too much to say, or nothing at all, hashtags—like *#RIPBree* and *#PrayforAngelina,* both used after the Willow Street shooting—proved useful, blending and conveying feelings including sorrow, respect, and defiance. When *#RIPBree* trended locally on Twitter, Aisha felt pleased, even proud. Teens revived hashtags on late peers' birthdays or the anniversaries of their passing—a statement of shared, ongoing remembrance.

Teens also built lost friends into the architecture of their online world. After Bryan died, for instance, many NC teens changed their Twitter handles to *RIP Bryan;* uploaded profile pictures or cover photos featuring his image; or added his name to a list of late peers in "bio" sections, along with other key information like their grade, star sign, and favorite sports teams. Seeta's Twitter bio read: *#TeamIndian #CRLS #TeamTaurus; RIP Jude, Sparks, Omari, Gabby, Bree & Bryan.*

But all memorials, on- and offline, were subject to politics of proximity. A peer's likeness on a pin or profile picture was sacred. Sacred objects, explains Randall Collins, are not only "treated with respect" and "emotionally and vehemently and self-righteously defended."[34] They also have "special qualifications as to who can approach."[35] Just like priestly books or chalices, the objects of teens' digital rituals were revered, and reserved for those deemed truly affected by traumas.

Digital rituals helped make grief legible. They also restated community resilience. Such digital rituals exist at all scales, even globally. Facebook, for instance, offered its hundreds of millions of users new profile picture overlays after momentous occasions, including the Tricolor's red, white, and blue after the 2015 terrorist attack in Paris. "When these flares of solidarity first go up," notes Vinson Cunningham, " . . . [t]he effect overwhelms; the uniformity of color and intent almost replicates a sung anthem."[36] Like an anthem, a popular hashtag or a sea of new profile pictures reiterated unity and bolstered peer groups threatened by trauma.

Shutting Down and Moving On

Each new trauma opened barely healed wounds. After Bryan's death, Stephanie told me, "I just hope nothing else happens, because it has been consecutive violence." Other teens tweeted:

I can't take seeing someone else I grew up with die.
RIP to all my fallen soldiers here Sparks, Jude, Omari & now Bryan ..
Way too many deaths in the past year. RIP KJ, Gabby, Omari, and
   more .. And now Bryan today? SMH[37]

Amid ongoing and cumulative grief, some teens worked to distract friends or help them move on. Friends tried to lift the spirits of Rosie and Leon after they lost their brother Bryan. Visiting their apartment the night the news broke, Stephanie found Leon outside with his boys. "They were tryna make him feel better," she recalled. "I did get a smile out of him, but you can tell, his eyes are just so fucking hurt." Stephanie also tried to cheer up Rosie. "You can't get depressed by all this," Stephanie related. "I said this to Rosie: It's okay to let it out and be sad and mad and angry at the world for a little bit. But you can't live your life in a dark place."

Days later, Florence took Rosie to play in the snow. "I tried to make jokes," Florence explained. "We were having a snowball fight. She was having fun. I'm just tryna make her smile." Florence paused and flashed her dimpled grin. "And girl," she said to me, "for the funeral, I got this suit. You should see my ass! Zora's mom was like, 'When they see how hot you look, they're gonna stop crying!'"

The imperative to "stay up" might have hampered mourning or stigmatized prolonged grieving. But after multiple traumas, it sometimes seemed to teens like a good way to cope.

This did not always mesh with adults' expectations, however. In Angelina's living room, she and Leti seemed to find Ms. Flores's overtures too solemn.

"How is your body feeling?" Ms. Flores asked Angelina.

Angelina lifted her leopard-print shirt and pointed to the scar running down her abdomen. "It looks like a zipper," she said. "I don't like it." Then she poked at her colostomy bag. "The reason I hate this is because look how *fat* it makes me look!" Angelina pulled her shirt back down, showing where she thought it made her stomach pooch.

We assured her otherwise.

"How is the rest of your body feeling?" Ms. Flores probed.

"Well, I have a lotta knee pain," Angelina said, matter-of-factly. "'Cause where the bullet went in, it went through my digestive system, but it also fractured my pelvis and went through veins and nerves and stuff."

Moments later, Angelina ran her hands through her hair. "My ends were so bad!" she said. "You shoulda seen it when I came out of hospital, it had been two weeks. It was so bad!"

As Ms. Flores made to talk, Angelina continued, "Today I did a treatment. I put cholesterol in it. ¿Me lo traes?" She asked her mom to bring over the bottle.

Throughout the visit, Leti helped distract Angelina with happier topics. When Ms. Flores asked another well-meaning question, Leti stamped her right foot down next to Angelina's. They were wearing the same sandals.

Similarly, after the marathon bombing, students quickly tired of the soul searching at school following the arrest of their classmate.

"They would not *stop* going on about it!" a senior said to Aisha and me over lunch. "Three periods in a row! I was like, 'If it carries on like this, I am not coming to school tomorrow.'"

"It was too much!" Aisha concurred, dipping a French fry into a pat of ketchup.

Online, classmates aired similar frustrations:

Um xcuse me Jahar ur interrupting my Dr Phil

If I hear Jahar's name one more time I'm gonna skip class for the rest of the day idc.

This case also stung for another reason: teens resented the huge police mobilization, given the fruitless investigations into their peers' deaths. The evening of the lockdown, as police found and hauled an injured Dzhokhar Tsarnaev from a boat parked in a Watertown yard, Rosie tweeted: *Y'all monkey cops didn't find out who killed my brother, it's been a month and more but y'all find these suspects in 5 days.* One classmate tweeted similarly, *AS MUCH AS IM PROUD IT'S JUST A DAMN SHAME WE DON'T KNOW WHAT HAPPENED TO BREE OR BRYAN,* and another wrote, *Find out who Killed Bryan and then MAYBE I will give a fuck about this shit.*

Adults rarely shared teens' hierarchy of traumas or their coping practices. While peers knew when to engage and when to distract, adults and teachers could be heavier-handed.[38]

Still, teachers and staff were often invaluable resources as teens processed traumas. Natty spent hours with a guidance counselor after her ex-boyfriend Bryan died. And many students appreciated Ms. Flores's sensitivity after the Willow Street shooting. As Joanne explained, "It's really hard to sit in class and be present when someone else's reality was just shattered. Ms. Flores wasn't trying to be like, 'Let's continue on with George Washington.'"

School officials also took special measures to involve Angelina in her graduation.[39] Bed-bound in the hospital, Angelina could not yet stand or walk. But, just like her friends, she had her hair styled and was helped into a cap and gown. She joined the ceremony through a video link, and her brother collected her diploma on her behalf.[40] The crowd roared for Angelina, projected onto big screens.

"You guys," she stirred, "We finally made it!"[41]

They roared too, for another graduating senior: Malachi, who had lost his sister, Bree. "You will never be alone," the senior class president told him. "You have four hundred brothers and sisters." As Malachi crossed the stage, they rose to their feet and clapped.

Technologies of Trauma

In the face of devastating tragedies, teens pieced together shattered worlds by making traumas manageable. After news "exploded" online, through thick tangles of connections, teens made sense of the senseless, collaboratively comprehending what had happened, to whom, and why. To cope, the girls drew boundaries that located danger elsewhere. Digital rituals helped them grieve and restated community resilience. And teens helped each other "stay up" and move on.[42] Teens' work to restore their safety, routines, and relationships often took place out of view of adults and teachers and sometimes clashed with institutional expectations for trauma management.

Dissemination, comprehension, and coping could all come quickly, like one Thursday night, weeks after Bryan's death, when Aisha, alone in her apartment, heard gunshots. At her desktop when she heard the bangs, she tweeted:

> *Multiple gun shots here .. ? Or am I hallucinating ?*
> *I mean do we have to live in terror ? Every other ducking week now*
> *They just found three bullets .. This shit is right under me ..*
> *About 6-9 shots fired .. It was a drive by type thing .. 2 secs later the*
>   *police came thru*

Aisha uploaded to Facebook a grainy photo of police searching the area with the caption, *From the window .. It's fucking law and order out here*. She sent an eight-second video of the same scene to her Snapchat contacts, voicing over the words, "Be safe."

Aisha's posts spread the news. Friends and neighbors online quickly established that nobody had been hurt. With her mom at work, Aisha's peers were her only outlet. They met her posts with empathy and suggestions. One neighbor commented, *same,* and a friend wrote, *Yep sleep with ur light on then ull feel better.*

Bigger traumas, however, could take months or years to manage. After her brother's death, Rosie became wary, particularly after dark. One night, Rosie's clique encouraged her to join them at a house party nearby in the project. The girls gathered for a drink beforehand. When we prepared to head over, Rosie hovered in the apartment's hallway as Faith opened the front door.

"I hate walking around in the dark," Rosie said. "You go first, I'm scared," she added, and pushed Faith into the street with a hand to the lower back.

Faith stepped encouragingly into the night. Rosie followed. Moments later, however, Faith's red cup slipped from her hand and clattered against the sidewalk. Rosie flinched, trembling.

Over time, however, the baby of the group grew into a self-assured and joyful young woman. Rosie inched, week by week, closer to the center of rooms. One Saturday night, Rosie's friends smiled as she strode out from the shadows and danced.

6 Dealing with Difference

Aisha decided to throw a party one weekend when her mom left town. She spread the word and asked her brother, who worked at Entertainment Cinema, to pick up a shift, leaving her home alone.

On the Friday evening, Aisha changed into the outfit she had chosen: blue denim overalls and a purple crop top. She took some selfies, capturing the tattoo on her waist: a woman's face over the continent of Africa. Then, with Brittani's help, she prepared the living room. The girls shoved the chairs against the wall to clear a dance floor.

Before long, Aisha's home filled with eager teens. Some sipped drinks they had brought along or that they had paid Vincent, Joanne's brother, to buy on a liquor run. Others smoked weed in the back stairwell. Aisha didn't smoke—in her clique, only Seeta did—and she drank only infrequently. But a party was a special occasion. So from a bottle stashed under the sink Aisha poured shots into paper cups for herself and her favorite friends.

While Aisha, Joanne, and Seeta got "wavey," Brittani sat on a chair by the wall, arms folded over a baggy gray shirt that read, "We Are College Bound." Brittani didn't drink; alcohol, she said, smelled nasty and burned her throat. But she didn't mind her friends drinking. Even when others, as she put it, got "pretty big into drinking, getting weed," they still hung out together, including at the "Riv," the clearing by the Charles River where teens gathered some weekends. Brittani felt no peer pressure. "I know I'm not going to do it, so I have nothing to worry about," she said.

Aisha surveyed the crowd from the corner of her living room. She snapped photos of people dancing in pairs and groups. Then she shoved her way into the middle of the room and parodied twerking. Aisha and her friends could dance with snappy talent but rarely did so in public. As her hands touched the floor and her thighs shook, Aisha ran back into the throng.

"No, suh! No, suh!" she laughed.

Her friends clapped and whooped.

Spurred by their laughter, Aisha returned to the center of the dance floor, this time crossing her arms over her chest and stroking her own shoulders to mime a couple's embrace. Again she cracked up and dashed back into the crowd. This wouldn't be *that* type of party.

As the hours passed, teens took turns hooking their iPods up to the speakers. They played songs they liked, singing or rapping along. Some teens flirted gently through the evening, but most seemed focused on having fun with friends.

Just after midnight, as steam speckled the windows, Aisha noticed the time on her iPod. Suddenly she cut the music.

"Listen up!" she hollered. "Y'all have twenty minutes until the last train. Thank you for coming!" She bowed dramatically. Teens laughed at her bluntness.

Those who had come from "East," "Port," and "Coast" bustled out first. The NC kids found friends to head home with and followed shortly after.

Once the guests had left, Aisha peeled the duct tape off her fridge. Then she perched on a chair, surveying the mess. She would clean up the party's physical traces before her mom returned, but first she wanted to upload digital ones. She scrolled through the photos she had taken, of friends and classmates from all over the city. The photos showed teens with diverse hobbies, habits, and hopes—teens who, despite their differences, had together made the most of this Friday night.[1]

This diversity existed even in Aisha's own clique. Some of the girls experimented with drinking and drugs, but others chose not to. Growing up, the NC girls had not faced such discrepancies, so these decisions forked a path they had long walked in lockstep. To protect their friendships, the girls found ways to deal with difference.

Homophily and Peer Effects

Many teens have friends like themselves. The popular trope of the socially segregated lunchroom—"jocks" at one table, "nerds" at another—is, in fact, supported by research.[2] The concept of homophily, meaning love of the same, suggests that the foundation of friendship—and many other types of relationships—is similarity. Most people's social networks, sociologists note, are largely homophilous in values, beliefs, and behaviors.[3]

Young people often act like their friends, not only on measures like whether they do their homework or apply to college, but also when it comes to what researchers call risk behaviors, like alcohol, drugs, and sex.[4]

Hundreds of studies in sociology, criminology, and psychology investigate these peer effects, aiming to capture how habits and outcomes end up shared.[5] Some emphasize the idea of *selection:* teens choosing friends who act like they do. Others claim that through *socialization,* peers encourage one another to adopt new behaviors.

But studies that try to identify whether peer effects work through selection or socialization have two key limitations. First, they flatten relationships into mere predictors of outcomes, like whether or not someone smokes.[6] They mark friendships as either present or absent, when in fact they are continually (re)negotiated. This can obscure the dynamic, day-to-day processes that animate friendships and blur the complicated forms that social influence really takes.

Second, researchers who study peer effects, particularly among low-income teens, often describe a "contagion" of risk behaviors.[7] This metaphor stigmatizes certain acts and even whole groups of people. It also elides the tremendous diversity that exists within cliques. While many studies explore diversity and heterogeneity in poor neighborhoods,[8] fewer consider how close friendships handle difference. How do groups of friends manage disparate beliefs and behaviors?

In NC, when some of the young women began drinking or having sex, there was no "contagion" of peer effects. Those who experimented did not *select* new friends with similar habits; that would have meant losing cherished relationships and important support. Nor did they *socialize* one another to start acting the same way. Instead, the girls protected their relationships pragmatically, by accommodating a degree of difference.

Dealing with Difference: Identity Claims

Personal Identity Claims

During adolescence, teenagers' personalities and identities rapidly develop. Social media has an impact on this process, giving young people new opportunities to define and portray themselves. In online bios, many of the NC girls chose to emphasize their social relationships, ambitions, and achievements. Zora's Twitter bio, for instance, read, *My motivation and purpose to succeed are my main prioritys. God got me!! College Student! Haitian Black, I'm educated, an educator, and role model. Reaching the stars.* Others tweeted photos of A grades marked on returned papers, or shared posts like, *Study Time Now! No matter what nothing distracts me from success.*[9]

On social media, the girls also expressed their views on things like drinking, drugs, and sex. Aisha, for example, tweeted *#soberlife* during periods when she shunned alcohol, and of her vocal sexual abstinence, she hashtagged *#nunlife*. Such tweets forced their authors to follow through or risk being seen as "fake."[10] Moreover, hashtags conjured a community, transforming personal choices—like sobriety or virginity—into shared social identities. They turned a choice not to *do* something into a decision to *be* someone.

Such identity claims offered pride, like when Aisha tweeted, *#DUMBESTMOMENTS: WHEN I ALMOST LOST IT TO A N***A THAT I DIDN'T EVEN CARE ABOUT AND STILL DON'T -____- DAMN #TEAMVIRGINS WE'RE SUPERIOR*. They also let the girls access positive and supportive feelings of group membership, even when their friends acted differently. Perhaps this made the girls less susceptible to peer pressure, helping sustain diversity within cliques.

Somewhat paradoxically, however, the girls resisted identity claims made by friends who *did* drink or smoke weed. Florence, for example, who smoked more than any of her friends, called herself a "hippie." When she had first tried weed as a high school sophomore, encouraged by her then-boyfriend, Vincent, she didn't like it very much. She liked it a little better when a friend gave her a blunt after she helped him with homework. By the end of high school, Florence posted Snapchat selfies blowing perfect smoky O's.

"I feel so spiritual when I'm high," Florence mused in Zora's kitchen, just after midnight one Saturday. Swiping two cookies from a drawer, she passed one to me and bit into the other. "I feel so spiritual and peaceful and humble," she said. "I could be a hippie."

But her friends viewed things differently. Faith, Florence's younger sister who had never smoked, said smoking was "not based off [someone's] character, it's just something they're doing." Brittani spoke similarly: "They're still the same person. They just do something that makes them feel better." When it came to things like smoking and drinking, the girls often cleaved the practice—something someone *did*—from the person—something someone *was*.[11]

The girls made personal identity claims that bolstered their decisions to avoid so-called risk behaviors. At the same time, they framed indulgence among friends as a choice, not an identity, making their differences seem superficial.

Group Identity Claims

Another way the girls made differences between them seem superficial was by claiming a unified *collective* identity for their entire cliques. By drawing group-level boundaries between themselves and outsiders, the girls raised their sense of internal similarity.[12]

Late one Saturday night, Florence, Faith, Zora, Rosie, and I sat around a picnic table behind the project.

"Go in the house, Jonny, you ugly ass!" yelled a thin Black woman standing in the long grass nearby. Jonny, a red-haired white man in a sweat-stained gray shirt, leaned out of a first-floor window and shouted down in response.

"Shut the fuck up, Jonny," the woman bellowed back. "Your momma fucked that Haitian so he could get a green card, and you *still* live in public housing!"

The girls laughed at the melee.

"My *God,* she's ratchet," Zora said, pursing her lips.

"She's from Boston, right?" Faith asked.

"Yes, she's from Boston," Zora said.

"Why are people from Boston coming over here? Like, is it that bad over there?" Faith asked.

"So ratchet," the girls chuckled.

The girls slammed neighbors who were raucous, who wore tattered clothes, or who used drugs in public as "ratchet"—a favored epithet meaning nasty and uncouth. The word marked a stark social distance between themselves and that group of others.[13]

The girls used "hood" and "ghetto" similarly, as class- and race-inflected slurs that deemed certain people less worthy and respectable. While they used the noun *hood* to describe NC, the terms, as adjectives aimed at other people, were meant disparagingly.

Walking to the movie theater another evening, Florence side-eyed two women who passed us on the street. "That weave, though," Florence whispered to Faith. "This one thinks she's Beyoncé!"

"*Maaad* ratchet!" her sister laughed. "Reminds me of those ratchet hoes that time in South Boston."

"Yeah, that was so ghetto!" Florence said. "It was like, 'Shaniqua, *heeey!*'"[14]

By contrasting themselves, explicitly or implicitly, to "ratchet" others, the girls played down internal differences, even as their own beliefs and behaviors diverged.

Dealing with Difference: Pluralism and Policing

Practicing Pluralism

The girls drew on other strategies when confronted clearly with their own disparities. Often they let difference slide, opting instead to "practice pluralism." Particularly when a friend was only *talking* about something challenging, proceeding with conversation could be less awkward than a confrontation.

One Saturday afternoon, for example, I strolled with Florence and Stephanie to the local strip mall. On our way to TJ Maxx, Florence brought up weed.

"I got so high on my birthday," she laughed. "I was caught in a storm, high as shit! It was so funny!"

Without pause, Stephanie, who had never smoked, replied, "The last time I got my hair done, I got caught in the rain! I wasted all my money."

Stephanie was smoothing over comments that highlighted the girls' dissimilarity. Such conversational creativity—which called for quick thinking and sometimes for clunky non sequiturs—sidestepped conflict, which can be costly in adolescent relationships.[15] This accommodation of difference helped preserve valuable friendships.[16]

The girls also practiced pluralism in more challenging encounters. They treated one another with grace and kindness, even when someone got "too turnt."

One Friday evening, I joined Florence, Faith, Rosie, and Zora as they drank together before a house party being thrown by an NC friend, Stevenson.

Between glugs from a glass bottle of sangria, Florence complained to her clique about Vincent. When she had run into her ex that afternoon, Vincent had high-fived the friend Florence was with but totally ignored her.

"He looks like a stupid little Ninja Turtle," Faith said, consoling her sister.

"Whatever," Florence sighed. She passed the bottle to Rosie.

Rosie took a small swig, and Zora scowled. Rosie had only recently started drinking when her friends did, and Zora still felt protective.

A while later, the girls stood to head to the party. They checked their phone batteries, took some selfies, and braced into the January night. Dodging heaps of snow graying on the sidewalk, Florence's black pumps slid over icy paving stones. She caught her balance and smoothed her black skirt.

We entered Stevenson's block and climbed three flights of stairs to the apartment. Inside, Stevenson nodded at us from the TV stand where he was DJing, his laptop propped beside a handle of Bacardi and a plastic pitcher of fruit punch. Behind him, a wall-mounted poster of Barack Obama sagged slightly from its fastenings.

The girls dropped their coats on one of the twin beds in Stevenson's room. Back in the living room, they hugged friends and classmates. Florence strode straight to her friend, Robenson.

"You got weed?" she asked. She gave Robenson two fives in exchange for a small baggie and passed another friend two bucks for a chocolate cigarillo.

Florence took her haul into the bathroom, trailed by Zora, Faith, Rosie, and me. She sat on the closed toilet seat and scored the cigarillo with her house key, dumping its contents into the trash. As Florence crumbled clumps of weed into the empty cigarillo, Faith crossed her arms, bored.

Florence fussed and fumbled, and Faith rolled her eyes. Eventually Faith went for help, returning with Leon, who had an unlit joint of his own in his mouth. Leon nimbly took over from Florence.

"Why y'all using a 'rillo?" he said. "This shit will burn up all your lungs!"

Florence shrugged.

Then, turning to his little sister, Rosie, Leon said, "Girl, you better not smoke!"

"Don't you dare ever smoke!" Zora said to Rosie, seconding Leon. "I will kill you!"

"It's okay, I don't want to," Rosie replied, smiling shyly.

Leon finished his work and passed Florence her rolled joint. We headed to the kitchen, where smokers lounged on the furniture that had been shoved in to clear the living room. Through the haze, teens acknowledged each other with quiet nods.

Florence lit her joint and passed it back and forth with Zora. Faith and Rosie hovered by the doorway, impatient to rejoin the party.

Minutes later, the girls formed a circle in the living room and danced to the Meek Mill song playing through the speakers. Florence felt everything, hard. She squeezed her eyes shut and flailed her arms. Faith raised her eyebrows at her sister.

Suddenly Florence turned her back on her friends, pivoting to face the crowded room's center. Then she bent over and heaved, retching a thick stream of sangria-pink vomit onto the floor. People screamed and sprang away.

Florence staggered toward the bathroom, shooting a second pink pool on the floor just outside. Zora grabbed Florence's arm and rushed her out of the apartment, past amused and disgusted teens. Faith, Rosie, and I followed them through the front door.

"I'm so high, I'm so sorry," Florence said, collapsing onto the block's interior stone stairwell. "I am Florence. I am at Stevenson's house. This is a party," she told herself.

Stevenson appeared, holding a roll of paper towels.

"Oh, we're fine. Thanks," Zora said.

Stevenson stood still, arm extended.

"Oh," Zora said, a moment later. "You want us to clean that up?"

Stevenson widened his eyes in confirmation.

Zora pursed her lips and drew in a long breath before heading back inside. When she returned, having mopped up the mess, she decided to take Florence home. But Florence was only wearing one shoe.

"Where's the other one, baby?" Zora asked.

Florence was incoherent. Zora lay a palm on her friend's clammy shoulder and asked again.

Faith sighed and went to search the house. When she emerged, shoe in hand, Zora hauled Florence to her feet.

"Alright, boo, let's go," she said.

We walked Florence down the stairs and back into the snowy project. The girls guided Florence, with no coat and one shoe, to

Zora's apartment, stopping when she grasped for the black metal railings to settle her stomach. They put Florence to bed in Zora's apartment, tugging off her other shoe and placing an empty trashcan by her head.

Before long the girls laughed about Stevenson's party. Florence smiled when her friends ribbed her. The night caused no resentment or changes in their friendship.

Pushback and Policing

At times the girls challenged each other or called one another out. Usually, they softened the sharp edges of criticism; the point seemed to nudge, not hurt.

In their senior year, Seeta was the only girl in Aisha's clique who smoked weed. One day after school, as Aisha, Joanne, and I watched YouTube videos in Aisha's living room, Seeta called Joanne's cell.

"Seeta's going to buy fudge, then she's gonna come over," Joanne explained aloud to Aisha and me.

Aisha nodded.

"Wait," Joanne said to Seeta, still on the line. "Where you going to buy fudge at?" After a pause, Joanne threw back her head, laughing, "Ohhh! You said *bud!* I thought you said fudge!"

When Seeta arrived, minutes later, Aisha looked her up and down.

"Don't tell me you have bud in my apartment," Aisha said.

Seeta didn't respond. Instead she rubbed her head and said, "I'm tired. I'm not going to school tomorrow."

"You better be careful before you can't go to prom," Joanne said gently.

"I have to baby-sit tomorrow anyway," Seeta replied.

"I can bring your work," Joanne offered. Seeta shrugged. A few minutes later, she headed home.

Aisha criticized Seeta for having weed. Joanne used the school rulebook to encourage her to come to class and do her work. Yet neither was stridently confrontational, and neither pushed Seeta when she ignored their challenges.

More forceful policing often involved siblings.

Francis, Florence and Faith's older sister, sometimes challenged Florence for drinking or smoking. One night, Florence, drunk and high, walked into her living room, where Francis was lounging with some friends. Francis frowned.

"You been drinking?" she demanded.

Florence rolled her eyes.

Francis then glared at Florence's baggy T-shirt, which read, "Free Breathalyzer, Blow Here," above a large red arrow pointing down.

"Is that a dude's shirt? God!" Francis said. "The fuck is wrong with you?" As Francis laughed and her company joined in, Florence sheepishly led me to the kitchen.

Friends too could be confrontational on occasion. Just after Thanksgiving, for example, Florence and I caught a late showing of *Best Man Holiday* at Entertainment Cinema. Then we headed to Zora's house, where some of their clique were hanging out.

In Zora's bedroom, Rosie sat cross-legged on a folding metal chair as Zora wove her some braids. Faith, Francis, and Faith's friend Pia sat on Zora's bed, sharing a Strawberita. Over on another chair in the corner, Florence's friend Diego swigged from a can of Bud Light.

Florence and I joined the girls on Zora's bed. As Zora did Rosie's hair, we half-watched a movie playing on a flickering television. The sides of the TV were scratched up with scissors and bore several "Zora"s in cursive white-out. A bare bulb on a long lamp pole cast a white-yellow glare; like all the bedrooms in the project apartments, there were no overhead lights.

"No STDs, Diego?" Zora cracked, during a lull in the movie.

"Not no more," he quipped back, grinning.

"Hey, let's go smoke," Florence said. Diego stood, but no one else moved.

"You coming, Jasmin?" Florence asked.

"I'm gonna stay here. It's cold," I replied.

"Good girl," Zora said, as Florence and Diego left. "Don't go burn up all your lungs!" Zora smoked in phases, and in her off-periods a little self-righteousness helped her abstain.

"Where'd they get that weed from?" Zora asked the other girls.

"No, they have no weed to smoke," Francis said, explaining that they were smoking tobacco.

"Ew!" Zora said. "They bugging with that black shit! They're tryna kill themselves!" Tobacco sat near the bottom of the girls' hierarchy of substances.

"You know hookah is 180 cigarettes or some shit?" Francis said.

"No, it isn't!" Zora replied. "You're just trying to scare us."

"It popped up on my Instagram the other day," Francis insisted.

"Why we watching this disrespectful ass movie?" Faith cut in. She didn't smoke—hookah, tobacco, or marijuana—and neither did she like these discussions. Rosie also ignored the conversation, fussing instead with her cell phone.

Meekly, Pia rose to join Florence and Diego.

"Make sure you stay outside with them too," Zora said, disdainful.

"Yeah, for a good thirty minutes!" Faith added.

"Last time, they came to the house smelling like straight-up marijuana," Zora said to everyone left in her room: Rosie, Faith, Francis, and me. "They had my house smelling like marijuana, and they were mad loud too! You know whenever Florence gets high she gets mad happy?" Zora continued.

Faith nodded.

"I was like, 'Yo, Florence. If my dad comes downstairs, I'm not getting in trouble for y'all. I'm straight snitchin','" Zora said.

When Pia returned minutes later, Zora narrowed her eyes.

"Let me smell you," Zora said. "Go sit in the corner! You're making me nauseous."

Pia obliged. As Faith's friend, not Zora's, Pia could not easily respond. But Faith did, on her behalf.

"I don't smell a damn thing," Faith said. Faith disliked both smoking and conflict.

"Nauseous," Zora reiterated. It was her house and her last word.

Such direct policing was not particularly common. Zora's comments—which marshaled multiple justifications: nausea, parents, health concerns—aimed both to cajole her friends and to restate her own commitments.

Limiting Difference?

Pushback and policing did not eliminate disparities between the girls. Still, nudges may have limited differences within cliques, making them more manageable.

One Saturday afternoon, I joined Florence, Zora, Stephanie, and their friend Neveah at a cookout in the project. At the folding table spread with silver trays, we loaded paper plates with chicken wings, tortilla chips, cheese puffs, and watermelon slices, then took seats on plastic chairs nearby.

As soon as we sat down, Florence slipped away to smoke weed. When she returned, Stephanie turned to the group and said, "Florence is *too* happy."

"She got so much worse this year!" Neveah seconded, laughing.

"At least I'm not having sex!" Florence cut back. "I have to substitute something. You know, like in that episode of *Sex and the City* when all she does is eat when she's not having sex. It's like that but not with food." "I don't even drink that much," she added. "I don't even drink hard liquor, just wine, and hello! Wine is good for you!"

The conversation moved on. But Florence's defensiveness suggested that her friends' words caused a twinge of discomfort. Florence, and all the girls, cared more about friends' opinions than adult judgment.[17] And counter to the conventional account of peer pressure—where risk behaviors are encouraged and abstention is ridiculed—Florence knew she might have to explain herself each time she lit up.[18]

Another evening, in Aisha's living room, Seeta regaled Aisha, Joanne, Brittani, and me with a story about a fight she had seen earlier. Her friend Kim had "gotten into it" on the street with another girl, Anais.

"Who won?" Aisha asked, without looking up from her phone.

"Well, Anais walked away, so," Seeta said, upbeat. "Kim barely had any cuts. Anais had a bump on her frikkin' *face* . . . Kim hit her so many times I was like, 'Oh damn, I'm proudda you!'"

Aisha and Joanne turned to Seeta.

"Look at you with your ghetto self," Aisha said, smiling ever so slightly.

Seeta went on: "After the second time, Kim wanted to go for a third time, but I was like, 'Let's go.'"

Brittani scrunched her forehead. "Anais is ratchet. She's irrelevant and stupid."

"But no, Kim's not a fighter," Seeta said, defensive. "This was her first fight."

"She fights with her sisters," Aisha said.

"Yo, have you seen her sisters? They are so deez," Seeta scrambled.[19]

Without criticizing Seeta, the other girls shared their views of fighting. This kind of gossip about other people was another way friends established what was tolerable, possibly limiting their differences.[20]

Growing Up and Growing Apart

Over the years, some of the girls experimented with so-called risk behaviors, like drinking or smoking weed. Some didn't. Others started, then stopped, then started again.[21]

Researchers rarely consider this kind of heterogeneity—either within cliques or within teens' own habits over time. Instead many have focused on a different task: creating tools to understand similarity between peers. They have sought to ascertain whether teens find new cliques who share their practices or adopt behaviors picked up by their friends. But the NC girls did neither. They did not curate their social lives based on fixed beliefs or behaviors. Nor were they powerless victims of group norms.[22]

Instead, the girls developed strategies to deal with difference. While some made individual identity claims based on resisting risk behaviors, they all claimed a unified group identity by contrasting their cliques to "ratchet," "ghetto" outsiders. This minimized their sense of internal variation. When faced with their disparities directly, the girls often practiced pluralism to keep conversations going. Sometimes, however, they pushed back against or, occasionally, more stridently policed their friends.

The choice of one response over another varied; sometimes the girls sanctioned friends, and sometimes they kept quiet. Sometimes they became impatient, and sometimes they were amused. Yet together these strategies—and the girls' use of a *practical consciousness*, responding creatively to situations instead of enacting fixed rules—helped them preserve their bonds day by day and year by year.[23]

This pragmatism helped protect relationships that the girls needed to survive both mundane and extreme hardships. More meaningful to the NC girls than a shared approach to drugs or drinking were other similarities, including their common experiences and mutual patterns of care. The girls liked each other and relied on each other, and although these types of affinities are less frequently measured or analyzed by social scientists, they helped friends stick together as their habits diverged.[24]

If researchers study peer groups only as variables—things that predict the likelihood of something else—they miss the real-life processes that drive social influence.[25] They also miss the strategies involved in adapting old friendships to new differences. In other words, they overlook *how* teens protect their relationships. Moreover, if researchers explore only those types of similarities and differences most interesting to themselves, they ignore countless ways in which teens feel closeness and community. In doing so, they miss *why* teens work so hard for their friendships.

3   *After Graduation*

7 Struggle and Support at College

"CONGRATULATIONS GRADUATES," read the sign over CRLS's auditorium doors. As family members of graduating seniors made their way inside the building, vendors hawked small bouquets and stuffed animals. A solitary police bomb truck idled across the street, but unlike the previous year's ceremony, a week after the Willow Street shooting, no TV news squads hovered with cameras.

In the auditorium, Joanne's mother, Carole, marshaled her four youngest children into a row of seats. The three boys wore satin vests, and Joanne's little sister had two braids finished with white clips. Around us, helium-filled balloons twirled in the AC breeze.

Everyone stood for the pledge of allegiance. Then, with the audience once more seated, teachers and officials gave speeches praising the graduating class.

"I will remember you most," the principal said, "as an innovative, focused, and resilient group that made the sweetest lemonade out of the lemons you encountered."

The superintendent said, "Three hundred sixty-five days ago, we gathered in this space and remembered Bree and Angelina. . . . This year, more big events—some natural, some man-made—hit us."[1] Up front, the girls nodded, somber.

But as diplomas were distributed, there was only happiness. Teens crossed the stage to cheers, gowns billowing behind their legs.

After the pageantry, girls posed for photos outside. Diplomas in one hand and phones in the other, they posted status updates and misty-captioned montages. Joanne tweeted, *Mad shit happened to our class as a whole in Senior year and to everyone individually. We are soldiers! #SOPROUD.*

Aisha posted a photo of herself, Joanne, Seeta, and Brittani with the caption, *LOOK MAMA WE MADE IT These are MY Girls since day 1. My high school experience, MY LIFE, my everything. These are my sisters if there's Anyone I could say has loved me more than my family it is these girls.*

Spirited by imminent separation, teens leaned into last-chance fun. Cookouts stretched through long days, parties through hot nights. And, in a flash of independence, Aisha and Seeta got their noses pierced together.

There were also formal celebrations, like the brunch at Aisha's church to honor the congregation's graduating seniors. To mark the occasion, Aisha's mom let her daughter invite her friends.

When the Sunday came, Aisha's brother drove Aisha, Joanne, Seeta, Brittani, and me to the business park that housed the church. We rode up together in an elevator. As soon as the doors opened, Aisha dashed off to mingle. Her friends stayed back, listening to the Luganda chatter and scanning the space. Rows of red-cushioned chairs were split by a center aisle. Crosses of grass and flowers hung on the walls.

An MC tapped the mic to start the ceremony. Aisha's mother sat with friends in the first row, and Aisha's brother and I took seats a few rows back. Once everyone had found chairs, Aisha and two other graduating congregants, along with Joanne, Seeta, and Brittani, were welcomed down the aisle to applause. The teens sat at a long table up front, which was covered with a blue paper tablecloth and decorated with blue balloons.

The pastor's low voice then filled the room: "What a huge honor it is to graduate high school in the greatest country in the world!"

As everyone clapped, Aisha's brother leaned to me, whispering, "Our mom got Aisha a laptop for a graduation present. No one knows, so don't say anything!"

"Let us pray," bellowed the pastor. Next he invited the mothers of the three church graduates to offer some remarks. Aisha's mom went last. The gold threads in her red dress shone under the overhead lights and her earrings shook with the vigor of her words.

"Aisha has been a very good little baby to me," she said to the room. "She's kind of spoiled, not through me, but through her aunties. But why I love Aisha? She knows God." The audience applauded. "As a single mother, it's not easy to raise up kids. Sometimes you come home when you're grumpy, you don't even want to talk to anyone. But I praise God because I've tried my best, and I'm still trying."

The girls spoke next. Usually buoyed by an audience, Aisha seemed bowed by the momentousness.

"I'm sorry if I cry, I'm very emotional," Aisha said, timidly palming the mic. "If it wasn't for my mom, I wouldn't be here." She then thanked two aunts, the pastor and his wife, and the church, before turning to the table beside her. "And I wanna thank my three friends, Joanne, Brittani, Seeta. I love you guys so much. They understand the in-between. Like, being Ugandan and being American. That is not easy. They understand." With tears rolling down her face, Aisha urged the children gazing up from the front row, "Have friends that understand you. Who've been where you've been."

Aisha's friends were similarly moved. Through tears of her own, Joanne said, "We've all had experiences. I came from another country . . . I also have a single mom. Sometimes people don't understand."

Seeta said, "I understand what Aisha feels and Joanne feels . . . I'm just very happy to be here."

Sniffing back tears, Brittani went last, saying, "Hi everyone. I'm really nervous. I thank God for getting me through high school with all my friends. I also grew up with a single mother . . . It's been a real great struggle, but we fought through it, my friends."

The girls wiped each other's smudged makeup before lunch: rice, beans, stewed meat, and fried greens, ladled onto styrofoam plates in a side room. The graduates ate at the decorated table and sipped grape juice from plastic flutes.

After the meal, the graduates cut a large cake shaped like an open book. Then the music began. As women kicked off their heels and danced, the girls let loose at the table.

Adults greeted the teens, offering the church graduates congratulations and, occasionally, a white envelope into which they slyly peeked.

Aisha's mother placed a heavy bag by her daughter's feet and walked away. Aisha glanced into the bag and gave a small nod.

"What is it?" Aisha's friends buzzed.

"It's a laptop," she said.

"What type?" Joanne asked, trying to prolong the excitement.

"Not a Mac," Aisha shrugged. "It's kinda ghetto."

"Girl!" Seeta said, "I don't even have a computer!"

It wasn't Aisha's dream, but it would do. It was the most grown-up thing she had ever owned.

Next Steps

After graduating from high school, the girls, like most teens nationwide, planned to attend college.[2] They shared an "ambition imperative" that encouraged aiming high.[3] Joanne judged some NC boys who, she said, did not "do anything or get anything." "You wanna live here your whole life?" College, by contrast, conjured pride and a bright future.

Yet while the landscape of postsecondary education has flourished in recent decades, it has also grown harder to navigate, particularly for first-generation students who often struggle to build effective trajectories.[4] Most of the NC girls' parents did not have the time, know-how, or English skills to help their daughters apply to college. Many of the girls selected schools with a slapdash pragmatism, adding, to price and location, scraps of information and intuition.[5]

"I only applied to dumb schools," Aisha told me. Although she had dreamed of college in California, far from her mother's discipline and Boston's winters, she only applied in-state. "I didn't know what to apply to," she said.

Still the girls jointly pursued the goal of making it to college. They toured campuses and shared insights from older cousins and friends: which schools were "popping" and which were a little too crazy. And they held each other accountable.

One Friday night while Vincent buzzed Aisha's hair with his electric razor, Joanne joined her best friend on the bathroom floor. "Did you do your scholarship application?" Joanne asked. "You know I'm a be on you about that!" The following night, Joanne offered to explain the online application portal to Seeta.

After submitting their applications, the girls waited.

One Saturday night, Joanne, Seeta, and I watched a pirated stream of the final *Twilight* movie in Joanne's living room. Midway through the film, Carole came home with the mail and passed her daughter an envelope. Joanne opened it carefully.

"Oh my God, I just got into college!" she exclaimed.

Seeta hugged Joanne, then tweeted: *Congrats to this hoe @Joanne she got into umass boston!*

Over the next several weeks, the girls posted screenshots of welcome emails and photos of acceptance letters, announcing their own and one another's achievements online. A few used social media to seek advice on which schools to attend. *Curry College or St. John's??*

Seeta tweeted, and a fellow senior posted, *University of Rhode Island or Bryant??? #imtorn.*

While some of the girls struggled to weigh options, they mostly agreed, however, that community college was an inferior choice. One evening I joined the girls at a banquet for graduating high school seniors enrolled in the city's Workforce program. We took seats at a round table, on which organizers had left a card printed with the colleges where enrolled students had won admission. Zora reached for the card and scanned the list.

"They really shouldn't put Bunker Hill," said Zora, who had herself started at the school before transferring to a private university. "It's a community college. Of course you're gonna get accepted! If you don't, you should really reevaluate yourself."

Heads turned to Faith, who would start at Bunker Hill in the fall. After a moment, Faith shrugged. "That's what Francis said," she said.

The girls who accepted places at community college explained their decisions differently. Brittani felt like she had no choice; she had been accepted by her first-choice school, but, she explained, her mom's debt stopped her from getting the loan she would need. Faith was longer-winded. "I wasn't ready for the big school, going away right away," she told me. "So I chose to stay home and do community college. 'Cause with me, money wasn't a problem, but at the same time it was a problem. I didn't wanna go to a big school where I knew I couldn't pay the rest and then be in debt for the rest of my life."

With limited guidance, the girls did their best. They encouraged one another to dream big and helped where they could.[6]

Girls without supportive friends often faced tougher choices. Natty, for instance, a cousin of Florence and Faith, had grown up in Cambridge with two brothers, a sister, and a mom who worked long hours washing dishes. Although Natty recalled a happy childhood, moves between elementary schools left her somewhat unrooted. In high school, Natty, like Florence, found that boys could make her feel secure. Also like Florence, an attraction sparked between her and Vincent.[7] The two started talking, and a while later Florence walked in on them in bed together. From then on, Florence called Natty her "ex-cousin."

"Natty doesn't have much close friends," Florence's best friend, Stephanie, told me. Natty didn't disagree. Most of her friendships had dissolved through high school—both cause and effect of her interest in boys' affection.

Natty started seeing another boy, Keshawn, who over time became her primary source of support. Keshawn comforted Natty when her mother was treated for breast cancer and when her friend Bree and ex-boyfriend Bryan were killed months apart.

"Keshawn's been there every step of the way," Natty explained. "If I need someone to talk to, he'll talk to me. He tries to take my mind off it."

Yet Natty felt like her relationship interfered with school. "Keshawn is like, 'Are any boys in class trying to talk to you?'" she related. "I'm like, 'Stop being jealous. I go to school for school.'"

Natty was ambitious, and her older sister tried to help her apply to college. "She's always kind of been like my mom," Natty said. "She goes to my school meetings. My mom stopped that like, seventh grade."[8] But Keshawn's complaints troubled Natty. "He's nervous because he knows I want to go away to school, not just live at home and go to school. He thinks crazy stuff like, 'You're going to cheat when you go to school.'"[9]

Natty relied on her boyfriend, who helped her through crisis after crisis. But while her former friends, including Florence and Stephanie, pushed one another to leave, Natty felt held in place. Ultimately, even though, as she put it, "going to a four-year was on my bucket list," Natty stayed home and enrolled at Bunker Hill.

Moving Away

All nine girls in both cliques graduated from high school. They all applied to college, received offers, accepted places, and enrolled. Aisha, Joanne, Stephanie, and Rosie started at public universities, and Florence and Seeta began in private colleges. Brittani, Faith, and Zora started at community college.[10]

All nine girls came from low-income homes. Most were the first generation in their families to attend college. These factors exposed the young women to well-studied financial, logistical, and emotional hardships on campus. Yet the NC girls would face another challenge too: leaving each other behind. Would their friendships survive the distance? How would the girls adjust without their best friends?[11] The following sections describe what happened to Florence, Joanne, and Aisha after they started college.

Florence

"I hate doing applications," Florence told me, grinning. "I'm just so lazy."

She applied to a single school, Colby-Sawyer College, a private university in New Hampshire that her counselor suggested. Florence knew the name—Zora's brother attended—and she loved the thought of leaving Massachusetts. Her mom opposed the idea, however, so Florence, after submitting her application, told a little lie. She had already been accepted, she said, and it was free. Luckily, Florence got in. She even won a scholarship, which she learned the same day her first nephew was born.

"It was kind of a magical day," she said.

Florence was excited. She looked forward to the parties, the "nature," and joining the dance team. She planned to major in nursing, since helping people came easily to her. Quick to laugh and doggedly optimistic, Florence loved to make others feel good.

As the semester approached, Florence started packing. She rode the Red Line to the Best Buy in Boston and, using money saved from work, hauled back a laptop in a big bag.

Along with the other scholarship recipients, Florence headed to campus a week before the semester began. "We got some tools," she explained. "Getting used to the library, knowing who to go to to help us out."

Florence met her five roommates assigned by an online personality quiz and settled in. On campus, the liberty was heady. "I was so happy to be away from anybody calling me, like, 'Where are you?'" she said. "And not having to worry about, 'Oh, I can't have this person over.'"

But before long came the first small disappointments. The dance team held no auditions to filter the skilled from the dilettantes. And she got a 1 out of 5 for a speaking presentation because she wore sweatpants.

"It was about hip-hop," Florence told me. "I was teaching them to dance. It was completely appropriate for that occasion."

On edge, Florence started to miss her friends, especially Stephanie. Stephanie was back in NC; she too had wanted to leave the state for college, especially when she got into a school that offered a business program she was excited about. But the school cost more than a local state university, and, Stephanie explained, "I kind of just got stuck with family, helping out, doing my part. A lot of life happened, and I had to be the backbone for a period of time." So Stephanie stayed home and commuted to UMass Boston. In New Hampshire, Florence missed her dearly.

"Just having someone to relate to certain things," Florence explained. "Like, if you're watching a show or a joke, like, 'Only Stephanie would get this.'"

Florence found that weed soothed her nibbling stresses. Often she lit up with a new friend, Diego, a classmate from Oakland who smoked hard and worked harder. Diego was kind and funny, and mostly their friendship was platonic.

Florence brought Diego to NC for Thanksgiving when he couldn't afford to fly home. I joined them both in Florence's bedroom one day during the break. Peering at the certificates for high school achievement and summer programs on Florence's wall, Diego wondered aloud about his major. "I write really good and present really good," he said.

"Really *well*," Florence corrected.

Later we met up with Stephanie. Diego said he wanted to smoke, and Florence asked him, "Are you gonna get a bag of ten, do twos?"

"Look at you, knowing all the words," Stephanie said, a little terse.

Back on campus after break, Florence's mood fell. She withdrew from her biology class—it was too hard—not knowing it would land her on academic probation.

"I kind of got depressed," Florence recalled. The college nurse blamed the weather.

At the start of spring semester, however, as little blossoms pushed through hard earth, Florence's grades inched up. She found a rhythm with work and tried to enjoy all college offered: zumba, yoga, peace and quiet.

But one March night, Florence's phone buzzed as she walked home from yoga. It was Zora; Bryan was dead. Florence remembered hearing the words in slow motion, "just like on the TV." She had been worried about Bryan all week. A few days earlier, an NC friend had called just as Florence woke from an eerie nightmare. "We're looking for Bryan," the friend had said on the phone. "Have you seen him? When was the last time?"

"I had a gut feeling," Florence recalled. "I knew it wasn't going to end well."

The grief hit hard. Florence kept picturing Bryan's light-up sneakers when he first moved to NC. In her mind she replayed their last meeting—outside his mom's house in the project—over and over. Florence ruminated on what Bryan might have gone through, what his last thought might have been. *I can't even study . . . I really want to go home :(* she wrote on Facebook. Her professor refused to excuse her from class; Bryan was not a blood relative. But Florence skipped anyway. Her friends needed her, and she needed them.

Then came midterms, and even her all-nighters couldn't make up for work she had missed. Then bombs exploded at the finish line of the Marathon. Then she watched a manhunt for a former classmate lock down her city.

Florence coped the only way she knew how: "I wake up, I smoke. And then like at 2 o'clock, we eat and relax and smoke again, and then dinner, and then we smoke."

At the end of the year, Florence got a D in a writing class for failing to submit the final; she had submitted it, late, but by then the adjunct had left the school. She decided to switch her major, figuring she should do something with her "heart all in it, to get those A's and stuff."

"Now I'm majoring in communications, like PR," she told me. "I could minor in like, child development? I want to be like, a teacher or something one day, or I could work in a hospital. *Mad Men* got me thinking about marketing. I could be good at that because I'm so creative. . . . I could do events, like for the White House." Florence quivered with undirected energy. Nobody helped her discern the realistic paths from the pipe dreams that flashed before her.[12]

Still, Florence attacked her sophomore year with zeal. She moved with friends into an off-campus house. The house, painted a beautiful blue, had a kitchen island and built-in living room shelves. Her new major also let her line up easier classes: media, history, and French, helped by her fluent Kreyòl.

"My professor was saying we're in the age of social media. My major is actually gonna be important, I'm gonna make money from it!" Florence gushed, her old grin dimpling her cheeks. "I'm excited for this new chapter of my life," she continued. "This is gonna be like, *How Florence Got Her Groove Back*." She planned trips she might take: "Puerto Rico for Spring Break, and San Jose 'cause my friend lives there, and for December, somewhere like Texas."

But college didn't get easier. Florence couldn't manage her time and didn't ask for help. Others with her scholarship struggled too, "mostly because of the culture and the professors," Florence explained. "I feel like a lot of the faculty weren't used to teaching people of color, because for so long they didn't have any." Florence felt estranged from her academic advisor, a white woman. "She didn't really care to push me to make it. Like, as an African American student. I can already tell she didn't want me here." Racism seeped into her social life too. "You would find yourself not being able to go to certain parties, because, 'Oh, Black girls,'" she related. There were students who had "never interacted with Black people" and students who used the N word. "It just didn't feel like there was much support," Florence said.

Around the same time, her ex-boyfriend Vincent got a new girlfriend. "That kind of stressed me out and made me sad. I didn't really want to do anything," she said.

When Florence returned home for winter break of her sophomore year, she decided not to return to Colby-Sawyer. She blamed the decision on the fact that her school "changed the communications department to media studies." "I didn't want media studies on my diploma," she said. "Like, what the fuck am I gonna do with that, be a paparazzi?"

For weeks Florence's belongings lay on her bedroom floor. Rehanging her clothes in her childhood closet was a defeat she would not yet concede.

Having missed the enrollment deadline for the local community college, Florence signed up for one in South Boston. She didn't see herself as a community college student, however, so she planned to transfer. But she couldn't get hold of a transcript. "It's mad technical, for no reason," she explained.[13] When the transfer didn't pan out, she got two jobs while deciding what to do next.

One afternoon, on a midshift break from her job at Panera Bread in Harvard Square, Florence and I walked down to the Charles River. She took off her uniform cap and smoothed the crease imprinted in her hair.

"This is my favorite place," she said, by the calm, teal water.

Her new plan, she told me, was to load up on classes at another community college and then return to Colby-Sawyer. Florence spoke to someone on campus about renewing her old scholarship; if she could combine that with grants and loans and commute home on weekends to her Panera job, she could, she thought, afford tuition. But she worried about the $257 health insurance bill from the first community college when her application wasn't processed before the waiver deadline.

Eventually, Florence reenrolled at Colby-Sawyer. Preparing for her return to New Hampshire, she had some loose ends to tie up. During the year and a half at home, Florence had met and married Samuel. The whirlwind of their courtship had felt like a glimmer of good amid all that was difficult. But week by week, the sheen had dulled.

"Relationships is like, they're hard," Florence said, some months after getting married. "That's the thing with Haitians. The stubbornness, the controllingness, that thing about being a man."

Florence wanted out. But they had already filed for Samuel's green card, and the bureaucracy was baffling. "You can't just call and say I want to cancel the process," she told me. "You have to write a letter, to whom it concerns, and all that."

Samuel yelled that she was heartless, but she had made up her mind. So on a ten-degree January afternoon, Florence and I rode the Red Line to meet him at the courthouse. She wore a black beanie and fuchsia lipstick and stood, straight backed, the whole way there.

"Children or no children?" asked the clerk, not looking up from her desk.

"No children," Florence said. The clerk slapped down a heap of papers.

In the elevator back to the lobby, Florence and Samuel stood in bristling silence. When the doors opened, she walked wordlessly into the snow. Samuel held the divorce papers to his winter coat and watched her leave.

"I'm glad that's over," Florence told me, toeing an Ugg into the powdery snow. "Well, almost," she said. "There's a fee to pay, and a summons, which is—well, I don't really know what that is." Florence's friend, a young mother, had received government assistance for her own divorce. "I should get it too," Florence reasoned. "I go to school. Plus, I live in public housing. Give me a break."

The ice crackled underfoot as the winter light leached from the graying sky.

At Panera, before her shift began, Florence and I took seats by the window. "It's easy to take time off school," she sighed.[14] "But it was a good experience." Her optimism strained as the day darkened. Across the street, Harvard's columns glowed gold under streetlamps. "I just want to end where I started," said Florence. The frost crept over the window, blocking her view.

Joanne

From her graduating class of over four hundred, Joanne was one of sixteen students selected by CRLS to be featured online as a "Super

Senior." On her profile, she listed as her career goal "CEO of my own non-profit for adolescents."

Joanne applied early action to Brandeis, her "reach" college. One fall afternoon, Vincent drove Joanne and me to visit the campus. In the backseat, Joanne bopped along to Miguel's *Adorn* on the radio and noted helpful businesses as we approached: KFC, Dunkin' Donuts, Walgreens.

Vincent parked in a visitor's lot. "Do Black people go here?" he asked, surveying the neat lawns around us.

"I'm hoping they're in need of Black people," Joanne laughed. "I did a net price calculator, and I can be going to this school for forty-four dollars. It's need based." She planned to do Work-Study, she told her brother.

"Work-Study sucks," Vincent said. He then warned his sister about hidden costs; Vincent had started college in New Hampshire two years earlier but moved home after his financial aid dried up. He suggested she choose a state school. "You could do grad school at Brandeis," Vincent offered.

"No, that's Columbia," Joanne replied, firm. "Grad school is Columbia University."

As Vincent began to object, Joanne went on: "Whatever. I'm used to working and going to school and doing a thousand other things."

We joined a group campus tour led by a peppy white undergraduate in denim shorts and a Brandeis T-shirt. Joanne marveled at the four-story library and the building that looked like a castle. She asked the tour guide what a typical day entailed.

"I don't know typical," answered the guide. "But today I had class, then a lecture, then lunch, now I have this tour, and then dinner, and after dinner another class."

"Oh, so you're not really that busy then?" Joanne asked earnestly, assessing where her one or two jobs might fit.

Joanne didn't get into Brandeis. It stung, but she was accepted everywhere else. Once her offers and scholarships had piled in, she selected UMass Amherst, a flagship state university. "I picked the one farthest away," Joanne said. "My mom wanted me to stay close. I wanted to *go*."

After graduating from CRLS, Joanne returned to her lab job for the summer, preparing for Amherst on days off. She planned expenses with a color-coded list on her cell phone: pillows, notebooks, and post-its were among the most urgent purchases; snacks, a raincoat, and toiletries went under "it can wait." She also handled administrative snags, like when, as she put it, "the government fucked up my citizenship status," jeopardizing her financial aid. Joanne spent a long day at the Social Security office to fix their error.

Joanne mapped out her semester: "I want to do poetry, and join this leadership for Colored women thing. . . . I enrolled myself in a psych class!"

But excitement and anxiety bubbled together. Joanne opted for a random roommate match but worried about racial dynamics after receiving her assignment.

"She's Chinese," Joanne said quietly. "She's from Northborough. Everyone's white. White, rich . . . She thinks I'm white, probably. I haven't told her that I'm Haitian or Black! I'm gonna break it to her slowly . . . I don't know if she's gonna be alright with that."

As Joanne's departure approached, she stewed about the distance. Aisha was moving twenty miles north of NC to Salem State, a public four-year university. Seeta and Brittani would stay at home— Seeta commuting to a private school south of the city and Brittani attending Bunker Hill. But Amherst was almost one hundred miles away. "I feel like I'm moving to Australia," Joanne said.

After an evening trip to Burger King, Joanne stood with her best friends and me around the open trunk of Seeta's car. Seeta had offered to move Joanne to Amherst, and the girls appraised her ride's storage.

"Don't underestimate how much stuff you need," Aisha cautioned, brandishing the half-eaten Whopper she had wrapped up for later. "Even bring toilet paper, because you never know."

In the end, Vincent and Carole drove Joanne to campus. They left her and her boxed-up things in her new room, nervous but brimming with promise.

Joanne's best friends sent her off with online tributes. Aisha posted a photo of herself, Joanne, and Brittani, their faces scrunched in theatrical emotion. The caption read, *SO WE'RE SENDING OFF OUR CHILD #JOANNE TO THE #ZOOMASS OUR LITTLE MONKEY!!! I WOULDN'T be surprised if you are in the top #1% you are brilliant and have so much to offer the world . . . I love you so much be perfect out there let everyone know YOU DAA BESTEST !! please please STAY SAFE!! I NEED YOU ALIVE !!*

Used to noise, Joanne slept soundly through parties in the parking lot outside her block. Partying was not a priority. "They'll be crazy animals, and I'm gonna be a nun," she told me. Instead Joanne found spots to hide away: "In the main library, the higher you go, the quieter it is."

But Joanne struggled to complete schoolwork between her other commitments. While she enjoyed her work-study job at the campus media lab—it was "kinda a perfect fit," she said—she disliked her paid gig at a wings joint, not because she didn't eat meat, but because the biweekly 4:00 p.m. to 1:00 a.m. shifts left her tired in early classes. "I can't wait for the day I don't have to wake up and go to work," Joanne said. She also volunteered to tutor children on Tuesdays and Thursdays.

Two months into the semester, I Skyped Joanne. She lifted her laptop to show me her room, pointing at her bed, planner, and snack drawer. "I'm so organized!" she beamed.

"That's great. Are you having a good time?" I asked.

Joanne paused. "Yeah . . . "

I waited.

"I mean, it's alright. It's an alright time." Her tone hardened. "I dunno if I'll ever have a really—I feel like there will be good moments, but I will always be stressed out. My main focus is academic," she said. "My goal is to graduate cum laude. I don't plan on partying unless you guys come to visit me."

Gradually Joanne became lonely. She missed her home friends, and her schedule made it hard to meet new people. Moreover, her living situation, as she had feared, was hostile. "I felt very much like I was a filthy Black kid . . . the exotic animal that everyone stared at," Joanne said. "I'm the only Black girl on the floor, and the only Black girl in the whole building . . . like, 'Oh, I'm your speck of diversity." At the psychology department too, Joanne noted, "I couldn't meet people of color older than me doing things."

Joanne requested new accommodation midway through her first semester. An acquaintance with a car helped move her across campus; in return, Joanne helped her write a paper. Joanne liked her new roommate. "She's very friendly, she's my kinda person," she said, cautiously optimistic. "She studies classical ballet. She's white, but she's whatever about it. She doesn't look at me."

Joanne quit the wings job and performed poems at open mics. She even found some study buddies who let her personality shine: "We'll be in the library doing homework, mad intellectual work, writing these sophisticated-ass papers, and then we're just talking mad smack! We be ratchet just to have fun. Then it turns into this intellectual response."

"I'm good now," Joanne told me, near the end of her first semester. "I wasn't good before, because living in that place I felt like I was on exhibit all the fucking time. I'm a normal person. I like conversation, and these people just would not talk to me."

When winter break arrived, Joanne returned to NC with a fiercer edge and a new ear piercing. The stud, twinkling in her tragus, "gave Grandma a heart attack," Joanne laughed. She added a star-shaped tattoo of her family's names on her back. All through break, Joanne basked in their company and that of her best friends.

In January, Joanne steeled herself and returned to Amherst. The second semester was worse than the first. Joanne was hardy; years of pain management and therapy meant she could "meditate on the spot." But although she could handle migraines, depression and anxiety were new and frightening.

Joanne was blindsided by the "ruminating thoughts" and "social anxiety." "It was like an out-of-body experience," she later explained. "There would be moments where I would just sit in my room and eat Cinnamon Toast Crunch, and my friends were like, 'Why are you sitting in your room eating Cinnamon Toast Crunch?' Because it is what I want to do. I want to sit in this room and eat Cinnamon Toast Crunch."

Over in Salem, Aisha grew alarmed. Her instinct told her what to do.

"I was just like, 'Honestly, I feel like you shouldn't be alone,'" Aisha explained. She crossed the state and spent a week at Amherst. "I just chilled there and did my homework and stayed for the week," she said.

But the trip unsettled Aisha. "You have to watch things you say," she told me afterward. "She gets easily like, anxiety, and she'll hyperventilate and spaz out and start crying. It's not Joanne at all. It's, no offense, the whitest thing that's ever happened to her."[15]

Aisha worried when Joanne refused to take the medication she had been prescribed. But then again she couldn't really gauge the situation's severity. "I didn't get diagnosed with anything," Aisha said, both joking and proud.

Nor could Joanne grasp what was happening, or why. "I was going through a lot mentally, which I didn't really understand," she reflected later. "I think it was always there, but it was magnified when I was by myself. I was one in a sea of a billion, even in the lecture hall." She went on: "I was always under this pressure by not letting my mom down. Academic-wise it was so go go go go go, and then keep going. I never took a pause, and I think it really affected my health, which is why my anxiety came out."

Joanne's GPA dipped into the 2.0s, precluding the extension of her first-year scholarships. As her freshman year concluded, Joanne put her things back into boxes. Driving away from campus, from its library and lawns, she knew she would not return.

Back home, she picked up a hostess job at Legal Seafood. There was a lot of time to think on the bus: forty-five minutes each way. At first Joanne hoped to keep up with classes online, unwilling to let go of UMass or Columbia or the nonprofit. But the commute and her hours and her anxiety were exhausting. The dreams would have to wait.

Aisha

Aisha was the first of her clique to leave NC. Shortly after graduating from CRLS, she began a six-week residential orientation at Salem State. On campus Aisha shared her new world with her old friends through dozens of daily tweets, like:

> *U know you are in Salem when you hear a rooster*
> *SALEM STATE needs renovating n new computers like damn*
> *THIS GIRL SAID SHES OBSSESSED WITH ME and has a girl crush*
> *   on me ayeee*
> *NOW GOING TO COMMEDY NIGHT :)*
> *I want to separate myself from the group but its like everyone is drawn*
> *   to me :/*

The orientation, which helped students settle in before the semester's strains and stakes, was "very systematic," Aisha said. "You had a time you had to be in bed. You'd go to classes, you'd go to study. It was teaching you mad time management and stuff."

From Cambridge, Joanne helped Aisha with challenging assignments. "Just ideas like how to start an introduction. Sentence structure. Things like that," Joanne explained.

Aisha found a routine and made friends. Before leaving NC, she had tweeted, *At salem all the friends I will have will benefit me somehow.. I hope i meet one with a beach house no lie.* And, true to her words, Aisha paid attention. "I'm not the most observant person," she told me. "Like, I won't remember what you were wearing. But I'm good at reading what kind of people are gonna benefit me."

Aisha found some classmates who piqued her interest. One girl's annual beauty spending, she figured, totaled thousands of dollars. "Her parents are pres . . . pris . . . prescription doctors," she related. "And in a private hospital too."

Aisha used social media to stylize herself into a covetable confidante; in several daily videos posted to Snapchat, peers surrounded her. The anthropologist Penelope Eckert found that students who *appear* to be having the most fun often end up as the most popular members of their social groups, a cycle Aisha catalyzed online.[16]

But as peers flocked to Aisha, she held most at arm's length. "If a girl opens up to you that quick, they've got a problem," she chided, talking about a certain classmate. "If they tell you how many abortions they've had, how many miscarriages, their body count . . .," she balked.

Seeking some space, Aisha went to breakfast alone one morning, without her group of seven fast friends. One hollered, "Why you sitting by yourself? This is our crew!" But Aisha was unimpressed. "I was thinking, 'I have friends back home,'" she explained. "I tried to stay low, but everyone knows who I am. Again. It's like high school." Aisha's practiced unavailability only raised her allure.

After the orientation, Aisha had a couple of weeks in NC before the start of the fall semester. A new friend drove her home. *Yo this is why you are friends with ten million people! i would've taken the train home .. but this shorty gave me a ride,* she tweeted.

Aisha went straight to her best friends, aiming to make the most of their days together before separating again—this time for much longer. Once the semester started, her clique planned to delay visiting each other until Halloween, when they would reunite at Salem State. This, they hoped, would help them all "get used to it," Joanne explained.

Back on campus for the fall semester, Aisha picked up where she had left off. She flourished, filling the new space allowed her. She even got faculty on her side; she told me how, after an English professor gave her a zero for talking in class, she approached him, and pleaded, quivering with fake emotion, "This class is really important to me." Aisha laughed, describing how she had unnerved him. "But you have to advocate for yourself!" she said. Aisha intuitively grasped what sociologists have demonstrated: schools reward the kind of self-advocacy typical to a middle-class habitus.[17]

Outside class, Aisha's Snapchat videos showed her at parties, lit by strobing lights; shrieking happily while trooping over campus at 4:00 a.m.; eating a carrot cake muffin and yogurt behind the caption, *college breakfast.* Her videos also revealed her evolving style: dark berry lips one night, eyes lined silver the next. Aisha's energy shone, as did the diamanté stud that she had pierced into the back of her neck.

Still, Aisha missed her friends. She tweeted at Joanne, *i just LOVVEEEE YOU WITH ALL MY HEART !! OK ?* And after Joanne and Seeta visited Salem, Aisha posted a Snapchat video with the caption, *I'll never ever vibe with my school friends the way I do with my home friends. I hate when my school friends try vibe with my home friends. Stay in your lane.*

But peers remained eager to please. So did boys. Tentatively, selectively, Aisha tiptoed toward the type of relationships she had avoided in high school. At a party near the end of her first semester, a classmate, Wilson, approached Aisha and said, plucky, "Yo, we have to dance together, you owe me a dance." At first Aisha thought him cocky.

"I don't owe you anything," she replied.

But Aisha gave Wilson a dance. Just one song, at first, then another and another, until the crowd around them seemed to vanish. After that they got close, fast. When a party they were at was busted, they fled together and stayed up until morning talking and laughing over PB&Js. Wilson started visiting Aisha; since her roommate had dropped out, she had the room to herself. Wilson brought Aisha her favorite snacks. "I told him he didn't have to," she related. "I hate when people feel obligated to do things for me."

But Aisha trusted Wilson. They made each other promises and their relationship became serious. Aisha had made it out of high school, she reasoned. She didn't need to wait until marriage.

After a while, classmates learned of their romance. Aisha was annoyed at the loss of privacy. Soon after that the two started squabbling. "Why do you drink?" Wilson asked Aisha disapprovingly.

"No," she remembered responding, "just because I sin differently than you doesn't mean that you're better than me. You're having sex with me! I went on the scripture thing. I hate when people try to play Bible with me."

When an ex-girlfriend tried to win Wilson back—bothering Aisha and making all sorts of claims—Aisha decided she was done.

To move on, Aisha did what she knew best: she cut Wilson out. She warned their mutual friends, "If you guys chill with him, I'm not chilling with y'all. You *know* I can make new friends in two seconds."

Others clamored to replace Wilson, but Aisha had more urgent concerns. Joanne was struggling over at Amherst, and back home, Seeta wasn't doing much better. Despite the distance, Aisha tried to be there for her friends.

Ultimately, Aisha finished freshman year proud of her 3.3 GPA and the new life she had built. When asked about college, Aisha told story after story about the *people*—in her dorm, in classes, at parties. Aisha found a wide range of support from a broad circle of friends, one of the very things that helped her get to college in the first place.

Sophomores Rising

As the new school year approached, Aisha invited her clique to her apartment one evening when her mom was out of town. Aisha wanted to host a "back to school" dinner before college split the girls again. This time, however, only she would be leaving.

I joined Aisha and Joanne in Aisha's kitchen, where Joanne stirred spaghetti and sauce on the stove. Both girls wore summer dresses, Joanne's white and Aisha's navy.

Brittani arrived, in jeans and a T-shirt, seeming a little glum. She missed Aisha when she was gone and was not looking forward to her upcoming departure. Social media helped somewhat with the separation. As Brittani explained, "Snapchat keeps me connected. Instagram keeps me updated. . . . We still talk to each other about anything. We know that whatever it is, we'll help deal with it." But it wasn't the same. Besides, she couldn't help but compare Aisha's college life to her own. At community college, Brittani felt like she had "missed a little freshman experience." She wanted more opportunities, like classes in African American studies, dance, and ceramics. To get them, she hoped to join Aisha at Salem State by transferring once she earned her associate's degree.

As Joanne finished cooking, Aisha set the table. First she laid gold plastic placemats around the centerpiece: a framed photo of Aisha, Joanne, Brittani, Seeta, and me, taken at Joanne's eighteenth birthday picnic in Danehy Park a year and a half earlier. Then Aisha set white ceramic plates on the placemats and topped each with a paper towel folded into an upturned V.

Next she fetched the fancy glasses from the kitchen.

"Do they go on the right or the left?" she asked. Her friends shrugged. "I think right," Aisha said, "'cause you reach with your right hand."

Joanne hauled through two plastic Tupperwares heaped with steaming pasta: one with meat sauce, the other al fredo with chicken and broccoli. Then she retrieved her own dinner, a specially prepared vegetarian pasta.

"And I got juice for y'all!" Aisha said, placing a handle of peach drink between the Tupperwares. For a final flourish, she dropped into each girl's cup a red cocktail cherry from a glass jar. The cherries wisped pink curlicues into the viscous juice.

Aisha, Joanne, Brittani, and I took our seats. But nobody would eat until the empty chair was filled.

The girls felt apprehensive for Seeta's arrival. Tension between the group had started shortly after Joanne and Aisha left for college. Aisha related how Seeta had protested, "You guys forgot about me!"

"We didn't," Aisha later told me. "But home is the last thing you think about."

Stuck in NC, Seeta had started seeing a neighborhood boy, Jay-Jay. Aisha was appalled. "He's just a bum," she told me. "He doesn't go to school."

Aisha also worried about JayJay's dealing, explaining, "Seeta will transport bud for him and hold bud for him. Not even like a no-big-deal-everyone-smokes. It's more like a you-get-one-to-two-years-for-it type stuff. The Seeta I know would not do stuff like that."

On Twitter, Seeta shared her struggles:

> *It's hard going from having someone to talk to all the time to not having*
> *anyone at all*
> *Damn I am really losing weight*
> *Just so fucking stressed . . .*

Suffering was etched on Seeta's body. Her cheekbones and clavicles poked through her formerly curvy frame. "She's been smoking a lot," Aisha explained. "You can see the scoliosis in her back."

Aisha felt JayJay was making things worse. "Seeta is so broken, like self-esteem broken, money broken, home broken," she said. "She needs somebody who will build her, not tear her down."

Aisha and Joanne decided to act. "We tried to stage an intervention," Aisha told me. "We started out like, 'Well Seeta, what I like about you is how you're very strong and willing to help anyone even though you're poor. And then I was like, 'Joanne, what do you like about Seeta?' That's how interventions go, right? I seen it in a movie. You start out with what they are good at, then you do the bad stuff, and then you end up with the good."

Seeta, Aisha related, had bawled, "I don't eat anymore. I don't feel good anymore. My parents don't have money for me."

The girls didn't know what to do.

"Seeta had a lot going on in terms of financing for school and having all of her friends be away," Joanne told me. Joanne had wanted to help but felt hampered by her own depression. "How do you know the signs of certain things when you are so caught up in your own world also?" she wondered.

Distance between the girls had continued to increase through the school year.

But at the dinner party, Aisha hoped they could forget the friction. When Seeta's car finally rumbled in the driveway, Aisha sprang up and threw open the door. She twerked ironically to greet Seeta, before ushering her to the table.

With everyone finally seated, Aisha reached out her palms. We all held hands while Aisha bowed her head and prayed.

Then we dug in hungrily. A few minutes later, Aisha tapped her glass with her spoon to get everyone's attention. She put three fingers to her lips, miming the war salute from *The Hunger Games* movie. Joanne and Brittani cracked up laughing. Seeta sat expressionless.

"Can you just get emotional so I can cry and run my eyeliner?" Joanne said.

"Okay," Aisha began, her voice low. "I wanted to have this dinner for the people I love, because you guys mean so much to me. You are so positive in my life . . . It's so difficult thinking about going back to school without you guys." "Okay. Don't cry, don't cry," Aisha told herself. "I just hope that we stay in contact during the school year. I just wanted to have a dinner, and that's my toast."

Aisha sat down, and Joanne dabbed her own eyes with a paper towel.

Next Aisha had an idea. Everyone, she suggested, should say "a goal for next year and one thing you accomplished this year." She paused, reflecting on this suggestion: "Wow, I'm getting whiter and whiter."

Seeta went first: "My goal is to gain weight. I need to pass 120, at least. And I need to bring up my GPA a lot."

"And what did you accomplish this year?" Aisha asked.

"Nothing," Seeta folded her hands in her lap. "This has been a bad year."

"You have accomplishments!" Joanne said.

"I can't think of one," Seeta shrugged.

"Something you feel proud of," Aisha said. "Taking care of your nephew?"

Seeta smiled, her recall prompted. "Oh, this is recent. My dad always tells me I'm irresponsible, but this week I got my car checked. I paid for my inspection, and now it doesn't make that sound anymore."

"There you go!" Joanne said.

Joanne went next: "My goal for the year is to save at least 75 percent of every check, and just, I don't know, be a bit more outgoing, a bit more optimistic. Accomplishments? I got a job, that shit was stressful." The girls applauded.

Next Brittani said, "I have a lot of goals . . . Number one is to get a job, and definitely keep my GPA up so I finish this year and transfer to Salem."

Aisha whooped.

"My accomplishment?" Brittani continued. "I guess actually making friends from Bunker Hill from volleyball."

Finally, Aisha said, "My goal is to travel for the school year and become more organized. Also, I want to make new friends from my school. And hey, I've accomplished a lot, let me tell you. I did the summer program, that's an accomplishment. I went to college, that's an accomplishment." She went on: "Anything that tried to break me, my brain has been in the right place." Her friends nodded.

"Okay, we have to take a family picture!" Aisha said, emotion catching once more in her throat. After selfies, the night ended with karaoke. We sat on Aisha's couch and floor, singing along to instrumental versions of pop songs played on YouTube.

Saying her goodbyes, Aisha hugged her friends, grasping them close, in turn.

Struggle and Support

College enrollment has ballooned for first-generation and low-income students like the NC girls. Yet, although almost half of low-income young people begin postsecondary education, just 11 percent will earn a bachelor's degree after six years—well below the 55 percent of more privileged students who do the same.[18] Some researchers argue that the challenge now facing low-income students is not college access but completion.[19]

Overall, low-income and first-generation students arrive on campus less ready for college-level coursework and less skilled at time management than their middle-class peers.[20] But even controlling for academic preparation, students from low-income homes still drop out at higher rates.[21] This means that on-campus hardships often limit students' ability to continue.

At college, the NC girls ran into many well-studied obstacles.[22] Most felt their biggest problem was money. Even with scholarships, work-study, need-based grants, and paid work, they had outstanding costs.[23] And just like in high school, financial strain took an emotional toll. But unlike when their friends were in similar situations, many girls felt excluded among new people and places. Joanne, for instance, met a girl, Shayla, at UMass Amherst, who invited her to join her Black sorority. The sisterhood appealed to Joanne, but the cost was prohibitive. "Joining is like, a thousand dollars," Joanne explained. "Shayla was like, 'I been have that money!'" Joanne did not.

Joanne worked two jobs just to get by. Students with heavy job schedules are, studies find, more likely to quit college.[24] Typically, researchers assume they can't keep up with classwork. Yet jobs take up other time too. As Joanne boxed up wings after midnight, her wealthier classmates might have been studying, but they might have been partying and making new friends. The time to build new bonds and enjoy campus life was a privilege Joanne could not afford.

The NC girls faced additional difficulties, including struggles with classwork and grades. When they did poorly, many blamed picky, "mean" professors. Perhaps academic expectations were unfeasible; perhaps girls could have tried harder. Either way, failures hurt. Compounding this, complex bureaucracies and campus alienation left many feeling isolated and ashamed. To convert *values* about education into academic achievement, research shows, students need to feel like they belong.[25] But many girls didn't. Their needs were neither understood nor met. Some professors were culturally insensitive; others refused to allow students to miss class for a friend's funeral. The sense that their schools didn't care made it harder to keep trying.

Moreover, the NC girls could not help each other through these new challenges. Many viewed their struggles individually, even when, as Joanne put it, "a lot of people flopped, and a lot of people staggered." Although the girls could lucidly condemn systemic inequality in general, they mostly attributed college hardships to their own failures.[26] Echoing cultural tropes lauding grit and drive, girls blamed themselves when they stumbled on the steepest of paths.

Over time, wells of resilience ran low—and sometimes dried out. Few girls gave up entirely; most moved between schools, like Florence, who carried along her rugged hope and whichever credits would transfer.[27] But this choppy trajectory denied Florence a new, anchored social life. This likely cost her the long-term professional benefits that college friends can offer; it also, in the short term, left her lonely.

By contrast, Aisha found new friends to meet her needs. Though she was not the only girl who made friends at college, Aisha was the most determinedly social. She was also the only one of the nine young women on track to get a bachelor's degree from one school. Rebuilding a peer group was far from the only factor that forked the girls' roads; each brought their own burdens and skills to campus. Aisha, for instance, also benefited from her summer orientation and from her unique ability to advocate for herself to adults.[28]

But making friends mattered. When the girls separated, they lost time-tested solutions to problems. They lost a multifaceted intimacy and the security of dependable support. And although social media was key to their closeness, cell phones alone could not deliver all of friendship's benefits.

Losing peer support shaped college experiences, both for the girls who moved away and for those who stayed in NC. Adults, however—researchers, policy makers, faculty members, and college administrators—do not always grasp what it can mean for teenagers to leave their friends behind. The girls struggled not just because they had limited resources, information, and help on campus. They also struggled because they had lost what had often been their most vital source of care: their best friends.

Conclusion

"I am tired of being poor," Aisha said, drizzling a syrup star over a buttermilk short stack. Back in Cambridge over winter break of her sophomore year, she contemplated her future from our IHOP booth. "I'm tired of being poor, but what am I good at? To start a business plan," she said. "I was watching YouTube videos by a bunch of people who were poor and made it."

Aisha was spurred, in part, by the semester's challenges. "First year was hard emotionally," she said. "Sophomore year is a struggle academically. I didn't eat. The doctor said I lost five pounds." Aisha picked at her pancakes. Then she sighed. "No one told us when we grow it gets so hard."

Just a few months later, however, Aisha felt reinvigorated. By the end of her sophomore year, she was enjoying her chosen major—mathematics—and thriving as a spoken word poet, even scoring an invite from Ilyasah Shabazz to perform at a fiftieth anniversary memorial celebration for her father, Malcolm X.

Aisha returned to NC for summer break. One late May afternoon, she and I strolled together down Rindge Avenue.

"I'm going to Tokyo," Aisha said, casually, as we walked.

"You are?" I asked.

"They gave me a grant for the flight," she said, breaking into a grin that betrayed her practiced nonchalance. Work wages would cover the rest of the trip, a six-week, school-led tour of Japan. As soon as she heard about the tour, Aisha was interested. She researched the Tokyo "scene," she explained, and felt sure that residents' love for Black music and culture would make her a "VIP," fostering "connects" to cash in later.

"I want the challenge," Aisha said. "School was too easy. I know everyone." Like high school, college had set her a somewhat solvable puzzle.

Many things had helped Aisha flourish despite the harms and hurdles she had faced growing up. She was driven, gregarious, and resourceful—perhaps uniquely so. She also attended a good public high school, where classes like photography honed her creative interests. Adults, like teachers, sports coaches, and pastors, cared for Aisha. And then there were her friends—girls who had shared their lives and their belongings, who had dreamed together of bright futures and reached for joint goals.

For Aisha and the other NC girls, friendships brought joy and comfort and mitigated some of poverty's hardships.[1] Friends helped meet one another's material needs and, in doing so, granted dignity and inclusion. Girls managed boredom by using their constant connection to pass time and make fun. They coped together with emotional challenges, including family conflict and stigmatization. And they tried to buffer stresses related to dating and sex, though friends had less sway in these realms than in others.

The NC girls fought for their friendships when they were threatened. After catastrophic neighborhood violence, the girls managed trauma together and protected their relationships. And when new disparities—like drinking alcohol or smoking weed—tested old bonds, the girls learned to accommodate difference.

Close friendships were one factor that helped the young women reach their shared goal of going to college. But there they all struggled when—along with the financial, logistical, and emotional obstacles that await low-income, first-generation students—they lost the peer support on which they had long relied.

In contrast to research that frames friendships as harmful for teens marginalized by racism and poverty—with peer effects spreading "deviance," derailing trajectories, and limiting life chances—this book shows how girls used connection, in person and online, to care for one another both day to day and under tremendous strain. In what follows, I consider what can be learned from the young women and their relationships.

Overlooked Needs, Overlooked Power

Poverty, typically, is defined as a lack of material resources. But financial deprivation has social and emotional costs; it can rob people of dignity, threaten their self-worth, and undermine their sense of belonging. These harms are not trivial; rather they profoundly threaten human flourishing. "No more urgent business in a life can exist," note Richard Sennett and Jonathan Cobb, "than establishing a sense of personal dignity."[2]

As such, researchers studying inequality must consider "not only ... questions of distribution (who gets what and how much) but also ... questions of recognition, inclusion, and voice," argues the sociologist Michèle Lamont and colleagues.[3] Considering facets of well-being that are noneconomic yet fundamental can help correct the historical overemphasis in social science on poverty's material dimension.

Doing so also illuminates the full breadth of support between the NC girls. The young women offered forms of care that—while often overlooked by academics—were, to them, profound. Social and emotional needs like dignity and inclusion can be especially critical during adolescence; as teenagers begin to form adult identities, they seek and depend on approval from peers.[4] In this context, the non-material support that girls shared—their mutual witnessing, love, and affirmation—felt as vital as the cash they pooled.

Some researchers use the term "social capital" to describe friend-ships' benefits. Yet this concept does not generally capture the pri-macy of socio-emotional support as an attribute of close relation-ships; rather it emphasizes the potential of connections to generate financial gain, as the economic metaphor of capital implies.[5] More-over, the most common definitions of social capital—which hinge on conventional forms of prestige, cohesive family relationships, or ro-bust neighborhood organization—do not recognize or include the girls' patterns of care.[6]

Research frequently ignores the care and strengths that exist among people living in poor neighborhoods. Places like NC are regu-larly described as sites of lack—not only of social capital but also of jobs, role models, and more.[7] Against this trend, critically oriented scholars seek to recenter the assets and agency of people in "socially marginalized groups."[8] The education researcher Tara Yosso, for in-stance, proposes the notion of "community cultural wealth" to fore-ground unique traditions of fostering aspirations, resistance, and more.[9] By showing how the NC girls identified and met a wide range of one another's needs, this book joins calls to "focu[s] on and lear[n] from the array of cultural knowledge, skills, abilities and contacts . . . that often go unrecognized and unacknowledged."[10] It also adds to critiques of the deficit-based lens through which poor neighborhoods, and their young residents in particular, are all too often viewed.

Supporting Young People

The girls' experiences underscore an insight long emphasized by queer theorists and feminist scholars: friendship can be powerful, transformative, and life-sustaining. As bell hooks notes, "Friendship is the place in which a great majority of us have our first glimpse of redemptive love and caring community."[11]

Despite this, cultural messages and social policy alike privilege family over friends. "Many of us," hooks notes, "learn as children that friendship should never be seen as just as important as family ties."[12] And policy at all levels—from federal tax benefits to campus rules like the one that penalized Florence for missing class after the death of a close friend—centers and validates the nuclear family.

Relatedly, research typically treats friendship as trivial, something with merely personal—rather than social—significance.[13] Moreover, researchers who *do* consider teens' social ties frequently stress the risks of close friendships, especially among low-income young people. This has an impact on the types of programs and interventions they design. As the sociolinguist Penelope Ecker explains, "Rather than encouraging and helping supportive adolescent networks, society focuses on their potential for delinquency and pressures them to disband."[14] Programs for young people generally seek not to build their capacity for mutual care but rather to boost adult intrusion in their lives.[15]

Teenagers absolutely need adult guidance and institutional resources. But they often engage such resources and opportunities together with their friends. In NC, for instance, the girls jointly enjoyed the youth centers and after-school programs funded by the city. Many enrolled in the Cambridge Housing Authority's Workforce program, where, Joanne explained, "there's homework hour, and they offer tutoring and help you get your taxes filled out and things like that." Joanne appreciated the varied programming, but her fondest memories involved her peers. "It's just one big happy family," she said. "Me and Seeta did Workforce together, and then I convinced Aisha to do it. We're all just this huge happy family." Brittani spoke similarly of a different program: "We were like a family basically. That's where I made my most friends."

Peer and institutional support work best reciprocally.[16] Given this, youth workers, educators, and practitioners could seek to facilitate friendships between young people instead of relying on traditionally hierarchical dynamics between adults and children.[17] For example, after-school programs, as the education professor Tanya Wiggins explains, should "make space" for young people to share their knowledge and resources and "make time" for durable peer relationships by offering long-term, consistent participation opportunities.[18]

Schools too can play a role. Currently, most young people experience adolescence in "cultural and institutional spaces (particularly schools) that provide virtually no systematic training for the task of constructing social systems of support," explain Ricardo Stanton-Salazar and Stephanie Spina.[19] To bolster young people's systems of support, schools could promote relationship building between students by expanding opportunities for academic and extracurricular collaboration. They could also reward nonindividualistic forms of achievement and success.

In turn, colleges could help mitigate the social loss many teens encounter when leaving home by expanding efforts to nurture campus friendships or even by considering helping friends attend college together.[20] They could draw inspiration from the Posse Foundation, which integrates scholarship recipients into supportive teams—posses—of ten students. Posse scholars, with a ready group of similarly situated peers, have a graduation rate of 90 percent.[21] This speaks, of course, to selection and programing but also testifies to the importance of friendships for navigating life transitions.[22]

Finally, young people and their friendships would benefit from more accessible, safe, and welcoming public space and from investment in places like youth centers where they can spend time together and have fun.

But peers are no panacea. Poverty's barriers are durable. Messages telling young people that certain steps—whether making friends, staying out of "trouble," or gaining credentials—will lead to economic independence are simply untrue. Moreover, such messages can be harmful.[23] They oversell individuals' power to surmount structural obstacles and fault people for failing to shake off poverty's shackles.[24] Likewise, encouraging personal skills like "grit" or "resilience" can elide the inequalities that make these traits necessary.[25] And, as hooks argues, "To be strong in the face of oppression is not the same as overcoming oppression."[26]

Absent vast systemic change, poverty will continue to harm young people. When researchers seek a magic, individual-level mobility bullet—the right program, policy, or attitude—to help people "get ahead," they must also ask, "Get ahead from whom?" And they must remember that others will always trail in their wake.[27]

Digital Natives

Young people feel ambivalent about social media's pervasive presence.[28] They describe several drawbacks, including intense social pressure, "fear of missing out," and constant comparison of themselves with others. More worrying, scientists see social media as a key contributor to the decade-long national decline in young people's mental health, a trend labeled "devastating" in a 2021 advisory by the surgeon general of the United States, Vivek Murthy.[29] Although researchers do not agree whether teens' heavy social media use *causes* or *reflects* mental health challenges,[30] the connection demands attention.

The stresses and anxieties tied to social media have likely only intensified over the years since the women in this book were teenagers.[31] The women did not use Instagram and other image-focused sites until their junior and senior years of high school; preteens today, however, spend their formative and vulnerable early adolescence swiping on such apps. Reflecting on the resultant pressures some teens face, Faith said recently, "I didn't have these problems, like social media problems. We were just living our life. Now kids are onto social media, have phones at eleven."

Without discounting these potential harms, constant connection nonetheless offered some meaningful benefits as the girls grew up. Social media helped them have fun without spending money. Online, they found comfort and entertainment and even processed trauma. Social media also gave young women space and voice, which not only support well-being, but can, in fact, be revolutionary for women marginalized by racism and sexism. "While domination may be inevitable as a social fact," Patricia Hill Collins explains, "it is unlikely to be hegemonic as an ideology within social spaces where Black women speak freely."[32] Hill Collins lists churches and community organizations as examples of such spaces, but the girls could also speak candidly to one another online.[33]

Relatedly, the NC girls used social media to craft and portray identities that opposed damaging tropes and "controlling images"—stereotypes used to justify Black women's degradation.[34] This too can be radical. "Far from being a secondary concern in bringing about social change," Hill Collins writes, "challenging controlling images . . . constitute[s] an essential component in resisting intersecting oppressions."[35]

As a vehicle for peer support, however, social media had limits—as the girls found once they moved apart. This explains why Aisha crossed the state to join Joanne when she struggled with depression at college. While posts and messages helped girls keep up with one another's lives, they less effectively transmitted the powerful care their friendships had long offered. Data gathered during the COVID-19 pandemic reveal a similar dynamic; social media provided people with meaningful connection, but the loss of in-person contact caused by lockdowns, social distancing, and remote school and work curtailed relationships' energy and intimacy.[36]

Ultimately, friendships and peer support among the NC girls depended on both in-person and online contact. Social media did not replace face-to-face interaction but rather strengthened connections rooted in shared physical experiences by laying further paths to engagement.[37] Physical and digital contact were friendship's joint foundations; together they offered more than the sum of their parts.

The ubiquity of social media challenges some long-standing theoretical assumptions. The often taken-for-granted online/offline binary, for instance, had little relevance for the NC girls, who experienced neither one as a fully independent space. Moreover, the girls' constant participation in several conversations over multiple media—and their ability to integrate their personal feeds into group hangouts—gave them a different view of interaction from that proposed by theorists like Erving Goffman, who emphasized mutual focus on a single flow of messages.[38]

Social media also complicate assumptions about poverty in cities. Starting with the ecological approach of the Chicago School—which in the early twentieth century theorized how communities affect individuals—neighborhoods' power to shape their residents' lives has guided a century of research and policy making. And, following William Julius Wilson's seminal *The Truly Disadvantaged*—which showed how the geographic clustering or "concentration" of poverty produced exponentially negative consequences—physical and sociocultural isolation have been viewed as defining features of urban marginality.[39] Currently, however, residents have through their cell phones instant and unlimited access to media, information, and cultural products. Young people today—including those growing up in poor neighborhoods—are members of history's most connected generation.

Place continues to matter, tremendously so. For the most part, teenagers in poor neighborhoods go to poor schools and experience place-based hardships, like local violence. Yet cell phones obfuscate the impact of "neighborhood effects." In perhaps the first urban ethnography of hyperconnected young people, the sociologist Jeffrey Lane notes, "Neighborhood based risks and opportunities associated with urban poverty are socially mediated through the use of popular communication technologies."[40] As social life takes place less on the "street corner" and more on the "digital street,"[41] a reliance on traditional field sites and methods will limit what researchers can learn, about cities, poverty, and the lives of young "digital natives."

Limitations

The young women in NC were, as a group, no more sociable, studious, or coddled than others in their neighborhood. Still there are limits on the light their experiences can cast on those of other teens. Boys, for instance, are rarely encouraged to build the type of emotional intimacy with friends that the NC girls shared.[42] Peer support among young men likely rests, then, on a different foundation and, as a result, takes different forms.

In addition, eight of the nine young women were second- or 1.5-generation immigrants. In Florence's clique, where all five young women were Haitian American, the girls often discussed or joked about their Haitian identity, sometimes peppering sentences with Kreyòl. In Aisha's clique, by contrast, the girls—whose families came from four countries over three continents—instead shared a more general experience of racial and ethnic othering.

Being the daughters of immigrants shaped more than the girls' friendships, however. Many young women felt, at times, suspended between two sets of norms or struggled with conflict stemming from their parents' cultural expectations.[43] Despite these challenges, studies have identified a "second-generation advantage" that the children of immigrants—even those in groups who have historically faced hostility and stereotyping, like Haitian Americans[44]—enjoy relative to local-born peers. The location of second-generation young people "between two different social systems allows for creative and selective combinations of the two that can be highly conducive to success," researchers argue.[45] The NC girls may well have benefited from this advantage.

While the children of immigrants are the fastest-growing segment of American youth, representing nationwide almost a quarter of those under the age of twenty-four,[46] future research could consider how dynamics of care vary in neighborhoods inhabited mostly by local-born white or Black Americans or by other groups.

Peer support undoubtedly looks different in different places and communities. Most teens find friendships helpful; the girls' wealthiest classmates surely leaned on their friends too. Yet peers with bigger allowances didn't have to help each other ride the train; those whose parents went to college didn't need friends' help with applications.[47] And in poorer cities with fewer institutional resources than Cambridge, peer support probably takes forms other than those described here.

Still, young people marginalized by structural inequality care for one another in ways that are often overlooked—and even sometimes undermined—by adults and institutions. Teenagers' creativity and resourcefulness deserve recognition and investment, as does the profound power of their friendships.

. . .

A few days before Aisha's trip to Japan, she and I headed to Brittani's apartment, where the girls planned to spend one last summer afternoon together. We walked a familiar route, through a changing NC. The city had begun knocking down Jefferson Park, the housing project where the girls had grown up, and demolition had scattered their families. Aisha's mom had already moved, earlier in the semester, to a new apartment a mile away.

Aisha stopped walking as we passed the construction site that had once been her home. Chain-link now fenced the development from the street. Aisha hooked her fingers through the wire and peered at the hole in the earth where her block had stood.

"Those old buildings," Aisha said of her former home. "They were dirty. You tried your best, but that thing was dirty."

She turned her back and walked away.

As we strolled down Rindge Avenue, Aisha updated me about her friends. Brittani was doing well at Bunker Hill, still planning her transfer to Salem State. Joanne had added a second job—morning shifts at a nursing home—to her Legal Seafood position and also started an Instagram account to show off her growing expertise with makeup. Aisha wanted Joanne to get back to school, but she worried her friend's family was "conditioned not to value women's education." Although they had taken out "mad loans" for Vincent to attend culinary school, Aisha said, they wouldn't help Joanne.

"But Joanne has *transformed* in self-confidence," Aisha said, stamping her feet on the sidewalk. "Let me tell you! Her confidence went from zero to a hundred. I love it. Something about having to figure it all out and being scared."

Aisha, Joanne, and Brittani were still "RODs"—ride or dies[48]—but they had winnowed from four to three. "I am done with Seeta," Aisha explained. "We used to work out because we understood each other's problems. But now Seeta's like, 'I have new friends. They understand me better.'"

Aisha related their final text conversation: "The last thing I said was: I hope you know I'm not mad at you. If I see you, I'm gonna say, 'Hi.' On your birthday, I'll tell you, 'Happy Birthday.' I hope you have a great and happy life."

Seeta had sent a reply, but Aisha ignored it. "She texted a whole paragraph, but I haven't read it," Aisha said icily. "When I'm done with things, I'm really done."

Aisha found her friends lounging in the sun behind Brittani's building. Brittani closed the notebook in which she was planning a Zumba workshop for the after-school program she was staffing over the summer. Joanne looked up from the makeup bag on her lap. Aisha ran to join the girls, and they fell into relaxed and happy chatter. All afternoon, Aisha took selfies and photos of her best friends.

A week later, Aisha took photos and videos as she dragged her suitcase through Boston's Logan airport.[49] She checked in for her flight, lined up for security, and boarded the plane, settling into a window seat. The engines whirred, then shrieked as the jet raced down the runway and peeled into the sky. The trees, the homes, the streets—her streets—shrank as they climbed. Rippled clouds snatched the old world from view, leaving Aisha with the racing in her chest.

A Note on Research and Writing

This book is based on ethnographic fieldwork I conducted over four years. In February 2012, when I was in graduate school, I began volunteering in CHANGE, a community-service-based elective class at CRLS. Over the semester, I met and got to know many of the young women who would become this project's participants. As summer break approached, I asked some of the girls whether we could hang out so that I could learn and write about their lives. Everyone responded with enthusiasm. Joanne, for instance, clapped her hands and said, "Yay, I'm gonna be in your book!" Many parents were welcoming too, inviting me to family parties and giving me nicknames.

Several of the NC girls grasped intuitively what ethnography entailed. They introduced me to friends, relatives, and neighbors, and brought me to social events and activities. Although I spent countless hours "hanging around"[1]—which was how the girls passed most of their free time—I also joined them at all sorts of gatherings and celebrations. After a few months, I moved into a rental apartment across the street from the project where everybody but Brittani lived. Sometimes the girls visited my place; more often we spent time at theirs.

For two further semesters, I attended and observed CHANGE classes. A party at Aisha's apartment, however, made me reconsider my presence at school. Aisha invited me in a Facebook message: *hey*

Jasmin Im having a highschool Party tommrow if you want to come might help with your book lols I hope it isnt a force but my moms gone and w.e and uhh yyea.

On the night, among the guests were teens enrolled in classes I was observing. While chatting with Faith, I overheard another student ask Joanne about me, "Isn't she a teacher?"

"No, she's a grad student," Joanne explained.

"Who knows her?" the other girl asked.

"Loads of people," Joanne said.

Soon after, I wound down my visits to CHANGE to avoid being seen as an authority figure and focused on fieldwork outside of school.

After many of the girls left NC for college, I moved out of the apartment. Yet we kept in touch on social media and met in person when they came back for breaks or permanently returned home. A couple of years later, as the fieldwork concluded, I met individually with several of the young women in coffee shops and restaurants. I set a voice recorder between us and asked questions about their lives—including those that might have felt too formal or unnatural to ask when we were regularly hanging out together.

On Digital Ethnography

The increasing ubiquity of social media has made digital ethnography—the method of including online spaces in field sites and using online posts as data—both more popular and more necessary.[2] As the sociologist Jeffrey Lane explains, "Assertions and behaviors cannot be evaluated exclusively within face-to-face situations because the social environment has evolved. Saying and doing are situated online and offline, which requires our attention to the overlap and tension between the two."[3]

Shortly after we met, many girls added me on Facebook or asked that I add them. At their encouragement, I also made accounts on

Twitter, Instagram, Snapchat, and Vine. The girls taught me how to use these apps and to send texts as they did; their laughter at my messages—too long, too delayed—schooled me in their rules. With these digital ties established, I regularly scrolled the girls' feeds and posts, adding information and screenshots to my field notes.

Digital ethnography presents researchers with new opportunities but also new challenges.[4] For example, social media helped me make and formalize connections with participants. The girls enjoyed the validation of friend requests, likes, and retweets, and they reciprocated such overtures. These interactions, which were largely public, solidified and expedited our relationships. They also eased my welcome into the girls' social world. Sometimes new people I met through the young women said they had seen me online, just as I had seen them.

As well as helping with relationship building, social media taught me a great deal about the girls' lives. I kept up with their daily broadcasts, and once I had grasped certain online codes, I learned how to infer information from other digital activity. For instance, when I noticed that Seeta consecutively liked a few of Faith's Instagram posts, I understood that the friction between the two girls had eased, even before this was confirmed to me by Florence.

Social media also let me observe the young women from a distance, which was especially helpful as they hung out in two distinct cliques.[5] Relatedly, it helped me keep in touch with the girls after they left NC for college. I followed their feeds, saw their journeys unfold, and could reach out online if cell numbers changed.[6]

Finally, I used social media to triangulate things the girls *said* with things they *did*. For example, I could cross-reference Florence's in-person claim that she had stopped drinking with her Snapchatted selfies sipping liquor.[7] Such moments of tension offered not only insight but also a valuable opportunity to consider what motivated the contradiction. Similarly, posts could cast light on what the girls were thinking or feeling. One afternoon, I joined Rosie, Zora, and

Stephanie at a cookout. The girls talked and giggled as the party pulsed, and Rosie seemed cheerful—dancing and cracking jokes. Later, however, I saw online that throughout the afternoon, Rosie had been tweeting about her grief for her late brother Bryan. The dual sources of information added a complexity that would likely have been inaccessible without social media.

Still, social media had drawbacks and limitations as a fieldwork tool. For one, it was not always obvious how to gauge posts' tone or intention. When the girls and I made plans by text, I sometimes struggled at first to understand messages like, *u can come if you want LOL.* Eventually, I learned how to decode these kinds of invitations. But such obscurity raised a broader ontological concern; without context or cues from in-person communication, statements' depth or meaning could be unclear. When, for instance, someone tweeted, *I hate my mom,* was this a deep confession or a quick line fired mid-fight?[8] Online, people can make all kinds of claims or comments, just as they can stage or manipulate photos. This underscores the value of triangulating information from feeds with face-to-face fieldwork.

Digital ethnography also raises questions about respondents' privacy—though perhaps no more than any type of ethnography. The girls did not perceive, as academics often do, online and offline as distinct worlds. As such, intimacy generally developed in parallel over social media and "IRL";[9] the first time I hung out in Seeta's room, for instance, was the same day she followed me on Twitter. As other researchers have found, the young women did not seem troubled by my digital presence during fieldwork.[10] And when I showed the girls the manuscript, they called the inclusion of tweets and other posts "genuine" or "real." However, just as I have changed participants' names for privacy, I have concealed social media handles. I have also, following social media researchers, including Jeffrey Lane and Forrest Stuart, "un-Googled" online data I present. This involves making minor syntactic tweaks that—without affecting the

overall meaning or style—ensure a quick Google search cannot uncover the data's source account.[11]

Social media can heighten participants' exposure. But it can also
hand them new forms of power. One is the ability to control researchers' access by, for example, delaying responses to texts or messages.
As Aisha once told me, "If I didn't want to [meet up], I would have
just deleted your text and been like, 'Oh, I never got your text.'" Another is the capacity to gaze back at researchers. Girls could use my
social media to see what I was up to, scroll through my old posts and
photos, and gather information about me as I did about them. Visibility went both ways.[12]

On Presence and Positionality

Ethnographers are often asked whether their presence alters participants' behavior. In some ways, of course, the answer is yes. Early on,
girls sometimes said things I doubted they would say to their friends;
Aisha once joked, as we took the muddy shortcut from the road to
Entertainment Cinema, "Don't worry, I'm not leading you down a
dark alley." Such comments, which alluded to my difference, and
specifically to my race and class privilege, suggested I increased the
girls' self-consciousness.

These kinds of remarks mostly stopped after a while, however,
and, over months and years, the girls' comfort around me grew, as
mine did with them. A few times someone followed a salacious story
with a laughing, "Don't put that in your book!"[13] More often, though,
they said things like, "Oh yeah, your book," when I referred to my
writing. I don't believe the girls generally censored themselves or
acted unusually around me, an intuition supported by their confiding
painful or embarrassing stories. Still I will never truly know.

But to the question of whether a researcher's presence necessarily and fundamentally changes the lives they seek to understand, I

believe, with other ethnographers, that the answer is no. As Mitchell Duneier explains, life's demands simply "are more influential than the social condition of a fieldworker being present."[14] Herbert Gans writes similarly: "Most people are too busy living to take much notice of a participant-observer once he has proven to them that he means no harm."[15]

Questions of presence, however, also gesture to questions of "positionality": the relation of the researcher to the social context they seek to understand. Positionality, in turn, implies at least two considerations. One is epistemological—how do researchers' identities shape their data collection?—and one is ethical—what power do they wield through research and writing? While "outsiders" can, in principle, sensitively and thoroughly portray people with different identity characteristics,[16] questions of ethics can be harder to answer.

As I discuss in the introduction, my identity guided and limited what I learned from the young women in NC. Some facets in particular—notably being white, being older than the girls, and having access to Harvard's resources and prestige—also gave me significant privilege and power. Yet acknowledging these inequities does not negate them.[17] Nor can listing demographic characteristics mitigate other forms of authority that fieldworkers hold, including the power to impose oneself in a place, to grab stories and bend them in the telling.[18]

The power dynamics between myself and the young women owed not only to my identity-based privileges. They owed also to my ability to write and share this book. Rather than ignore these inequities, the young women and I discussed them. Just as we talked about my whiteness in conversations about their experiences of race and racism, we talked too about the kind of book this would be. I expressed my gratitude for the girls' company and expertise. Still, although I view everything I learned from the young women as knowledge we co-created, as the author, I had—and have—authority.

In what follows, I discuss the decisions I made in writing this book and describe sharing it with the participants.

On Writing

To inform these chapters, I drew on my field notes, as well as interview transcripts, screenshots of social media posts, photographs, and some news stories. I used NVIVO, a coding software, to organize over twelve hundred pages of typed field notes, adding descriptive "tags" to themes that began to emerge. Poring repeatedly through the data, I "sift[ed] and resift[ed] . . . the evidence until a pattern ma[de] itself known."[19] Then I started writing.

Ethnography means learning about people by spending time with them. It means building relationships and trying to put lives on paper. It means—literally—*writing* about *people*. And writing about people presents choices: linguistic, scholarly, literary, and ethical. Had I made different choices, I would have told different stories; language does not transmit reality so much as create it. In this sense, ethnographies are, as Clifford Geertz notes, fictions—things *made*.[20]

In making this book, I chose to use the past tense to capture real, discrete events. Things I describe someone as thinking or feeling were reported to me as such. There are no composite characters. Some of the young women asked me to use their real names, but I stood by my initial promise to conceal them. I do, however, name North Cambridge. Following Mitchell Duneier—who, against a long tradition of ethnographic pseudonyms, argued that anonymity often protects researchers more than participants—scholars have weighed the risks and benefits of naming field sites and even people.[21] In this case, I considered the risk of compromised confidentiality against the benefit of specificity. I decided to name NC to avoid conjuring racialized stereotypes of an urban "ghetto."[22]

A commitment to specificity also guided my choice to write about only a few young women. I hoped that by spending time with fewer girls, I could learn more about—and better depict—their lives. I wanted to avoid bland tropes, like *good kids trying hard,*[23] and instead convey young women in their fullness. But this too raised important questions about representation. Would, for instance, including certain material, particularly about girls' romantic lives, propagate racist myths about Black girls' sexuality? In the end, I decided, in concert with the young women, that since sexuality is intrinsic to humanity, I should not exclude this real, relevant part of growing up.

This close focus on a small number of participants also left me unable to compare social dynamics among the NC girls with those among other teens.[24] Instead, however, of considering the young women as representatives of social categories,[25] I sought to craft portraits they themselves might recognize. Perhaps at the cost of generalizability, I follow Katherine Boo, who notes, "When I settle into a place, listening and watching, I don't try to fool myself that the stories of individuals are themselves arguments. I just believe that better arguments, maybe even better policies, get formulated when we know more about ordinary lives."[26]

On Returning

At the start of fieldwork, I asked the teens I spent most time with to sign consent forms indicating their willingness to participate in the research. Those who were minors signed an "assent" form and had a parent sign the consent form.[27] I trusted the young women—in most cases, seventeen- or eighteen-year-old high school seniors—to make thoughtful decisions. But I also invited them, years later, to read and reflect on the work in individual meetings before it was published.[28] For each meeting, I printed two copies of all passages in which they featured, and, over lunch or coffee, we went together through the pages.

I first met Stephanie at a restaurant in Boston. By then I had moved out of the city, and although I was excited to see Stephanie, I was unsure how she or any of the women would feel reading these stories. Across from me in a booth, she read silently through the manuscript.

"This is a trip down memory lane," Stephanie said, after several minutes.

"Yeah?"

"Yeah," she said, and kept reading.

Once she was done, she smiled and shook her head.

"What do you think?" I asked.

"You did a good job getting down everything that happened," Stephanie said. But then she grew tearful, describing how she had grown estranged from Florence and the others. "We follow each other on Instagram, but we don't look through stories,"[29] she explained. Still, she said, she would always care about her oldest friends.

When Stephanie circled back to the book, I asked whether she had read anything she disagreed with or would like me to remove. She didn't ask me to take anything out—nobody did—but she did offer a minor factual clarification here or there, and I incorporated these edits.

All the women were interested and thoughtful, and I was humbled by their eagerness to engage with my characterizations and ideas. They called the inclusion of their tweets and texts "true to life," and some considered how newer technologies have further had an impact on adolescence. Faith, for example, noted that Uber has changed—and expanded—her younger neighbors' experience of NC.

The meetings were more emotional than I had anticipated. I was moved by the nostalgia of facing the girls as women, and moved too by their excitement about being in a book. Some offered to promote it on social media, and Brittani even suggested, half-jokingly, that she should introduce me to her new friends so I could "write a sequel."

Brittani, like many of the women, was stirred by depictions of her teenage clique, as they too had since drifted. Reading the manuscript at a table in Harvard Square's Starbucks, she dabbed her cheeks with a stack of scratchy napkins.

"Why is it gone now?" Brittani wondered aloud. "Why is adulthood being apart? Friendship is like a marriage without papers. You don't get that kind of loyalty anymore."

Brittani apologized for crying. Then, laughing, she said, "I didn't know you were paying attention like *that*. You captured this time of life perfectly." She laid the pages on the table and placed her hands on top. "This is what we made of what we had," she said. "We didn't need everything to make special moments. We made things cherishable."

I met Joanne at Bertucci's restaurant in the Boston suburb where she lived with her husband and ten-month-old daughter, Micaia. Micaia had been a quiet, easy baby, Joanne said, at least after a stressful, four-month hospital stay following her premature birth. Micaia's sparkling brown eyes drew coos from servers and nearby diners. Joanne held her daughter and asked me to read the manuscript aloud. She listened carefully, nodding and sometimes crying as she reflected on the writing and her own memories.

Joanne was not the only woman to have left NC; Florence was living with her boyfriend in Boston, where we met at a café for breakfast. Florence was feeling under the weather that morning, but, characteristically earnest, she spoke excitedly about her future plans. Currently, she told me, she was working at Starbucks and hoping to move into a new apartment.

When we turned to the manuscript, Florence asked me to read the sections aloud as she sipped a chai latte.

"How do you feel?" I asked when I finished.

"I was so lit!"

"What do you mean?"

"You know, it happened," she said. "I seem thirsty for a man, but I feel like a lot of people can relate to that—to trying to have someone there." Florence then shared with me more stories she thought I could include—about NC and CRLS, about college, racism, and obstacles to opportunity.

Finally, I met Aisha at a seafood restaurant in Boston's newly developed Seaport district. After graduating from college, Aisha was living with her mom in the NC apartment she had moved to after Jefferson Park was demolished. Their relationship had eased somewhat, and Aisha's mom didn't mind her taking some time to figure out next steps. Recently, Aisha had returned from spending a few months in Uganda, where she was considering launching a business importing cosmetics and skin care products.

Aisha and I sat together at the restaurant for several hours, as I read aloud dozens of pages. She reacted throughout, sharing thoughts and adding updates or asides about people referenced.

"*Okurr!*" she trilled at the parts she liked. "Wow, I was funny!"

When Aisha grew teary, she first deflected her emotion with a witty quip or by Snapchatting her glazed salmon. But as we kept going, she let the tears fall.

"What are you feeling?" I asked, as she pressed the edge of her linen napkin to her lash line.

"You know, that's how I lived," Aisha sniffed. "Reading this makes me feel like I'm going to be okay. It makes me feel I'm going to be okay in life." She leafed through the printed pages. "There's not a false story in here. Thank you for reminding me of me."

·　•　·

During fieldwork and writing, I thought often of some words from Clifford Geertz. Ethnographers' "essential vocation," Geertz wrote, "is not to answer our deepest questions, but to make available to us answers that others . . . have given, and thus to include them in the consultable record of what [humanity] has said."[30]

I recalled these lines once more as I sat in Starbucks with Brittani. She said something that I feel captures what the girls taught me and what—if nothing else—I hope this book conveys about young women's determined caregiving in the face of inequality and exclusion.

"At the end of the day," Brittani said, "nobody wants to be alone. Everyone needs someone to make them feel like they exist. We made each other feel like we exist."

Final Reflections
Ten Years Later

Shortly before this book went to press, I caught up with most of the central women over Facetime and Zoom. The women, ranging from twenty-six to thirty years old, shared what life had held since we last spoke. Many had graduated from college, embarked on careers, left their parents' homes, and started families of their own. They had all survived a global pandemic and worked to build fulfilling lives.

Few close friendships remained among the women, though some kept in touch online or saw each other from time to time. Just three women—Brittani, Stephanie, and Rosie—still lived in Cambridge. Most of the women's parents had also left NC after the city demolished the Jefferson Park housing project.

On our calls, the women reflected on their lives; discussed adulthood's joys, struggles, and surprises; and revealed what they hoped the future might hold. Below I offer snapshots of what the women shared, not only about their experiences, but also about the shifting role of friendship and connection as they have grown older.

Zora

Zora was living in a Massachusetts town twenty miles from Cambridge, with her fiancé, Ray. Zora enjoyed taking care of their shared home, intentionally making the space a refuge from the world.

After finishing high school, Zora had spent two years at Bunker Hill Community College before transferring to Colby-Sawyer College. She graduated three years later with a bachelor's degree in sociology and began working at a nonprofit focused on ending neighborhood violence. Zora ran the youth program. She was motivated, she said, by her own experiences growing up in NC, by "the sad reality of growing up in the hood," and by "the people we've lost along the way, from gun violence to drugs to addictions."

For Zora, the losses had been personal. "I understood what it was like to lose someone through violence," Zora explained, referring both to her own stepbrother, Sparks, and to close friends, including Bryan. She wanted to help the young people she worked with "utilize their pain for something greater than themselves," she said.

After a while, Zora left the organization, frustrated by the leadership's funding decisions. She worked at both a restaurant and a gym, before contacting a temp agency, which offered Zora an internal administrative support position. Zora accepted the role, was promoted several times, and now worked in employee relations.

Zora, the oldest of the women, had recently turned thirty. The birthday had made her pensive. "Two days before, I literally sat down and started crying," she told me. "I'm like, 'You really are about to be thirty. You are in a good career path, you are about to get married. Financially, you are in a decent space. . . . You are making things work. You are understanding the value of everything and just looking back at every little thing that has happened. . . . You have come far." Still she said, "I feel like I could do more."

In the future, Zora hoped to launch a podcast, where people would share difficult stories to help others through hardships. "All of us have had fucked up things happen to us, right?" she said. "Things that we don't talk about or are ashamed to talk about. . . .

The most beautiful thing about our pain is that someone else is going through the same thing. And if we're strong enough to speak up about it, imagine how many lives you can change."

Rosie

Rosie, the youngest of the women, was twenty-six. She was living in her parents' apartment in Jefferson Park; COVID-related construction delays had meant more time in their home, but they too planned to move within months.

When we spoke, Rosie had just finished a long day of school at UMass Boston; after spending one semester at Worcester State University and two years at Bunker Hill Community College—and also taking some breaks from school—Rosie had eight classes left to earn her bachelor's in management finance. After graduating, she told me, she was considering an online master's in management at UMass. She was also considering moving to Maryland, where her boyfriend lived.

"I'm ready to leave NC," Rosie said. "Everyone's gone. And it's a bunch of new people in the new apartments. Most of them are from Boston, and they're just a little ghetto," she laughed.

Stephanie

Stephanie, twenty-eight, was living with her mom and stepdad in a town neighboring Cambridge, where they had moved after the demolition of their home.

Stephanie spent a couple of years at UMass Boston before deciding to withdraw from college and focus instead on work. From an office administrative role at a real estate branch, she transitioned into office management and then into her current position as an executive assistant at a global environmental firm, a job she found through a staffing agency.

Stephanie was happy with how things were going. At home, she was enjoying new freedoms. Being "more grown and more adult," she told me, "I live my life how I live it, and [my mom and stepdad] just live their lives." Still, she did hope to leave her parents' apartment before too long. She too was contemplating a move out of state, possibly to the DC area, where she had some friends.

Faith

Faith, who had started college at Bunker Hill and later transferred to UMass Boston, earned a bachelor's degree in social work. She had felt some pressure to finish college faster, seeing peers graduate in four or five years. After a while, though, she realized, "I'm taking forever, but as long as I get it done, it doesn't matter to me."

Once she graduated, she quickly moved out of her parents' house, deciding to "jump straight into it." When we spoke, Faith, twenty-seven, was living alone in an apartment just south of Boston, enjoying the privacy and freedom of her own space.

After college, Faith said, "I went through a couple of jobs, trying to get my life together." She found her first job online: working as a behavioral technician for children with autism. From there, she began working at a daycare and preschool facility. Faith liked the role but hoped ultimately to work with children in a "helping" rather than a "learning setting." Ideally, Faith said, she could find a job that would pay for her to complete a master's degree in social work.

I asked Faith about her hopes for the future. "Wherever God sees me, that's honestly where I'm going to be at," she said. "Only he knows the plan."

Still she shared one goal: to become financially comfortable enough to go a week without checking her bank account. Other than that, Faith said, she was happy to "go with the flow" and see what life had in store.

Brittani

Brittani transferred from Bunker Hill to Salem State, where she earned a bachelor's degree in accounting. After graduating, she moved back into her mother's Section 8 apartment in NC and found a job at a health and human services nonprofit. After leaving that position—poor management left her pulling all-nighters—a friend from college volleyball helped Brittani find her new job: financial aid adviser at Roxbury Community College. Having herself attended a community college, Brittani found the position a great fit.

In her free time, Brittani made paintings and shared her bold, colorful art on a new Instagram page. When we spoke, however, Brittani told me the art was temporarily "on hold"; she still carried a sketchbook in her purse, but her canvases were in storage as she navigated the purchase of her first home.

The purchase, Brittani explained, had been both stressful and serendipitous. Brittani had been forced to leave her mother's home when her own salary pushed their household income over the eligibility threshold for Section 8. In a letter the city warned Brittani's mother that she would soon lose her housing voucher, without which she could not afford the cost of rent. Brittani hurriedly applied for her own affordable rental housing in Cambridge and Boston. She also, after seeing a tweet posted by the City of Cambridge's official Twitter account, entered an affordable home ownership lottery. Brittani wound up first on the wait list, and when another entrant passed on a sale she seized the chance to buy a one-bedroom apartment. The program helped Brittani with closing costs and qualified her for a 1.5 percent down payment, which she covered with wages saved from work.

Brittani was anxious but excited to move; except for her time at Salem State, she had never lived outside of her mom's house. After getting settled, Brittani hoped to increase her income enough to avoid government assistance altogether and live, as she said, independently.

Seeta

I was unable to schedule a call with Seeta, twenty-seven, but we messaged one another online. She was living in an apartment south of Boston with one roommate and the American Staffordshire terrier she had adopted as a puppy.

Florence

Florence, twenty-eight, was living near Atlanta, Georgia. After re-enrolling at Colby-Sawyer and then leaving for a second and last time, she returned to her parents' NC apartment and started working full-time at Starbucks. Florence tried two other community colleges before deciding, as she explained, "I don't have to finish college to be successful." She considered various careers, including becoming a doula, training as a dental hygienist, and working in medical billing.

Florence met her boyfriend, Miko, on a dating app. Her parents did not approve, however, and after an argument she left their home to move in with Miko. They lived for a while in Boston, then moved to Rhode Island. Florence transferred to a new local Starbucks, where she worked until COVID shuttered the store.

As the world changed around her, Florence wondered what to do next. Online, she sold candles she made at home; she also took a real estate class. After Miko was offered a job near Atlanta and the couple moved south, Florence first worked as a bartender. Then she was hired as a technical recruiter—a job similar to Miko's and one she had slightly padded her résumé to get. To thrive in the role, Florence completed a tech boot camp and also drew on the skills she had gained at Starbucks and Panera. "Customer service, working with people for all these years . . . it's not so different," she said.

Florence was enjoying the position, which involved spending hours every day talking on the phone, including, she told me, with people who inspired her with new ideas for the future. Florence's next goal was to save and invest some of the money she was earning. She also said she would like to marry Miko but, after her experience with Samuel, felt no rush.

Joanne

Joanne, twenty-seven, was living thirty miles from Cambridge, with her husband and their four-year-old daughter, Micaia. The couple, who had met at a graduation cookout for Aisha's college roommate, had been married almost five years when we spoke.

Joanne was a full-time mom for two years after Micaia was born. She started working again, part-time in customer service for a Boston-area catering company, but the COVID pandemic began after weeks in the role. A year later, Joanne enrolled in online IT classes and gained certifications in cybersecurity. She had recently started two new jobs: one helping a home health agency near where she lived and one conducting remote IT support work.

Joanne felt pleased by the achievement, which, she said felt especially poignant given her difficulties at UMass Amherst. After leaving campus, she told me, she had taken some local classes in early childhood education. But formal schooling felt challenging. "I was dealing with lots of anxiety," she said. She struggled with "the concept of going back to school and sitting . . . I went to therapy after that. I had to work through that. It was tough."

As Joanne gained experience in the IT field, she hoped to transition from more entry-level work into bigger positions. Family remained her focus, however. Joanne was proud to see Micaia growing into a self-assured girl. Joanne planned to give her daughter a little more "room" than she had when she was young. "Growing up from another place, your parents have different expectations for you because they're immigrants," she explained. "And so, while we can honor those expectations, we should also have some form of balance."

Aisha

Aisha, twenty-seven, was living in Uganda with her two-year-old daughter, Joy. After graduating from Salem State four years earlier with a bachelor's degree in mathematics, Aisha moved back in with her mom in NC. She then spent some time in Uganda before returning to Cambridge and starting work as an engineer's assistant at a company that manufactured electronic chips.

A friend invited Aisha to a youth event at a church, where she met a man, John. The two started talking, then dating. John asked Aisha to be his girlfriend, but, she explained, she wasn't sure she could trust him. A few months later, Aisha realized she saw no future with John. Around the same time, however, she found out she was pregnant.

Aisha didn't know what to do. Her mom, worried about the cost of another child, suggested Aisha was too young to have a baby. Aisha agreed but worried that if she terminated the pregnancy, "it would mess me up to always think about what could have been." Warned by her doctors that she was at high risk for a miscarriage, Aisha decided to wait and see what happened. The pregnancy proceeded healthily, though for months Aisha had a hard time keeping food down.

With parenthood approaching, John proposed to Aisha. Everyone, Aisha told me, pressured her to accept. But she said no. She didn't feel "good" or "secure" with John, she explained, and she sensed that his proposal was motivated by "control." Urged by relatives to reconsider, Aisha stood her ground. "Most marriages are bad in real life and good on social media," she said. When Aisha and I spoke, Joy was two, and Aisha was proud of her resolve. "Had I chosen the societal way of doing things," she said, "I wouldn't be talking to you right now. I'd be crying."

Aisha gave birth in Cambridge, then returned to Uganda, where, she said, she would stay for the foreseeable future: "The lifestyle out here is better for children than it is in America." Like Joanne, Aisha wanted her daughter's childhood to differ from her own. "I was meant to be a kid," Aisha said, "but I was always on hustle mode." She wanted better for Joy. "I prayed to God that she won't lack," Aisha said. "That's the one thing I asked for."

Aisha also planned to parent differently than her mother. When Aisha was eight months' pregnant, she told her mother, during an intense conversation, "I won't raise my child the way you raised me." But their relationship had improved since Joy's birth. Aisha appreciated her mother's presence and understood her in a new way: "I've actually been like, wanting to do stuff for her. I'm not resentful towards her."

John, who had since gotten married and had another child, helped out with Joy and paid child support. Aisha diligently put aside the cash John and his family sent for her daughter. Along with the child support, Aisha earned money through a car-sharing app. Back when she was working at the chip manufacturing company in Cambridge, Aisha had leased a Toyota Corolla, which she now remotely rented out via the app. "It ain't no Benz," she joked, "but don't worry, we're coming." She was saving up to lease a second car to list on the platform.

Aisha also had other plans. The goal, she said, was to have a few businesses that earned passive income. She also looked forward to feeling challenged again.

Friendships in Adulthood

On Facetime and Zoom, many of the women said they felt warmly toward their old cliques, even though few remained in close contact. More generally, friendships looked different in the women's late twenties from their late teens. Three of the nine lived with boyfriends, fiancés, or husbands. Many said their closest friends were women they had met at college or work; sometimes these new friendships had harmed old ones.

Other women had struggled to make new friends as an adult, like Brittani, who said, "People are very, like, wall up." Joanne too said, "Friendship is hard for me now, I will say . . . Friendships have to meet certain criteria . . . I find that protecting my peace is more important." Joanne was close with her sisters-in-law, though, and liked to host teatime together over video-chat for their daughters.

Many of the women described standards they now have for social relationships. Florence, for example, told me, "I'm not really in a hurry to make new friends . . . I know it will come to me. I don't want anybody that's gonna be in my life not being consistent and whatnot."

Stephanie spoke similarly: "Because I'm more mature and I'm a little bit wiser, I've been creating more boundaries for myself. . . . Also, just having more discernment and being more selective with the type of friendships that I want to have that will help me find more peace or just elevate my lifestyle a little bit."

Like Stephanie, Zora said she hoped to cultivate friendships that could be valuable. Friendships were assets, she explained, that could benefit not only her, but others she cared about. "I feel like the older we get, the more we view friendships in a more business way," she said. "That's how I'm being a beneficial friend to you. Because at this point in our lives, you might not need the emotional support I was able to provide when we were young. Our needs change."

Rosie echoed the idea that needs have changed over time. "I think friendships, they meant more to me back then," she said. "Now I don't really depend on it that much."

Aisha also viewed friendship differently. These days, she told me, she prioritized good feelings. "Once it feels warm," she said, "that's how I make my friendships. I'm big on security. Like, feeling safe at all times." Aisha had found that friendship could demand a little forgiveness. "Now I've grown older and really self-reflected," she told me, "I've learned to forgive a little bit more . . . It's not about perfection. I think it's just about somebody feeling warm. And then understanding that we're all doing life." Still, she too had standards. "Not everybody gets to experience my light," Aisha said. "Not everyone deserves to be around it."

Social Media

Over time, the role social media played in the women's lives had changed too. Many felt it had become less fun. In high school, Brittani explained, "we'd just post funny stuff." In college, however, "people started posting to distinguish friendships, like whose best friend was whose, and stuff like that." Since then, social media had shifted further: to "the business side," Brittani said. This had some utility for Brittani, whose art had acquired an online following; she was even hired by a local café to host a paint night after an employee found her page.

Stephanie viewed this shift less positively. "In the earlier days," she said, "you could just post a picture of your food, or you just hanging out with your friends doing the most basic shit. But now it's like, 'Alright, I'm running this business,' or 'I'm a fashionista, a relationship guru, I'm a therapist, I'm an astrologist, I'm an entrepreneur.'" Nowadays, Stephanie said, social media feels like a "moneymaking machine. . . . It's literally about making money and creating a brand for yourself."

In part for this reason, many of the women's interest had dwindled. Few used social media with any avidity. "I don't really use social media much," Rosie said. "Like, I'm on Instagram and everything else, but I don't post much. I don't follow a lot of people. Even if I'm friends with you in real life, I don't care to follow you or add you as a friend on social media. . . . I used to post a lot. But now I just don't care for people to know about my life like that."

Some women even defined "real" friendships against "online" friendships, like Brittani, who bristled at how social media enabled— or encouraged—the performance of intimacy between friends. "As far as like, having to post on their birthdays, it's like, no, I'm taking you out to dinner!" she told me. "We're gonna celebrate you, and it doesn't have to be on social media."

Others described intentionally limiting or eliminating their use of social media. Joanne, for instance, had not used Instagram for years. "I let go of social media right when I was pregnant," she told me. "I had anxiety and stuff, and I feel like looking at other people wasn't really helping."

Aisha spoke similarly. "I kind of toned back on social media," she said. "Being a mom and also postpartum, I felt like I didn't look good. I would post pictures, and I'd have anxiety through the roof." Recently, however, she had been feeling more settled and confident and was reconsidering her online presence. "Now I'm trying to rehab social media again and be back more often," she said. Aisha had also started an Instagram page for her daughter, Joy. She didn't launch the account right away, however. "I started posting Joy when she was good-looking," Aisha said, laughing, not when "she was a blob."

"Unprecedented Times"

As they built their adult lives, the women endured the COVID-19 pandemic. Nobody was spared the impact: Faith graduated on

Zoom; Joanne lost her first job since having her daughter. COVID also affected the women's relationships with friends and family. Yet since they were in their midtwenties when the pandemic struck—and had far outgrown the teenaged friendships whose dynamics are the focus of this book—I cannot speak to how lockdowns and social distancing influenced the types of peer support outlined in these chapters. Other researchers, however, have looked at this question.

The data, while preliminary, look bleak.[1] Unsurprisingly, many young people suffered enormously when the pandemic all but destroyed in-person socializing for months. Zoom lessons could not replace classrooms' dynamism, or the bustle and banter in school hallways. The loss of in-person social contact cost countless teens the entertainment, engagement, support, and more that they had previously found from peers.

Amid the upheaval, social media appears to have had a mixed effect. As this book and other research describes, social media can help young people give and get care.[2] And during COVID, certain uses of social media—particularly one-on-one digital communication, self-disclosure between friends, and funny online experiences—mitigated young people's loneliness and stress.[3] At the same time, however, some of social media's negative impacts—including anxiety and self-comparison—were exacerbated when in-person contact was curtailed. As a result, researchers identified social media use both as a protective factor and as a risk factor for psychological well-being during the pandemic.[4]

Ultimately, data gathered during COVID further support the idea that both face-to-face and online interaction are vital for young people's friendships. The pandemic's disruption showed that digital connection could enable much more than many people had imagined, but it also confirmed that cell phones and computers are no substitute for embodied, visceral social lives.

Final Reflections

On our calls, some of the women said they felt sentimental about having a written record of part of their youth. "It's like, wow, there's some type of historical information out there about me, if I ever wanted to go back and reflect," Brittani said. Florence said, "I felt that it was a blessing that we have something to look back on, and see how much we've grown, or what we can learn from each other. To have this documented."

I also felt sentimental; it is a strange and humbling privilege to learn about people's lives over many years. Reconnecting with the women in a new phase of our adulthoods, I was newly grateful for their welcome and all they taught me. I hope that despite the quandaries and reductiveness inherent in writing about other people, these pages do some justice to the women's experiences, skills, and personalities.

Acknowledgments

To the women from Cambridge, thank you for all that you shared with me. Thank you for your insights, your tolerance, and your friendship.

Matt Desmond, you taught me about ethnography, not just as a research method, but as a sensibility, a way of moving through the world. Your vision and confidence, when I often lacked both, are why this book exists. Over the years, you marked up thousands of pages, and your marginalia—as Haikus, lyrics, and doodles—made me a better writer and thinker. It has been an immeasurable privilege to learn from your contagious brilliance. Thank you for advising me with no agenda and for helping me find my voice.

Michèle Lamont, you have been an extraordinary and generous role model. Your majestic command of social science and your tireless commitment to others have been a joy to encounter. Thank you for the opportunities you brought me, for the thrilling conversations you facilitated—at conferences, dinners, and more—and for your warmth and support.

Mary Waters, thank you for asking tough questions. You encouraged me to push deeper and to consider the full implications of this research. Thank you for modeling a type of scholarship that is engaged, rigorous, and, crucially, compassionate.

Many faculty members and colleagues gave me comments that sharpened my analysis. Others offered encouragement that I needed and took to heart. For these contributions and more, warm thanks to Laura Adler, Asad Asad, Stefan Beljean, Monica Bell, Steven Brown, Bart Bonikowski, Brianna Castro, Curtis Chan, Philippa Chong, Matt Clair, Mitchell Duneier, Gary Alan Fine, Kelley Fong, Maggie Frye, Alice Goffman, Tamara Kay, Eric Klinenberg, Jeremy Levine, Tey Meadow, Chris Muller, Orlando Patterson, Sam Plummer, Jennifer Silva, Mario Small, Natalie Smith, Robert Smith, Iddo Tavory, Mo Torres, Van Tran, Adam Travis, Joseph Wallerstein, Bruce Western, and Chris Winship. I also thank the participants of Harvard's Culture and Social Analysis Workshop, Michèle Lamont's ISF Group, and the 2014 and 2015 Craft of Ethnography Conferences.

For close readings, incisive feedback, and intellectual and moral support, I thank my inspiring colleagues and friends Eleni Arzoglou, Carly Knight, Jeffrey Lane, Ekédi Mpondo-Dika, and Eva Rosen. Thanks too to my cheerleader and trailblazer, Tom Wooten.

To the sociology department staff, thank you for your endless work: Lisa Albert, Odette Binder, Nancy Branco, Deb De Laurell, Dotty Lukas, Jessica Matteson, Suzanne Ogungbadero, Michael Van Unen; and, at Princeton, Katie Krywokulski. Special thanks to Laura Thomas, my American mom, for Hershey's Kisses and belly laughs.

For funding, I thank the National Science Foundation, the National Academy of Education / Spencer Foundation, Harvard University's Joint Center for Housing Studies, and Harvard University's Center for American Political Studies.

Brielle Bryan, Theo Leenman, and Jared Schachner, thank you for your wit, nihilism, and camaraderie. Our dinners and group-chat were a solace. Theo, from our windowless office days to our transcontinental japes, your limber intelligence and wicked humor have been—and always will be—vital.

Across the pond, I thank the brilliant and multitalented Stephanie Edwards for fifteen years of laughing, learning, and travel disasters, and for helping me through two tough writing spots. What fortune to have found each other on the first day of college and to have held on ever since.

For friendships long and life affirming, I thank Kerala Adams-Carr, Maddy Bernstein, Anya Broido, Lydia Dallett, Phillipa de Lacy, Holly Graham, Myra Gupta, Esther Hindley, Louisa McIndoe, Sophia McNab, Diego Reinero, Ashley Sanders, and Liberty Timewell.

For teaching me about writing, I thank Chloe Caldwell, Chelsea Hodson, Jonas Hassen Khemiri, Parul Sehgal, and Tony Tulathimutte; and for teaching me about living, I thank Michelle Gallant and Ellen Westrich.

To Naomi Schneider and the team at the University of California Press, thank you for engaging with this research and bringing it to life.

To Charles Dellheim, Laura Gross, Alexandra, and Caroline, thank you for being my home away from home in Boston. Thank you for the shelter through snowstorms, homecooked meals, and lively conversations; you were over and again a refuge.

Beth, Gary, and Andy Gross, thank you for your love and welcome. I so appreciate your interest in my work and the respite you offered from it.

Gina, Victor, Reuben, and Isabella Oreffo, thank you for your presence, kindness, and care, now and forever. I am so grateful for each moment we can spend together.

Mark Sandelson, your support kept me warm (when I moved to New England with no winter coat) and kept me going. You made this project possible. Thank you for your big-hearted enthusiasm and all the adventures.

Jess, my wiser younger sister, I could have done none of this without you. Thank you for your insights, both sociological and psychotherapeutic, and for all the memes. You are perfect, even when you hang up on me midconversation. And thank you, Joe, for joining and bettering our family.

To my parents, thank you for raising me to ask why. Thank you for your politics and commitment to justice. Thank you for all of it: for your inexhaustible support, for the many transatlantic flights, and for letting me find my way.

Finally, Paul, whose love changed everything. Thank you for your deep and essential goodness. For the safety, joy, and witnessing. What a chapter that was.

Notes

Epigraph from Audre Lorde, *Zami: A New Spelling of My Name* (New York: Crossing Press, 1982).

Preface

1. Throughout, people's names and social media handles are pseudonyms. Place-names have not been changed. I discuss these decisions in "A Note on Research and Writing."
2. I capitalize "Black" to dignify the history of people descended from the African diaspora. Almost a century ago, W.E.B. Du Bois campaigned for newspapers and magazines to capitalize the "N" in Negro (Tharps 2014); he regarded "the use of a small letter for the name of twelve million Americans and two hundred million human beings as a personal insult" (in Lewis 2009, 234). I follow scholarship and style guides that apply Du Bois's thought to the word *Black*. By contrast, I leave "white" uncapitalized when referring to white people. Although some suggest that lowercase "w" risks eliding whiteness as a racial category, I am persuaded by those who argue that uppercase "w" propagates the symbolic violence of white supremacists who capitalize the word.
3. As Aimee Meredith Cox, professor of African American studies and anthropology, writes, "I do not consider Black girls units of analysis I need to romanticize to counter negative representations. Black girls are not the problem. Their lives do not need sanitizing, normalizing, rectifying, or translating so they can be deemed worthy of care and serious consideration" (2015, 8; see also Ladner 1971, xxiv).

Introduction

1. Aisha used filters not to alter her appearance—to change her face or body—but to add signifiers of "cool." Teens criticized as "fake" peers who overedited photos. See Goffman (1959) on how people perceive inauthenticity as immoral.

2. Sociologists have long studied social network-based resource transmission (e.g., Domínguez and Watkins 2003; Edin and Lein 1997; Granovetter 1973; Mazelis 2017; Newman 1999; Small 2009). Researchers studying urban poverty, from Stack (1974) to Desmond (2016), have shown how people lean on members of their social network—including friends, family, and strangers—to survive. This book adds a focus on the nonmaterial but indispensable goods that friends offered one another.

3. On the benefits of friendships for adolescents, including their power to promote development, boost emotional intelligence, buffer stress, and raise college aspirations, see, e.g., Bukowsi, Newcomb, and Hartup 1998; Masten and Coatsworth 1998; Stanton-Salazar and Spina 2005; Winiarski-Jones 1988. Scholars since Mead (1934) and Vygotsky (1978) have shown the essential role peers play in development and growth.

4. Extensive research explores contextual influences on young people's trajectories. Neighborhoods can affect young residents' outcomes (for reviews of the "neighborhood effects" literature, see Johnson 2010; Leventhal, Dupéré, and Brooks-Gunn 2009; Sampson, Morenoff, and Gannon-Rowley 2002). Schools matter too; among factors found to shape students' experiences are school size, violence levels, mean student socioeconomic status, and mean student achievement (Bryk and Driscoll 1988; Coleman and Hoffer 1987; Hoxby 2000; Mayer 1991; Paulle 2013). Even more than schools and neighborhoods, however, families are framed by researchers as critical to adolescent development and success (Burton and Jarrett 2000; Elliot et al. 2006). Studies show that family income, poverty, and resources—along with household dynamics like parenting styles, parental involvement, and child monitoring practices—have an impact on measures that include children's educational achievement, drug abuse, and physical and mental health (Duncan et al. 1998; Furstenberg et al. 1999; Laub and Sampson 1988; Spencer and Dornbusch 1990).

5. E.g., Corsaro and Eder 1990; Everhart 1983; Willis 1977.

6. Young people "do not perceive, interpret, form opinions about, or act on the world as unconnected individuals. Rather, they do all these things in concert with their peers, as they collectively experience the world" (Adler and Adler 1998, 206; see also Corsaro 1985; Thorne 1993).

7. Research into peer effects dates at least to James Coleman's *The Adolescent Society* (1966), which suggested that different peer cultures are tied to various levels of achievement.

8. E.g., Akers et al. 1979; An 2011; Brooks-Gunn et al. 1993; Elliot, Huizinga, and Menard 1989; Haynie 2001; Jensen 1972; Kandel 1978; Matsueda and Anderson 1998; Shaw and McKay 1942; South and Baumer 2000.

9. Crane 1991, 1227. See also Case and Katz 1991; Jencks and Mayer 1990.

10. In low-income neighborhoods, researchers find that increased peer support predicts increased levels of "antisocial behavior" (Leventhal and Brooks-Gunn 2000, 327).

11. See e.g., Morris 2015; Rios 2011.

12. Ray 2018b, 11.

13. Kasinitz et al. 2008, 350.

14. E.g., Bourgois 1996, 196; Edin and Lein 1997; Jarrett 1997; Waters 1999, 235.

15. E.g., Rainwater 1970, 73; Richardson and St. Vil 2016; Williams and Kornblum 1988.

16. Kotlowitz 1991, 31.

17. Jones 2009; see also Fader 2021.

18. Jones 2009, 54.

19. E.g., Thrasher 1927; Whyte 1943; Cloward and Ohlin 1960; MacLeod 1987; Sullivan 1989; Bourgois 1996; Kaplan 1997; Anderson 2000; Harding 2010; Venkatesh 2008; Contreras 2013; Goffman 2014. Importantly, however, what counts as "deviant" is historically variable and socially constructed. As the sociologist Joyce Ladner (1971, xx) explains, "Deviance is the invention of a group that uses its own standards as the *ideal* by which others are to be judged" (original emphasis). Howard Becker (1963, 9) writes similarly, "Social groups create deviance by making the rules whose infraction constitutes deviance, and applying those rules to particular people and labeling them as outsiders."

As a group, teenagers have long been studied through a lens of deviance. "Research on adolescence," Cox (2015, 12) explains, "has largely been written from the perspective of fear. . . . Throughout the history of academic work on youth, the idea of control and containment is a recurring theme" (see also Best 2000; Palladino 1996). Racist tropes and assumptions have exacerbated this tendency in research about young people of color.

20. E.g., Bourgois 1996; Edin and Kefalas 2005; Kaplan 1997.

21. As Ray and Tillman (2019, 4) note, studies that "sympathetically highlight why those living in marginalized communities participate in risk behaviors via

structuralist explanations" contribute to "an excessive emphasis on risk behaviors among scholars." Such research, in turn, has "strengthened policies and practices that focused on risk behavior prevention, and reinforced narratives about marginalized communities as social problems."

22. Ray 2018b, 229–30. Ray critiques the "at-risk" label that is pervasively applied—by government agencies, schools, and community organizations—to young people of color from low-income families. This labeling, she shows, encourages institutions to allocate resources to the prevention of "risk behaviors" rather than to the provision of holistic support for young people's transitions to adulthood. Ray notes, moreover, that describing young people marginalized by poverty and racism as "at risk" obscures the structural nature of inequality. Sharing Ray's critique, I hope this book shows how, even among young people labeled "at risk," there exists competent, creative peer support worthy of recognition and investment. While Ray reveals the unsolvable "mobility puzzles" facing such young people, I focus instead on the contours, details, and limitations of teens' mutual care.

23. E.g., DeLuca, Clampet-Lundquist, and Edin 2016; Ray 2018b.

24. Both academic and policy research disproportionately center boys and men. For example, the notion of the school-to-prison pipeline, explains Monique Morris, "has been largely developed from the conditions and experiences of males. It limits our ability to see the ways in which Black girls are affected by surveillance . . . and the ways in which advocates, scholars, and other stakeholders may have wrongfully masculinized Black girls' experiences" (2015, 9).

25. Jones 2009, 20.

26. Popkin, Leventhal, and Weismann 2010, 716.

27. East 2010.

28. E.g., Anderson 2000; Bourgois 1996; Contreras 2013; Dance 2002; Fader 2013; Goffman 2014; Harding 2010; MacLeod 1987; Rios 2011; Venkatesh 2008; Willis 1977. For exceptions, see, e.g., Bettie 2003; Jones 2009; Miller 2008; Ness 2004; Ladner 1971.

One reason for the relative dearth of women's stories is that historically most ethnographers have been men. Jay MacLeod (1987, 468) describes how his gender directed his focus in *Ain't No Makin' It:* "I felt totally incapable of considering adolescent girls in Clarendon Heights, whose situation was so far beyond my own experience." Relatedly, Herbert Gans (1962, 409), in his appendix to *Urban Villagers,* notes, "Even though my wife participated in the field work and told me about the female social gatherings, my report does tend to place greater emphasis on the male portions of the peer group society."

Beyond urban ethnography, a well-established field of girlhood studies de-centers boyhood and masculinity in research on youth (e.g., Best 2000; Caron 2011; Cox 2015; Harris 2004; McRobbie 2000; Ward and Benjamin 2004).

29. Cox 2015, 14. The academic focus on "urban poverty, migration, and the resulting shifts in neighborhood composition"—a focus that motivated many seminal urban ethnographies—partly reflects, Cox argues, "concerns about the stability within and reproduction of the male-headed nuclear family" (14).

30. E.g., Domínguez and Watkins 2003; Edin and Lein 1997; Nelson 2000; Stack 1974.

31. Jones 2009; Miller 2008; Ness 2010. As Cox (2015, 120) notes, "The litera-ture on Black girls emphasizes the ways in which they disrupt community through competition and physically fighting one another as opposed to the strategies they use to support and care for one another."

32. Pew Research Center 2018a. Although teens from different racial and so-cioeconomic groups are equally likely to own a smartphone, class differences ex-ist in access to computers: 96% of teens from households earning over $75,000 per year have access to a computer at home, compared to 75% among teens in households earning less than $30,000 per year.

33. Pew Research Center 2018a.

34. Spotty Wi-Fi was infuriating. After school one day, as Aisha angled for a free frappe from a classmate working the evening shift at Dunkin' Donuts, her cousin Afiya and I took seats at a nearby table. Afiya tried to connect to the Wi-Fi and after several failed attempts, banged her iPhone on the table. Beside us, a sticker on the window read "FREE WIFI!" Underneath the words, someone had scrawled in black ink, "A lie! And, FUCK YOU!"

35. See, e.g., Kelly et al. 2018; Sales 2016.

36. Turkle 2011. New technologies have always caused social anxieties; Plato, in the *Phaedrus,* famously worried that the invention of the written word would destroy people's memorization skills. Adults' anxieties shaped early research about young people's use of technology (Pascoe 2011; Third et al. 2015). More re-cently, however, scholars have identified young people's digital aptitude, compe-tencies, and creativity (boyd 2014; Byron 2020; Ito et al. 2010).

37. E.g., Baym 2015; Boyd 2014.

38. E.g., Bourgois 1996; Liebow 1967; Stack 1974.

39. Lane 2018; Patton et al. 2016; Stuart 2020; Urbanik and Roks 2020.

40. Byron (2020, 2) notes, "Despite a tendency to locate care in actions, such as actively helping or supporting somebody through a health issue or difficult time, care is also mundane. That is, when we read, scroll, and drift through our

social media feeds, we are seeing and remembering the people, practices, and things we care about. We scroll because we care." See also Ito et al. 2010.

41. Often, studies about online social support spotlight one aspect, platform, or medium—for instance, how people find comfort in internet forums or how Twitter users coordinate responses to natural disasters. Yet, as Hampton and Lu argue (2017, 863), "to focus on the exchange of support through any one medium at any one moment in time risks missing the broader role that communication technologies play for social support."

This book explores the latter: the broader role social media plays in peer support. "Peers" and "friends" are not, as Byron (2020) explains, analytically identical. Yet I use the term "peer support" to encompass not only care between close friends but also the broader benefits teens sourced from a wider peer group, particularly online.

42. Before participating, the central girls signed consent forms approved by Harvard University's Institutional Review Board (IRB). For those who were minors at the time, a parent—in all cases, a mother—signed a consent form.

43. Since roughly 30% of Cambridge's residents were foreign born (US Census 2013), being the daughters of immigrants did not place the girls in a small minority. Yet the conclusion considers how being 1.5- and second-generation immigrants shaped the girls' social dynamics, obstacles, and opportunities.

44. The Cambridge Housing Authority (CHA) administers both public housing and a Section 8 housing voucher program. At the time, CHA owned and managed twenty-nine projects, containing 2,334 rental units, and administered 2,814 Section 8 vouchers (US Department of Housing and Urban Development 2014).

45. American Community Survey 2016.

46. Typing in a notes app, I could capture conversations, including verbatim quotes, in real time, together with things like gestures and body language. Holding and using a phone while hanging out was normal if not expected. In fact, not having a phone (and thereby signifying the ability to entertain oneself) was sometimes read as unduly demanding attention.

47. See Desmond 2012; MacLeod 1987.

48. Positivist scholars argue that researchers are—or should be—objective. Yet researchers' identities shape each part of their work, as feminists, critical race theorists, and academics in the poststructural and postcolonial traditions have shown (e.g., Abu-Lughod 1986, 1990; Crenshaw 1991; Harding 1991; Hill Collins 2000; Mohanty 1991; Oakley 1981; Smith 1987). The notion of a universal subject who observes free of values and biases is a myth. Rather, because subjectivity is forged

within structures of power (Zuberi and Bonilla-Silva 2008), researchers' identities and experiences direct their consumption and production of knowledge. These important ideas, also engaged by sociologists of science and technology, have an intellectual history that traces at least to the hermeneutic theorists of the 1800s.

49. As the sociologist Jamie Fader (2013, 11) writes, "The strength of ethnographic methods comes from the close, personal relationships formed with the people being studied. This approach is a self-conscious departure from the positivist premise that scholars should remain detached and distanced from their subjects in order to reduce the potential for bias."

50. Being relatively short—five feet three inches—also placed me in the girls' height range, making me less conspicuous. Joanne once told me, "You blend in, you're like our height."

51. Other researchers have described how their foreignness affected their racial classification by research participants. Loïc Wacquant (2005, 10), for instance, explains, "French nationality granted me a sort of statutory exteriority with respect to the structure of relations of exploitation, contempt, misunderstanding, and mutual mistrust that oppose blacks and whites in America" (see also Lamont 2000, 255).

52. An extensive literature in anthropology explores care as both a resource and a relational practice (e.g., Black 2018; Buch 2015).

Chapter 1

1. During fieldwork, nobody explicitly asked me for cash, train fare, or any other money. At times, however, I participated in the girls' regular trade of small sums, particularly when contributing to food or drinks we would all share.

2. E.g., Desmond 2012; Edin and Lein 1997; Mazelis 2017; Nelson 2000; Newman 1999; Small and Gose 2020; Stack 1974; Venkatesh 2006.

3. Jencks 1997, xiv.

4. Milner 2015, 34.

5. E.g., Patillo-McCoy 1999.

6. For young women, consumption is presented as a path to social power (Best 2006; Harris 2004; McRobbie 2000). In addition, consumption, as an assertion of status, can also be a strategy for dealing with racism (Lamont 2000; Lamont and Molnar 2002). Yet consumption can be fraught for Black and brown teens, who experience racism and discrimination while shopping and are also stereotyped in the media as "combat consumers," determined to acquire brand-named goods by any means (Chin 2011; see also Nightingale 1993).

7. Ray (2018b) shows how some teens from low-income homes with no realistic mobility prospects perform a middle-class identity through conspicuous consumption. See also Anderson 2000; Drake and Cayton 1945; Sullivan 1989; Williams and Kornblum 1988.

8. Theorizing about the links between consumption, identity, and group memberships dates to Veblen ([1899] 1994) and Marx ([1867] 2010). As the sociologist Julie Bettie (2003, 44) explains, "The expression of self through one's relationship to and creative use of commodities . . . is a central practice in capitalist society." See also Bourdieu 1984; Chin 2011; Lamont and Molnar 2001; Palladino 1996.

9. Pugh 2009, 7; see also Pugh 2011.

10. Best 2006, 2017.

11. As a white person, I opt not—even in reference or quotation—to write in full a racist word historically used to brutalize Black people.

12. On the ties between gifts and social relationships, see, e.g., Mauss 1967; Sahlins 1972.

13. Defining the concept of affordances, the psychologist James Gibson (1979, 127) writes, "The affordances of the environment are what it offers the animal. For instance, a flat surface is 'stand-on-able.'" The concept was later developed in science and technology studies to capture the interplay between a technology's inherent features and the innovative, flexible functions devised by users (e.g., Hutchby 2001).

The concept of affordances offered a theoretical middle ground between, on the one hand, the determinism that had characterized much research on new technologies—in which human agency yields to omnipotent machines—and, on the other, hard social constructivism—in which human agency is near-absolute.

The notion of affordances recognizes that technologies can simultaneously enable and constrain. For instance, a keyboard, designed to type words, affords users the ability to combine punctuation marks into representations of facial expressions, like smiling :), frowning :(, crying :'(, shocked :O, and more. While users can transcend a keyboard's intended function and infuse text with emotion, a keyboard does not afford the ability to send pictures or sounds.

14. Social exchange theorists would see Aisha's posts as "return," or reinforcement, exchanging symbolic prestige for material goods (e.g., Emerson 1976; Homans 1961). Instantly expressing thanks might have freed Aisha from a protracted gift-giving relationship. "In every society," Bourdieu (1977, 5) argues, "if it is not to constitute an insult, the counter-gift must be deferred and different." While Aisha did respond with a different counter-gift—a Twitter shout-out—this was typically not "deferred," but neither was this seen as an insult.

15. See Desmond 2012.

16. The materiality of the money jettisoned the only acceptable excuse for withholding: being broke. Adrian Nicole LeBlanc (2004, 146) describes a similar dynamic in *Random Family:* "Sometimes Coco"—a young mother living in a supportive housing facility—"spent down her money just so she could be the one to use it, which allowed her to maintain her integrity. 'This way if the girls in my house come to ask me for money, I tell them no, and I ain't lying,' Coco said."

17. See Best 2017.

18. None of the girls openly discussed or pursued romantic relationships with women or people of other genders.

19. Ray (2018b) found that young women believed they could gauge a man's commitment by his willingness to spend money on gifts and dates. Young people often equate care with financial provisioning and seek possessions as indicators that they are valued (Pugh 2009).

20. Keeping up with pop culture, particularly music, is a path to status for adolescents (Carter 2005), and the internet removes the cost of access earlier generations of teens faced.

21. Making money, at whatever scale, offers social and emotional benefits. In the underground economy of Chicago's Robert Taylor Homes, Sudhir Venkatesh found that "money-making schemes gave residents a sense of belonging and respect" (2000, 106). In fact, "in some respects, the cultural valence of hustling overrode its material significance, given that most underground ventures provided minimal earnings" (106).

22. Economic and relational realms mutually shape each other; meanings attached to money can shed light on cultural values, and vice versa (e.g., Zelizer 1997, 2011).

23. hooks 2003, 113.

24. As Karl Polanyi (1944, 46) has argued, "Man . . . does not act so as to safeguard his individual interests in the possession of material goods, he acts so as to safeguard his social standing, his social claims, his social assets. He values material goods only in so far as they serve this end." Similarly, the sociologist Randall Collins describes how socio-emotional motivations drive people's pursuit of economic resources. "The entire social-interactional marketplace for IRs"—i.e., interaction rituals, or encounters with others that produce positive emotional energy—"is what drives the motivation to work, produce, invest, and consume in the material market," he argues (2004, xv).

25. E.g., Giordano 2003; Hatch and Wadsworth 2008.

26. See Pugh 2009.

Chapter 2

1. See e.g., Anderson 2015; Chin 2011; Loebach et al. 2020

2. Sorokin and Merton 1937. Much sociological theorizing about time follows Durkheim ([1912] 1995, 492), who showed the links between time and social order. Researchers in this tradition explore how temporal rituals and/or time systems structure social organization (e.g., Zerubavel 1981). A separate body of theorizing pulls from the phenomenological tradition to probe how and why people experience the passage of time in different ways (e.g., Flaherty 1999, 2011).

3. The sociologist Amy Best shows how teens' experience of time differs across social contexts. At McDonald's after school, "the standard chunks of time between a ringing bell are cast aside. At McDonald's, kids linger, stretching not just dollars but time" (2017, 133). The NC girls also experienced time differently in various contexts, and they deliberately used social media to manipulate how hours passed.

4. Flaherty 2011, 2.

5. Conrad 1997.

6. The aversion to doing nothing is so strong that study participants choose to self-administer electric shocks rather than be left alone with their thoughts (Wilson et al. 2014). The discomfort of boredom is partly why long wait times at bureaucratic state agencies can be so dehumanizing and burdensome (Auyero 2012).

7. Periods of time represent larger percentages of young people's lives, explaining the "impatience of youth and their tendency to perceive time passing slowly" (Flaherty 2014, 175).

8. Many affluent parents spend considerable sums on after-school activities and opportunities for their children (Lareau 2003). Access to informal time-filling activities also often costs money, leaving students from low-income families with more free time.

9. The district's 2014 per-pupil expenditure rate of $27,163 was higher than almost any other district in Massachusetts, and the school's student-teacher ratio of 10:1 was far above the nationwide average, 16:1 (Massachusetts Department of Elementary and Secondary Education 2018).

10. Free lunches and reduced-price lunches were available, respectively, to students from families earning up to 130% or between 130% and 185% of the federal poverty level (Cambridge City Government 2018).

11. Wealthy and white students may often inflict—even unintentionally—class injuries on their peers (Bettie 2003).

12. Pattillo-McCoy 1999, 206; Steinberg 2004. Boredom is associated with many types of "boundary testing" and "risk taking"—including drug use and unprotected sex—that are often defined and punished as deviant (Mahoney, Larson, and Eccles 2005; Maimon and Browning 2010; Osgood and Anderson 2004). And boredom, more than material need, can also compel petty crime. In an early ethnography, Clifford Shaw's (1931, 7) young protagonist explains, "I did not steal for gain nor out of necessity for food. I stole because it was the most fascinating thing I could do. It was a way to pass the time." Jack Katz (1988, 79) notes similarly, "The initial experiences in sneak thefts of poor, working-class, and middle-class youths, alike, appear to be more clearly projects in constructing sneaky thrills than efforts to satisfy previously defined material needs." The young women in NC did not steal. But such research shows the powerful emotional compulsion to alleviate boredom among teens from all backgrounds.

13. E.g., Morris 2015; Rios 2011; Rosich 2007.

14. Lareau 2003, 44–45. See also Snellman et al. 2015 on the growing class gap in extracurricular activities.

15. Csikszentimihalyi 1990; Polly et al. 1993.

16. Flaherty (1999, 158). Perhaps the most seminal sociological account of people manipulating time is Donald Roy's study of workers who invent and play games to battle the "formidable beast of monotony" on the factory floor (1959, 158). See also Cohen and Taylor 1972; Roth 1963.

17. As the ethnographer Elliot Liebow (1967, 31) found among men in Washington, DC, "the comparison of sitting at home alone with being in jail is commonplace."

18. Communication among teens was often "phatic," which is defined by linguists and anthropologists as contact that serves primarily to cement and reassert social bonds rather than to convey information (Malinowski 1923; Makice 2009).

19. Durkheim ([1912] 1955) showed that rituals and collective effervescence foster social solidarity, ideas on which interaction theorists like Goffman and Collins later built.

20. Largely, they did this on specific sites; the girls shared norms for the proper use of each platform. Typically, these norms were tacit, until broken. (See, e.g., Goffman 1959, 1966, 1967; and Garfinkel 1967 on how day-to-day socializing hinges on taken-for-granted assumptions about how interactions should proceed.)

"I hate it when people use their Facebook like a Twitter," Seeta said one evening, scrolling through her phone. Facebook posts, she meant, should be relatively infrequent, unlike Twitter or Snapchat, whose respective length cap and impermanence (Snapchat posts disappeared after twenty-four hours) teens found perfect for sharing brief but unlimited updates.

Twitter felt differently, however, restricting users to 100 tweets per hour. Teens who hit these limits met a temporary posting ban, which they called "being in Twitter jail." *Im In Twitter Jail Because Of All My Beyonce Tweets & RT* [retweets], Faith announced on Facebook, after live-tweeting Beyoncé's halftime performance at the Superbowl. This let her redirect and continue conversations.

21. Only a few girls "protected" their Twitter accounts, restricting tweets' visibility only to approved followers. Many adults balk at teens' seeming disregard for privacy online, but many young people "simply see no reason to take the effort to minimize the visibility of their photos and conversations" (boyd 2014, 65).

22. Many young women feel intense pressure to constantly respond to each other online (Sales 2016).

23. Czikszentmihalyi 1990. boyd (2014) reframes the adult perception of teens' "addiction" to social media as an instance of "flow."

24. A portmanteau of *Twitter* and *watch*, to "twatch" is to attend to others' virtual behavior, with or without their knowledge.

25. Gershon 2010, 39.

26. The most frequent catalysts for online drama among teen girls include unliking posts or sharing messages sent by other people (Sales 2016, 133). Other researchers find social media can be a platform for the provocation, expression, and magnification not only of gossip but also of lethal gang beefs (e.g., Lane 2018; Patton et al. 2016).

27. Marwick and boyd 2014a, 5.

28. boyd 2014, 138.

29. Goffman 1967, 117, 167. The girls' social media use clashed with much classical theory about small group interaction, as the conclusion discusses.

30. Goffman 1967, 35–36.

31. Working as what Goffman would call an "interactive team" (1959, 82), the girls used their "bond of reciprocal dependence" to experience and portray fun.

32. With Uber and Lyft not yet popular, only one of the nine central girls had access to a vehicle: Seeta sometimes drove her dad's Dodge. On the link between transportation, cars, and freedom for adolescents, see Best 2006.

33. Storytelling gives events meaning and builds collective identity (Polletta 1998). The girls' digital storytelling—sharing pictures and fragments of experiences—made moments more meaningful.

34. Collins 2004, 112.

35. As Collins (2004, 63) explains, online interactions lack "the rhythm of immediate vocal participation, which . . . is honed to tenths of seconds." Evaluating his own theory during the COVID-19 pandemic, Collins (2020) found that social relationships and emotional energy indeed largely suffered when social distancing, mask mandates, and remote school and work limited face-to-face interaction. The "Final Reflections" chapter considers this further.

36. Researchers argue that online interactions can and do sustain emotional energy (e.g., DiMaggio et al. 2019; Ling 2008)

37. Lareau 2003. People's sense of agency ties to their feelings of control over time (e.g., Emirbayer and Mische 1998; Mische 2009).

38. The anthropologist Penelope Eckert (1989) shows how high school socializing prepares young adults for the class realities they will likely face as adults. Middle-class children often prepare for professional lifestyles through peer socializing styles that share the norms of corporate environments. Teens from low-income homes, by contrast, often socialize in ways that hone the loyalty and mutual support necessary for survival as a low-income adult.

Chapter 3

1. Aisha was not the only NC teen who viewed Officer Jacks fondly. Others, however, were skeptical. For instance, one senior, Ariana, told me she disapproved of Jacks "high fiving all the kids." "You have to act professional when you're in that role," she said.

Stephanie had a graver critique. When, one summer, Rosie's brother Bryan was beaten in the project, Stephanie recalled that Jacks was present but failed to act. "He didn't call for backup or do anything," she said. "He's sketchy. Cambridge police is very sketchy." Much of the fieldwork for this book took place before the Black Lives Matter movement and the conversations about police brutality that it catalyzed.

2. Call and Mortimer 2001, 7.

3. Chapter 6 shows emotional support given and received in the aftermath of traumatic neighborhood violence.

4. Call and Mortimer 2001, 3.

5. Ibid.

6. E.g., Elliot et al. 2006; Werner and Smith 1992

7. The 1996 Personal Responsibility and Work Opportunity Reconciliation Act profoundly changed how low-income families received assistance. Mandated work requirements forced many parents, mothers especially, to take low-wage

jobs with shift schedules that cut time with their children. Critics charged that by making adults accept paid work outside the home, the law failed to value unpaid domestic labor and ignored the difficulty of raising children in poverty (Ehrenreich 2003). Critics also argued the law was "anti-family," because pressuring parents to accept a job—"no matter how dangerous, abusive, or poorly paid" (Ehrenreich 2003, 504)—left them less time for parenting.

Two decades after the passage of welfare reform, studies traced its negative impact on household dynamics and child well-being (Dodson et al. 2012; Duncan, Huston, and Weisner 2007; Kalil and Dunifon 2007). For instance, although maternal employment usually associates positively with adolescent outcomes, mothers who work long or nonstandard hours, like shift workers in the low-wage labor market, have less time to support their children emotionally (Johnson et al. 2010). Some studies link having a parent who works nonstandard hours with lower test scores and more behavioral problems among children (Han 2005; Joshi and Bogen 2007).

8. Burton 2007; Dodson and Dickert 2004.

9. Many of the girls faced conflicting sociocultural expectations. Haitian immigrants—six of the nine girls were daughters of Haitian immigrants—often have high levels of parent-child conflict (e.g., Rumbaut 1997, 28).

10. Klebanov, Brooks-Dunn, and Duncan 1994; McLoyd 1990.

11. Burton 2007; Elder et al. 1995; Furstenberg 1993; Jarrett 1995, 1997.

12. The girls, who mostly "subtweeted"—or obliquely referenced—arguments with friends, could be more explicit when conflict involved family members, who were generally not on Twitter.

13. A dominant form of self-disclosure on Facebook is the expression of emotional states (Manago, Taylor, and Greenfield 2012). In part for this reason, studies find a positive relationship between frequency of Facebook use and perceived social support (Goulet 2012; Hampton, Goulet, and Rainie 2011). Social media facilitates a "pervasive awareness" of the resources embedded in one's social network (Hampton 2016). In particular, short, frequent, asynchronous exchanges—like status updates that receive likes or comments—make users perceive high levels of social support (Lu and Hampton 2017).

14. On trust and distrust in poor neighborhoods, see Smith 2007.

15. Further factors may have motivated this narrative. For instance, Nikki Jones (2009) found that some teen girls in a poor Philadelphia neighborhood labeled peers "associates" rather than "friends" to avoid having to fight in their defense. Although the NC girls never spoke this way, and rarely fought physically, they generally reserved their full loyalty and generosity for their closest friends.

16. According to the 2010 Census, 57.3% of Cambridge residents were white.

17. School discourses of "diversity" can be superficial (Carter 2005). Moreover, teens can capably grasp the difference between diversity and integration in their schools (Shedd 2015).

18. One day at CRLS, Latinx seniors Ariana and Val discussed body image and school dress codes. Val rolled her eyes describing girls who wore high heels and short skirts to school.

"I'm like, 'You're sixteen!'" she said.

"But also, they get away with it more," Ariana said. "They won't get in trouble for short skirts, but some people will."

"Who gets in trouble?" I asked.

"Plain and simple?" Ariana said. "The Black girls and the white girls. The thick girls and the skinny girls," she said, tying race to body shape to explain which bodies she believed the staff punished. White staff members often problematize and punish minority femininities (Morris 2015).

19. E.g., Kaplan 2013; Ladson-Billings 2002; MacLeod 1987.

20. See Chin 2001 on how race and class can structure humiliating and even dehumanizing consumer experiences for low-income youth of color.

21. See also Chin 2001 and Bettie 2003 for accounts of young people of color dressing smartly for the mall to try to avoid intrusive surveillance by security guards.

22. Kaplan 2013. The girls often articulated the negative stereotypes they knew others held. For instance, walking home from basketball practice one afternoon, Aisha accidentally bumped into and knocked over a bicycle locked to a streetlight. As she reset the bike, metal jangled loudly. Two white passersby across the street slowed as they passed and squinted in Aisha's direction. "They think I'm stealing it," Aisha said to me wryly.

23. Kemper 1978. For a review of theoretical approaches to emotion's role in daily life, see Turner and Stets 2006.

24. Gómez 2015; Nadal et al. 2017; Sue 2010.

25. For empirical examples, see Anderson 2000; Bourgois 1996; Kaplan 2013; MacLeod 1987; Scheff and Retzinger 1991; Willis 1977.

26. Building on Goffman's dramaturgical approach, scholars show how situational "feeling rules" constrain displays of emotion (Hochschild 1979, 1983; Rosenberg 1990; Thoits 1991).

27. Turner and Stets 2006.

28. "A simple 'like' of a friend's post can be felt and understood as an act of care—by that friend, by the liker, and by others who witness this gesture" (Byron 2020, 2).

29. Hirsch 2014; Lamont et al. 2016.

30. Hill Collins 2000, 184.

31. Introducing a logic of exchange into a relationship of care turned something *sacred*—support—into a *profane* object of instrumental maximization. Many people view close relationships and economic transactions as two separate "hostile worlds" (Zelizer 2005). This belief—that monetization depletes care relationships—persists even though in practice the two often overlap.

32. The description of this confrontation comes from Aisha's and Joanne's recollections.

33. Goffman (1971, 79) describes the nonrecognition generated by an unreciprocated "goodbye," which leaves an interaction unresolved. Micro moments of nonrecognition and exclusion can cause shame, which can, in turn, spiral into anger (Scheff 1990; Kemper 1978).

34. Collins 2004.

35. See e.g., Collins 2004; Goodwin, Jasper, and Polletta 2001; Honneth 1995, 2014; Scheff 1994. As the sociologist Victor Rios (2011, 39) explains, "Working for dignity has to do more with a sense of humanity than a sense of power."

36. As hooks (2003, 183) notes, "The poor . . . are daily assaulted by messages in mass media that say they are depraved, unworthy, criminal."

37. E.g., MacLeod 1987; Willis 1977. Some such studies, however, sit adjacent to the empirically discredited claim by the anthropologists Signithia Fordham and John Ogbu (1986) that Black high school students develop an "oppositional culture," characterized by the rejection of academic achievement, to avoid being seen as "acting white."

38. Many studies about young people's responses to stigma focus on boys. A notable exception is Monique Morris's (2015) analysis of how Black teenage girls experience school discipline. Morris shows how the justified frustration that Black girls express when they feel disrespected is often misread as "attitude" and punished.

39. Shame, when repressed, can morph into rage and trigger aggression (Scheff and Retzinger 1991).

40. Bourgois 1996, 8–9.

41. The sociologist Alford Young critiques the use in research on race and poverty of a mythic "mainstream" as a normative referent. Starting in the 1960s, Young (2008, 184) explains, many studies argued that "structural constraint, best exemplified by limited employment prospects, prevented low-income Black Americans from realizing their values, thus provoking their adaptation of norms, attitudes, and behaviors that contrasted with those fostered and upheld in mainstream

America." In the 1990s, this trend of blaming structural inequalities for "subcultural adaptations" yielded to research asserting that "members of the 'underclass' function just like members of the 'mainstream'" (187). Both bodies of work, however, conjure and perpetuate an imagined but empirically baseless image of "mainstream" America, one that is white and middle class. See also Rios 2011.

42. "Privilege and power is not simply a result of unequal material and cultural resources. It is a flow of emotional energy across situations" (Collins 2004, xiii; see also Hall and Lamont 2013; Lamont 2019). The conclusion, below, discusses further the importance of dignity, inclusion, and recognition.

Chapter 4

1. On colorism, see, e.g., Featherston 1994; Hunter 1998, 2002.

2. hooks 2003, 28.

3. Ibid., 45–46.

4. Cooper 2018, 115. As the sociologist Tressie McMillan Cottom (2019, 44) notes, "Beauty isn't actually what you look like; beauty is the preferences that reproduce the existing social order."

5. E.g., Shisslak, Crago, and Estes 1995; US Department of Health and Human Services 2001. Although young women of color have historically had lower rates of eating disorders than white girls (e.g., Lovejoy 2001; Milkie 1999; Schooler and Daniels 2014), harmful "self-objectification" exists among girls and young women from all racial and socioeconomic groups (Calogero, Tantleff-Dunne, and Thompson 2010).

6. Cooper (2018, 21) depicts women's mutual validation as a form of resistance to racist denigration: "These days, on what one of my homegirls has deemed #ThottieThursdays, it has become customary for my girls and I to sext one another slyly seductive pics of our asses, or thighs, or cleavages, sometimes bare, or sometimes clothed in the perfect way that all our curves are accentuated. And the tacit agreement is that we share to be affirmed, in our sexiness, in our beauty, and in our glory."

7. I never heard the girls express homophobic views (as in, e.g., Pascoe 2007); peers, however, occasionally did. Still queerness seemed excluded from the girls' "space of possibles"—the set of potential actions enabled by their social structures (Bourdieu 1993, 2000). The "compulsory heterosexuality" (Rich 1980) communicated by cultural and media messages was likely compounded by the sexually conservative views of many immigrant parents (see, e.g., Foner 2014; Stepick et al. 2001).

8. At the time, the girls did not use online dating apps, which were not fully mainstreamed in 2012–13 (they were also likely too young). Nor did they use social media to find local strangers to date (as in, e.g., Lane 2018). Instead, social media shaped romantic relationships that girls developed with people they knew "in real life."

9. "Subs" are one way teens command privacy online. As boyd (2014, 76) explains, "Rather than finding privacy by controlling access to content, many teens are instead controlling access to meaning" (see also Marwick and boyd 2014b).

10. This description comes from Faith's recollection.

11. Seeta later posted a montage of selfies, in which she stood hands on hips, gazing into the camera. "She'll never be me," the caption read. This kind of sub was common after a breakup. The girls posted self-loving selfies or shared screenshots of texts or Facetime calls with new partners.

12. The description of Florence's relationships with Vincent and Robensen comes from Florence's recollections.

13. Joanne graciously granted my request to use her poem.

14. The description of Joanne and Andrew's relationship comes from Joanne's recollection.

15. As bell hooks (2000, 160–61) writes, patriarchal thinking "sets up a gendered arrangement in which men are more likely to get their emotional needs met while women will be deprived."

16. Another danger girls face in relationships is intimate partner abuse. During my fieldwork, I did not know of any of the girls being in romantic relationships that they or their friends viewed as abusive. But for many young women, abusive boyfriends "wreak havoc with whole lives" (Armstrong, Hamilton, and England 2010).

17. Tolman and McLelland 2011. "Sexual subjectivity," explains the sociologist Jessica Fields (2008, 110), is "fundamental to young people's sense of agency in all aspects of their lives." Moreover, sexual agency and pleasure can be revolutionary (Lorde 1984). As Hill Collins (2000, 139) explains, "When self-defined . . . Black women's sexualities can become an important place of resistance . . . [R]eclaiming and self-defining. . . . eroticism may constitute one path toward Black women's empowerment." Brittany Cooper (2018, 133) notes that when women of color embrace their sexuality, this can constitute "a critical and intimate dissent from the wholesale American demonization of Black women's sexuality."

18. Schalet 2000; US Department of Health and Human Services 2016.

19. Schalet 2004, 1. See also Fields 2008, 169; Pascoe 2011; Russell 2005; Tolman 1994. More than merely disempowering adolescents, adults' denial of young

people's sexual agency obscures how broader social conditions and inequalities shape their experiences with sexuality (Froyum 2010).

20. Barcelos and Gubrium 2014. Much research on sexuality—particularly about Black and Latinx girls—has conflated sex and pregnancy, feeding a stigma about teen pregnancy that young people can internalize (Garcia 2012). Women of color feminist scholars challenge this kind of research and reject any academic definition of "sexual agency" as the right to live up to white middle-class ideals, like delayed childbirth (for a review, see Ray 2018a).

21. Fine 1988, 33. Almost two decades later, Fine revisited her seminal research on girls' "missing discourse of desire" and found that although many adolescent girls now perform desire—as depicted in mass media—there remains a lack of genuine, "thick" desire, whereby they can engage in "the political act of wanting" (Fine and McClelland 2006, 297).

22. Davis 1981; hooks 2014a; McBride-Murray 1996; Tolman 2005. Hill Collins (2000) shows how "controlling images"—stereotypes used to justify Black women's marginalization, like tropes of the sexually uncontrollable "Jezebel" or "Welfare Queen"—stigmatize Black women's sexuality.

23. Heteronormativity, sexism, and racism structure the content and delivery of school-based sex education (Fields 2008; Garcia 2009; Irvine 2002; Luker 2006).

24. Some teen girls decline to share information with peers for fear of gossip (Garcia 2012; Tolman 2005). This may also have limited the NC girls' mutual disclosures.

25. Gendered double standards around sex and stigmatization are well documented (e.g., Bogle 2008; Kreager and Staff 2009; Miller 2008).

26. The standardization and commodification of sex over the past few decades have transformed the semiotics of sexiness into a largely "formulaic visual vocabulary" (Esch and Mayer 2008, 7), on which the girls could draw (see also McRobbie 2008).

27. See also Garcia 2012.

28. Abbreviation for "I don't care."

29. Morris (2015, 121) writes, "Girls experience sexual assault, objectification, or being seen as hyper sexual in . . . their homes, in the street, on buses and subway systems, in their places of worship, and in schools. . . . Black girls describe conditions in which their bodies are scrutinized, touched (often without permission), and objectified in ways that make them feel self-conscious and constantly defensive."

30. Hill Collins 2000, 200. Other studies find a widespread "female fear" in some poor neighborhoods, caused by "the demoralizing effects of omnipresent

and constant harassment" (Popkin, Leventhal, and Weismann 2010, 716; see also Kling, Liebman, and Katz 2007). This is partly why moving girls out of poor neighborhoods can lead to a sharp reduction in their rates of distress and depression (Popkin, Leventhal, and Weismann 2010, 717). Jody Miller (2008) shows qualitatively the prolific sexual harassment faced by girls in a poor neighborhood.

31. Constraining deference norms meant girls rarely challenged men directly. The only time I saw girls "talk back" was to a man who was not a neighborhood resident. It was also on my behalf. At a summer cookout in the project one Saturday, some girls and I sat enjoying the late sun behind Florence and Faith's apartment. As the crowd thinned and the grill's charcoal ashed, the father of the DJ—roughly fifty, with long dreads and few teeth—walked drunkenly from woman to woman. At first the girls laughed as he grabbed a woman near his own age and pressed his body against hers. But when he sat down by Zora, the girls stiffened. Then he turned to me.

"I'm very glad to know you," he said, touching my arm. I nodded a perfunctory acknowledgment, then resumed my conversation with the girls.

"You need to tell your mom to make him go home!" a friend told Faith.

Faith shrugged, and we tried to ignore the man. But when he pressed his thigh against mine, Francis—Florence and Faith's older sister—sprang to her feet.

"Go home!" Francis said, hand on hip. "Go home to your wife. Go. Home!" She kept a hint of a smile on her face the whole time.

32. Many teens report that their strongest emotion is being in love (Miller and Benson 1999; Subrahmanyam and Greenfield 2008).

Chapter 5

1. The description of this scene—which I did not witness—comes from accounts of friends and classmates of people present and from reportage in local newspapers.

2. Ballou 2012.

3. Levy 2012.

4. I visited the sidewalk memorial several times, including with girls who wished to see or add to the tributes.

5. Ballou and Ellement 2012.

6. ilovedahatersz (2012).

7. FOX25 News, July 15, 2014.

8. Collins et al. 2010; Schwab-Stone et al. 1995; Schwab-Stone et al. 1999.

9. DuRant et al. 1995; Singer et al. 1995.

10. Collins et al. 2010; Peterson, Sarigiani, and Kennedy 1991.

11. The sociologist Mario Small (2004, 143) explains that rare but shocking events like shootings are not only "powerful, disheartening, and debilitating" but also attach scarring memories to the neighborhood, its resources, and its public spaces.

12. A lack of security threatens routines, relationships, and individual development (Hirsch et al. 2000; Stevenson 1998). Berger and Luckmann (1967), in the Durkheimian tradition, explain the significance of routine and ritual for daily life; society, they argue, cannot exist without a basic sense of "taken-for-grantedness." When fundamental, tacit assumptions are tested—including by disruptive and traumatic events—people often do not know how to respond. This can both strain individuals and undermine their social networks. See also, for example, Van der Kolk 2015.

13. On fear of strangers in poor neighborhoods, see, e.g., Anderson 1990; Merry 1981.

14. The urban theorist Jane Jacobs ([1961] 1992) discussed how residents' and strangers' "eyes on the street" promote neighborhood safety. See also Duneier 2000.

15. Cobbina, Miller, and Brunson (2008) find that girls in a poor St. Louis neighborhood relied on members of their social network, particularly boys, for company on journeys.

16. Similarly, Best (2006, 68) finds that when young women trade stories about getting into cars alone with boys, their stories serve both as warnings and to establish shared experiences.

17. See also Jones 2009.

18. This description comes from conversations with Rosie, Faith, Stephanie, and Florence.

19. Short for "timeline," meaning each user's main feed of tweets.

20. After hearing online about traumas, teens often sought one another out in person. Although digital communication could generate something like collective effervescence and provoke strong feelings, co-present bodies—with their physiological attunement—can heighten the emotional intensity of connection (Collins 2004). These feelings are likely more necessary than ever in the aftermath of trauma.

21. While social media can help coordinate mass mobilization after national events or natural disasters (Lotan et al. 2011; Sutton, Palen, and Shklovski 2008; Yates and Paquette 2011), the NC girls focused, typically, more on sharing information than organizing any kind of action.

22. Aisha did not have a cell phone at the time and instead paired an iPod with Wi-Fi to access social media.

23. Reports in a local newspaper also referred to the rapid spread of information via social media, as compared with official channels: "While Middlesex District Attorney Gerry Leone and Cambridge Police Commissioner Robert Haas gave information resulting from the shootings and 911 call at a careful pace Sunday, people on Twitter and other social media were reporting almost immediately afterward that [Bree] and [Angelina] were the girls shot" (Levy 2012).

24. As W.I. Thomas (1923, 42) wrote, "Preliminary to any self-determined act of behavior there is always a stage of examination and deliberation which we may call the definition of the situation." Goffman (1959, 9–10) elaborated this social process: "Participants contribute to a single over-all definition of the situation which involves not so much a real agreement as to what exists but rather a real agreement as to whose claims concerning what issues will be temporarily honored."

25. Turn taking—"sequencing"—and relating speech to prior utterances—"meaning adjacency"—are core components of in-person dialogue (Sacks, Schegloff, and Jefferson 1974). But teens could join online conversations without following these rules. On Twitter, the "interplay between the normative structures of conversational interaction and the communicative affordances offered by [the] technology" let teens form new conversational norms, which sometimes mirrored and sometimes differed from rules governing in-person talk (Hutchby 2013, 13).

26. Some early internet advocates championed the democratization of speech online. Yet structural inequalities constrain all forms of expression and participation, including online. No form of public talk is free from power dynamics, as noted by feminist scholars who critiqued Habermas's (1989) idealization of a democratic process characterized by the free exchange of ideas (e.g., Fraser 1990).

27. Most of the traumatic violence the NC girls faced was local. However, the marathon bombing centered Boston as a site of identity and belonging. This made the girls, temporarily, less residents of a segregated neighborhood than members of a city united by public grief.

28. The teens shared, for instance, photos of their bloody, excised wisdom teeth; selfies from hospital beds showing IV drips taped into arms; and pictures of unconscious relatives hours before their death. These uploads often communicated a need for care, a need that was reliably met. Peers—with their likes, favorites, and comments—offered attention, a form of support.

Yet the teens were also members of a generation that grew up jostling for attention, on- and offline. As boyd (2014, 148) notes, "The advertising culture that teens witness reveals a market-driven valuation of attention. . . . While society derides attention, gossip, and drama, teens also receive clear signals that these behaviors are normal. Teens may mock peers for being 'attention whores,' but they also recognize that attention can be—and is often seen as—valuable" (see also Marwick and boyd 2011).

29. That same afternoon, Malachi—noting that Dzhokhar Tsarnaev's Twitter account had gained seventy thousand followers in one day—joked online, *Damn that's all I gotta do to get followed on Twitter?*

30. Van der Kolk 2015.

31. Between themselves and participants in "that life," the girls drew a "symbolic boundary," defined by the sociologists Michèle Lamont and Virag Molnar (2002, 168) as "conceptual distinctions made by social actors to categorize objects, people, practices, and even time and space." Boundaries "separate people into groups and generate feelings of similarity and group membership" (168). For the NC girls, this created feelings of distance from people in "that life" and similarity with friends and peers outside it.

32. Collins et al. 2010; Kiser et al. 1993; Overstreet and Braun 2000; Schwab-Stone et al. 1999.

33. On the anniversary of Bryan's death, Zora texted Rosie: *I know today is a hard day for you but as always stay strong. Understanding that the physical body isn't there but the soul forever lies with your heart and body every where you go. Keep grinding and making him proud like you're making us proud. Make sure you give your mom a call and know I'm here for you if you want to talk or just cry. I Love you!!* Rosie screenshotted the message and shared it with her Snapchat contacts, adding her own caption: *My main is better than yours.* Rosie used Snapchat to thank Zora publicly for reaching out and caring for her.

34. Collins 2004, 97–98.

35. Ibid. Collins builds on Durkheim's *Elementary Forms of Religious Life* ([1912] 1995), which argues that rituals foster the moral solidarity on which society rests. Rituals strengthen the collective, often using totems: objects imbued with a sacred force that represent and embody the social group. Teens' sacred objects—like hashtags, pins, and T-shirts—were totemic too. The objects carried the power of the group and had rules governing their use.

36. Cunningham 2016.

37. Abbreviation for "shaking my head," expressing disapproval.

38. Adults are often confused by young people's social media use in times of trauma (see, e.g., Sales's [2016] account of adults' shock when the teen kidnapping victim Hannah Anderson detailed her experience online).

39. The description of this graduation, which I did not attend, comes from recollections of students and staff who were present, along with news articles about the event.

40. Parker 2012.

41. Ibid.

42. As Van der Kolk (2015, 81) notes, "Social support is the most powerful protection against being overwhelmed by stress and trauma. . . . No doctor can write a prescription for friendship and love."

Chapter 6

1. None of the girls' classmates who had what sociologists call high socioeconomic status (SES) were present, however—a boundary that overlapped largely but not entirely with racial divides.

2. E.g., Eckert 1989.

3. For reviews of homophily across social domains, see McPherson, Smith-Lovin, and Cook 2001; Kalmijn 1998.

4. Even if "risk behaviors" are not intrinsically problematic, they do expose young people living in poverty and particularly young people of color to risk, because these teens are disproportionately surveilled and punished. This chapter does not explore why some of the girls did or did not experiment with such behaviors but rather charts how the girls defended their relationships when faced with new discrepancies.

5. The peer effects literature spans sociology, psychology, criminology, education, public health, and more. See, e.g., Akers et al. 1979; An 2011, 2016; Borsari and Carey 2001; Brooks-Gunn et al. 1993; Case and Katz 1991; Elliot and Menard 1996; Elliot et al. 2006; Kandel 1978; Metzler et al. 1994; South and Baumer 2000.

6. Giordano 2003, 257.

7. Case and Katz 1991; Crane 1991; Jencks and Mayer 1990. Social disorganization theory, which considers the impact of place on crime and "deviance," even suggests that peer influence may be the primary way that community socialization adversely affects adolescents (Sampson and Groves 1989; Shaw and McKay 1942).

8. While earlier sociologists studying heterogeneity in poor neighborhoods suggested that social isolation produced a singular, adaptive, and often oppositional "ghetto" subculture, subsequent research outlined the diversity of beliefs and behaviors in poor communities (e.g., Anderson 2000; Gans 1962; Hannerz

1969; Kuper 1953). Extending this work, the sociologist David Harding (2009) identified heterogeneous "cultural repertoires"—sets of skills, knowledge, and tools for social action—that coexist in poor neighborhoods. The notion of repertoires—on which people can agentically draw—corrects earlier misconceptions that behavior was driven either by certain "types" of people or by rigid "codes" of action.

9. By crafting their own narratives online and choosing what to highlight on their digital "front stage" (Goffman 1959), girls resisted harmful tropes and "controlling images" (Hill Collins 2000).

10. Among the teens, "fakeness" was a generalized insult for anything or anyone bad. Goffman (1959) finds that people judge inauthenticity as a moral failure.

11. The sociologists Bruce Link and Jo Phelan (2001, 370) show that stigma is more acute when people are perceived to "be" the thing that they are labeled. Being schizophrenic, for example, is more stigmatizing than having schizophrenia.

12. Boundary drawing is key to identity formation (e.g., Fiske 2000; Gieryn 1999; Jenkins 1996; Lamont 1992, 2000; Tajfel 1974; for a review, see Lamont and Molnar 2002). Ethnographers show this dynamic in practice. For instance, Jay MacLeod (1987, 266) writes of two groups of teens he got to know, "Peer groups define themselves in relation to one another. The character of the Brothers' peer group is in some measure a reaction to distinctive attributes of the Hallway Hangers."

13. Symbolic boundaries "separate people into groups and generate feelings of similarity and group membership" (Lamont and Molnar 2002, 168). Sociologists have long documented the "boundary work" by which residents of poor, urban communities divide neighbors into categories of worth (see, e.g., Anderson 2000; Newman 1999; Pattillo 2007).

14. Ray (2018b) shows how this kind of boundary drawing can perpetuate oppression. When teens marginalized by racism or poverty *other* peers to assert superiority, they help reproduce the same systems of meaning that marginalize them in the first place.

15. Laursen 1998.

16. Adults also avoid conflict by practicing a "moral minimalism" (Baumgartner 1989). Lamont (2000, 45) identified a kind of pragmatism among workers and managers who have a "flexible moral code with a weak core that is highly adaptable to situations."

17. As Joyce Ladner (1971, 108) has written, "What one's peers regard as appropriate behavior is usually taken very seriously—that is, such conceptions are rarely dismissed."

18. Florence saw herself as a worthy, aspirational young woman, and needed her friends to verify this identity claim. As G. H. Mead (1934, 138–40) explained, "The individual experiences himself... not directly, but only indirectly from the particular standpoints of other members of the same social group" (see also Garfinkel 1967; West and Zimmerman 1987). People look to others to affirm their identities. When other people validate our sense of self, we feel positive emotions like pride; when they don't, however, we experience negative emotions like guilt and shame (Turner and Stets 2006), which can alter behavior. This suggests that even limited pushback could, over time, generate enough discomfort to change teens' acts.

19. Short for "diesel," meaning muscular.

20. Gossip often has negative connotations. But gossip, with its powerful social regulatory function (Vaidanathan, Khalsa, and Ecklund 2016), can be prosocial, increasing group cohesion (Feinberg et al. 2012).

21. Point-in-time, binary behavioral measures—typical of the statistical peer effects literature—rarely identify such nuances. Ethnography can better capture variation, including within people's own practices and predilections over time. As the sociologist Cindy Ness (2004, 46) explains, "The observation of variation that ethnography as a method can accommodate permits a researcher to highlight a range of reactions and competing outcomes and does not force him or her to promulgate the existence of only one local view, of one set of inferred meanings and emotions, and of a coherence of response that ordinarily defies intuition."

22. Cultural sociologists caution against "morphological determinism"—the idea that structure compels individual action (e.g., Emirbayer and Goodwin 1994; Vaisey and Lizardo 2010). They refute the analytical privileging of structure over culture, whether structure is defined either as durable social institutions or as the social networks in which people are embedded.

23. The sociologist Stephen Vaisey (2008) also found that teenagers make moral judgments using a "practical consciousness" rather than a decontextualized reasoning process. Pragmatists have long emphasized the importance of creativity, context, and situations in driving social action, generating meaning, and solving problems (e.g., Dewey 1938; Emirbayer and Maynard 2011; Joas 1996).

24. Superficial similarities are most important in a relationship's early stages. Once a bond has been established, however, "other criteria related to the provision of social and emotional resources become significant" (Aboud and Mendelson 1998, 88).

25. The sociologist Lothar Krappman (1996, 36) explains, in "survey studies ... it is difficult to realize many of the ambivalences, conditions, and counter-

arguments that can occur within these relationships. This . . . obscures the true impact of friendship, which is exerted not only by harmonic friendships, but also, or even more, by friends who fight their way through all the complications and contradictions that characterize different kinds of friendships in real peer life."

Chapter 7

1. He referred to Hurricane Sandy in the fall and the Boston Marathon bombing in the spring.

2. Snyder and Dillow 2013; Snyder, de Brey, and Dillow 2017. In recent decades, a "college for all" discourse has proliferated (Goyette 2008; Rosenbaum 2004), and today most young people, including racially and socioeconomically marginalized teens, aspire to a college degree (Nielsen 2015). In part their motives are economic; compared to people with only a high school diploma, college graduates earn more and are less likely to face unemployment (US Department of Education 2014). In addition, most jobs, including those in the fastest-growing occupations, now require postsecondary credentials (Carnevale, Smith, and Strohl 2013; Goldrick-Rab and Shaw 2005; Institute for Higher Education Policy 2005). But college has other motivations too. For instance, education supports positive identity claims, particularly as traditional markers of adulthood like home ownership have become delayed or unattainable (e.g., Alexander, Bozick, and Entwisle 2008; Deterding 2015; Silva 2012). Expanding admissions also owe to the commodification of higher education, including by for-profit colleges that treat students as consumers (McMillan Cottom 2017).

3. Young people use their educational ambitions to claim moral worth in the face of marginalization (Nielson 2015). As Ray (2018b, 129) shows, a "college-goer identity" allows young people of color from poor neighborhoods to differentiate themselves both from less successful peers and "from dominant discourses and stereotypes that construct economically marginalized black and brown youths as unambitious and lazy."

Decades ago some researchers claimed to have identified an "oppositional culture" among Black high school students who allegedly disinvested from education when faced with blocked opportunities (Fordham and Ogbu 1986). But teens from all backgrounds value schooling. In fact, not only are high-achieving students of color seen positively by peers, but African American young people report some of the highest levels of commitment to education (Ainsworth-Darnell and Downey 1998; Carter 2003; Harris 2011; Tyson 2011).

4. Roska et al. 2007. Unlike many low-income teens, the NC girls had school counselors. They also benefited more generally from the resources and norms at CRLS, where the rate of college attendance among low-income students (79.6%) differed only fractionally from the schoolwide rate (80.9%) (Cambridge Public Schools 2018; Massachusetts Department of Elementary and Secondary Education 2018).

5. Some girls spoke similarly when selecting majors for themselves or their friends. "I think Rosie should do criminal justice," Florence said. "Whenever she wants to find something out, she'll go to Instagram, Facebook, and she'll be like, 'What's happening with this guy?' She'll be able to find out."

6. Often research shows young people from poor neighborhoods distancing themselves from peers to succeed academically. In *Street Corner Society,* for instance, William Foote White (1943, 107) noted, "Both the college boy and the corner boy want to get ahead. The difference . . . is that the college boy either does not tie himself to a group of close friends or else is willing to sacrifice his friendship with those who do not advance as fast as he does."

Over seventy years later, DeLuca, Clampet-Lundquist, and Edin (2016, 123) described two adolescent respondents, "Bob and Bridget," who were "on a path to college." Yet this path, the authors note, "involved hard choices." Bob and Bridget "had to draw a bright line between themselves and their peers." Similarly, Bettie (2003, 165) found that low-income girls of color who were on the "college track" in a California high school befriended middle-class peers; were often busy and introverted; and "did not have the social life that is considered to typify the high school experience" (see also Chetty et al. 2022 on how friendships across socioeconomic groups promote social mobility among young people growing up in poor neighborhoods). For the NC girls, however, socioeconomically similar peers supported academic aspirations; friends were not constraining but supportive.

Moreover, studies about how peers promote academic achievement often focus on indirect influence. For instance, having a best friend with a college-educated mother (Cherng, Calarco, and Kao 2013) or having a peer group characterized by high levels of parental education (Crosnoe and Muller 2014) can promote college readiness and completion. But the NC girls supported one another independent of adult actions or characteristics.

7. Florence provided this account of the relationships between herself, Natty, and Vincent.

8. Ray (2018b) and Bettie (2003) show the role of support from siblings among young people from low-income homes. Sibling support was less common among

the NC girls, however. Florence, for example, did not know which schools her sister, Faith, applied to and did not help her prepare applications.

9. See Hamilton and Armstrong 2009 on how heterosexual romantic relationships can negatively affect young women's college experiences.

10. None of the NC girls went farther away from Massachusetts than New Hampshire. There are many social, emotional, and financial reasons that first-generation and low-income college applicants chose schools nearer home (Armstrong and Hamilton 2013).

11. I did not visit the girls on campus. This chapter's descriptions of the girls' college experiences come from conversations we had during and after their time at school.

12. Ray (2018b) also shows a lack of clarity among some low-income students about feasible pathways. Teens expect that shift work at a local bakery will help them climb the ladder in the "food industry," or that "working as floor crew at a clothing store while taking a fashion class at a community college will lead to a successful career in the fashion industry" (91; see also DeLuca, Clampet-Lundquist, and Edin 2016).

13. Colleges are complicated bureaucracies. Students must file baffling paperwork and work with unfamiliar adults, tasks that low-income students—even controlling for high school achievement—often find challenging. While middle-class students are typically raised to believe that institutions will solve their problems, students from lower-income homes are usually less confident advocating for themselves. This limits their access to resources and also, since teachers reward middle-class, proactive interaction styles, hampers academic achievement (Lareau 2003; Lohfink and Paulsen 2005; Pascarella and Terenzini 2005; Pike and Kuh 2005).

14. Many low-income students "stop out"—stopping and starting schooling over many years—rather than drop out. In fact, 25% to 35% of all undergraduates stop out (Park 2013). The probability of eventual graduation is low, but students hold close to their hopes.

15. Aisha was being glib, but she was referencing a powerful cultural trope that frames mental health conditions and treatment as the domain of white people. This trope owes, in part, to the limited health care resources available in many communities of color. It also owes to the fact that Black people, Black women in particular, are stereotyped as strong, causing their health needs—physical, mental, and emotional—to frequently be ignored (Bankhead 2015; Golden 2021).

16. Eckert 1989, 87.

17. E.g., Lareau 2003. Wealthier students are more often socialized to engage authority figures in academic contexts, which promotes their acquisition

of cultural and social capital, their educational experiences, and their postgraduation mobility (Calarco 2011; Carter 2005; Collier and Morgan 2008; Rivera 2015; Stuber 2011).

18. Goldrick-Rab and Roksa 2008.

19. Just 5% of low-income, first-generation students at public two-year colleges earn a bachelor's degree within six years, although two-thirds plan to (Engle and Tinto 2008). Low-income, first-generation students are nearly four times more likely—26% to 7%—to leave college after the first year than students with neither of these "risk factors" (Engle and Tinto 2008). While low-income and first-generation students concentrate in less selective, underresourced schools with lower graduation rates (Alon and Tienda 2005; Bowen, Chingos, and McPherson 2009; Light and Strayer 2000), disparities exist even within college types. In public four-year institutions, for instance, 34% of low-income, first-generation students earn bachelor's degrees in six years, compared to 66% of their wealthier peers (Engle and Tinto 2008). Private, not-for-profit, four-year schools have an even bigger gap: 43% to 80% (Engle and Tinto 2008). Statistics also reveal racial disparities: at four-year institutions, 63% of white students receive bachelor's degrees six years after college entry, compared to only 41% of Black undergraduates (Snyder and Dillow 2013; see also Rosenbaum et al. 2015).

20. Nunez and Cuccaro-Alamin 1998; Warburton, Bugarin, and Nuñez 2001.

21. Chen 2005; Choy et al. 2005.

22. Stressors bundle together, creating cumulative adversity. Developmental psychologists show the harms tied to this kind of "stress proliferation" (Dupéré et al. 2014; Evans and Schamberg 2009).

23. Many students leave college because of financial hardship. Students from low-income homes typically face greater unmet financial need throughout college than their wealthier classmates. Aid packages can help, but federal Pell Grant and Work-Study programs have not kept pace with rising tuition and living costs (Chen and DesJardins 2010; Engle and Tinto 2008; Kim 2007).

24. Students who work over twenty hours per week have lower college persistence than those who work less; yet up to 60% of low-income, first-generation students work over that amount (Engle and Tinto 2008; Pascarella and Terenzini 2005). While low-income students often prefer to work rather than borrow money (Cunningham and Santiago 2008), jobs can interfere with coursework and campus integration.

25. Carter 2005. First-generation students more often view faculty as unsupportive (Pike and Kuh 2005; Terenzini et al. 1996) and report experiencing discrimination on campus (Richardson and Skinner 1992).

26. Ray (2018b) shows that low-income students of color internalize the idea that failing to attend college owes to individual deficiency. She charts the symbolic violence inherent in the myth of meritocracy given that opportunities are so unequal.

27. On losing credits, see McMillan Cottom 2017.

28. Orientations can promote students' academic and social integration to college (Lotkowski, Robbins, and Noeth 2004; Pascarella and Terenzini 2005; Upcraft, Gardner, and Barefoot 2004).

Conclusion

1. Recent big-data research by the economist Raj Chetty and colleagues finds that for children growing up in poor neighborhoods, friendships with wealthier peers—what the authors call "economic connectedness"—help promote economic mobility (Chetty et al. 2022). The NC girls went to a diverse school also attended by teens from much higher-income homes; this likely exposed them to some of the benefits Chetty and colleagues identify, even though most of their friendships were with socioeconomically similar classmates who lived in their neighborhood.

Regardless, this book focuses not on long-term social mobility but on the daily dynamics of support among teens whose creativity and power have long been overlooked by researchers and policy makers. It shows how young women met one another's vital needs and underscores the power of the peer group. As Joyce Ladner (1971, 105) wrote half a century ago about Black girls growing up in St. Louis's Pruitt-Igoe housing project, "The adolescent peer group can be viewed as a solidifying agent: one which welds them together to combat the many problems, fears, despairs, etc. which confront them in daily situations. It is also a source of many of the positive things that happen to them as they grow up."

2. Sennett and Cobb 1993, 171. Audre Lorde (1984, 55) describes the "horror" of any system that "defines human need to the exclusion of the psychic and emotional components of that need."

3. Lamont et al. 2016, 273. Distribution and recognition are the two axes of social inequality; moreover, they reinforce each other (Lamont 2018). "Recognition gaps"—defined as "disparities in worth and cultural membership between groups in a society" (Lamont 2018, 421-22)—could be narrowed if not closed, Lamont argues, through the social process of destigmatization. But researchers' heavy emphasis on inequality's economic dimension has hampered this goal (422). On recognition and inclusion, see also Fraser 2000; Hodson 1996; Honneth 2014.

4. Teens spend much of each day at school—a bounded, age-segregated social enclave—vying for approval from peers (Milner 2015).

5. E.g., Coleman 1988. Some research, however, does point to social capital's affective dimension. Xavier de Souza Briggs (1988, 206), for instance, parses "access to social support that helps us cope with life's stresses and challenges ('get by')" from "access to social leverage, the key to mobility or 'getting ahead'" (see also Wellman and Wortley 1990).

6. For Bourdieu (1986), social capital flows only through ties that confer legitimated social goods, honor, and privilege; socioeconomic and racial marginalization excluded the teens from such relationships. Fraught relationships with parents also denied the girls social capital under Coleman's (1988, 111) definition, wherein "there is a lack of social capital . . . if there are not strong relations between children and parents." Portes (2000) too emphasizes social capital as a family asset. And a lack of common language skills among parents limited social capital qua "expectations for action within a collectivity" (Portes and Sensenbrenner 1993).

7. Studies, for instance, outline the lack in poor neighborhoods of social organization (Shaw and McKay 1942), collective efficacy (Sampson, Morennoff, and Earls 1999), jobs (Wilson 1987), role models (Jencks and Mayer 1990), and more.

8. Yosso 2005, 69. See also, e.g., Black 2018; Robbins 2013; Sharpe 2016.

9. Yosso 2005, 69.

10. "The main goals," Yosso (2005, 82) notes, "of identifying and documenting cultural wealth are to transform education and empower People of Color to utilize assets already abundant in their communities."

11. hooks 2000, 134.

12. Ibid.

13. Sociology regularly centers "the 'family' and the heterosexual couple in our intellectual imaginaries." Yet "much that matters to people in terms of intimacy and care increasingly takes place beyond the 'family' . . . and within networks of friends" (Roseneil and Budgeon 2004, 135; see also Adams and Allan 1998; O'Connor 1992; Roseneil 2004; Weston 1991). "Care" itself is often viewed as a duty of families or formal institutions, eliding informal—yet deeply meaningful—forms of care (Black 2018; Byron 2020).

14. Ecker 1989, 179.

15. Kaplan 2013, 164.

16. Following dozens of teenagers from poor Baltimore neighborhoods over a decade, DeLuca, Clampet-Lundquist, and Edin (2016) found that the most successful young people were teens who had an "identity project." Defined as "a

source of meaning that provides a strong sense of self and is linked to concrete activities to which youth commit themselves," identity projects gave young people the chance to "be about something" (66). Importantly, it was not just the activities that boosted well-being and mobility prospects. Rather identity projects linked young people to like-minded peers (76). The most effective identity projects both connected young people to peers and had institutional backing. On the reciprocal connection between institutional and peer support between adults, see, e.g., Mazelis 2017; Small 2009; Small and Gose 2020.

17. Linds, Goulet, and Sammuels 2012.

18. Wiggins 2018. On peer ties and "collective identity" as a youth programming asset, see Futch 2016. Los Angeles's Neighborhood Academic Initiative, a precollege enrichment program for low-income students, also fosters strong friendships between participants (Kaplan 2013).

19. Stanton-Salazar and Spina 2005, 409.

20. Some of the NC girls initially considered applying to the same schools. Joanne remembered, "We were real naïve for a little bit and thought we could go to the same school and be roommates." In the end, however, the girls submitted different applications based on their perceived academic prospects. As Aisha explained, "We knew Joanne was going to Harvard or something. Seeta was okay, so we knew she could get into the state schools."

21. Posse Foundation 2018.

22. Research validates the beneficial role of peer relationships in institutional programs, interventions, and transitions, ranging from adolescent STI/HIV prevention programs (Harper et al. 2014) to the experiences of young people aging out of care (Snow and Mann-Feder 2013).

23. Cox 2015; Fader 2013; Mazelis 2017. Academia can be complicit in the perpetuation of these harmful narratives. Studies that attempt to "account" for behaviors that hamper mobility—asking, for instance, why teens deal drugs or have babies—often assume that had young people from poor neighborhoods avoided these behaviors, they would have achieved mobility, when this is in fact not true (Ray 2018b).

24. Narratives of individualism can also discourage people from embracing and developing support systems in their social networks (Cox 2015; Mazelis 2017).

25. As Cooper (2018, 266–67) argues, "Celebrating the resilience of poor folks is a perverse way of acknowledging the unreasonable demands placed upon people who already are struggling to make it. In fact, in this moment, when a broad-scale conservative backlash threatens to absolutely gut the social safety net, 'resilience' is a dangerous word." See also Stanton-Salazar and Spina 2000.

26. hooks 2014a, 6. This ties too to the romanticization of Black women's "strength"—a trope that plays down racism's and sexism's harms (Golden 2021). As Hill Collins (2000, 306) explains, "Presenting African-American women solely as heroic figures who easily engage in resisting oppression on all fronts minimizes the very real costs of oppression and can foster the perception that Black women need no help because [they] can 'take it.'"

27. Lamont (2018, 433–34) argues, "A society that is increasingly organized around the pursuit of socioeconomic success and the achievement of middle-class status is doomed to condemn at least the lower half of the social pyramid to be defined (and worst, to define themselves) as 'losers.' That so much of our disciplinary knowledge has been oriented toward making middle-class status (and college education) available to all is troubling."

Given dignity's role in well-being, Lamont (2019) suggests researchers focus less on promoting pathways to "get ahead" and more on diversifying "social criteria of worth," thereby multiplying the paths to social esteem. This, Lamont explains, would entail "valorizing social contributions that are not directly tied to production and consumption, such as caring, educating, consecrating, and other types of activities, without subordinating them or justifying them by profit maximization" (685).

28. While 81% of US teens say that social media helps them feel more connected to friends and 68% say they feel that people online will support them through tough times, 45% feel overwhelmed by online "drama" and a similar percentage feel pressure to post content that makes them look good to others (Pew Research Center 2018b).

29. Many teens' mental health worsened through the COVID-19 pandemic, and some research suggests that increased social media use through this period exacerbated these declines in well-being (e.g., Guessoum et al. 2020; Magson et al. 2021).

30. Charmaraman et al. 2022.

31. As I discuss in "Final Reflections," below, some of the young women share this view.

32. Hill Collins 2000, 111.

33. Scholars have explored "Black Twitter" as a space for intimacy, connection, and identity construction among Black users (e.g., Clark 2014; Graham and Smith 2016).

34. Hill Collins 2000.

35. Ibid., 123–25. As hooks (2003, 150) writes, the "inability to shape how we see ourselves and how others see us is one of the major blows to collective self-

esteem." On the links between identity creation and self-worth, see, e.g., Lamont 2000; Snow and Anderson 1987.

36. While online socializing could boost mental health by raising people's perceptions of social support (Sahi et al. 2021), many relationships suffered when in-person interaction was lost (Bozic 2020; Collins 2020).

37. Generally, young people use social media not to make new friends but to engage with existing friends (Baym 2015).

38. Goffman 1967, 99. Goffman's assertion that "an individual's activities must occur either in social situations or solitarily" (67) was blurred both by the endless hours that the girls spent apart but communicating and by time spent together while focusing mainly on their own phones.

39. Liebow 1967; Sampson 2012; Sharkey 2013; Stack 1974; Wilson 1987.

40. Lane 2018, ix.

41. Ibid. "The street" has long been a metaphor used to describe the staging ground for social life in urban neighborhoods (e.g., Anderson 2000; Jacobs [1961] 1992).

42. "What bonds girls," Bettie (2003, 29) explains, is often "the disclosure of emotional injuries and insecurities" (see also Furman and Buhrmester 1992).

43. Haitian immigrants have among the highest levels of parent-child conflict (Rumbaut 1997, 28).

44. Stepick 1998; Zephir 2001. Other studies show some Haitian American people expressing shame about their identity (e.g., Stepick et al. 2001). In NC, however, while some of the girls made disparaging comments about Haitian men, they posted celebratory photographs online for Flag Day and shared memes about Haitian food, Haitian parents, or "Haitian people problems."

45. Kasinitz et al. 2008, 354. Early research suggested that some children of immigrants—particularly those who lived in poor, urban neighborhoods near local-born African American people with whom they could be (mis)identified—faced a "second-generation decline" relative to their parents, caused by "downward assimilation" into the urban "underclass" (Gans 1992; Portes and Zhou 1993). More recently, however, researchers have found a second-generation advantage enjoyed by the children of immigrants (Kasinitz et al. 2008). Some scholars challenge this optimism. Haller, Portes, and Lynch (2011), for instance, reiterate the prevalence of "downward assimilation" among second-generation immigrants. Nonetheless, argue Alba, Kasinitz, and Waters (2011, 766), most children of immigrants "have made significant progress relative to their parents," something researchers miss if they conceptualize upward mobility or success only as having graduated from a four-year college and obtaining a stable, professional job.

46. Woods and Hanson 2016.

47. "The peer group," Ladner (1971, 63) notes, of girls growing up in the Pruitt-Igoe homes, "seems to serve a somewhat different and broader function with these children than with their middle-class counterparts. There is more unsupervised contact with peers and peers also provide some of the non-tangible resources that parents are usually expected to provide. At a very early age many children begin to rely on their peers for company, emotional support, advice, comfort and a variety of other services that parents ideally are expected to offer."

48. Meaning "best friends."

49. This description was developed with Aisha after her return from the trip.

A Note on Research and Writing

1. See Bettie 2003, 29.

2. I distinguish digital ethnography—combining in-person with online field methods—both from solely online ethnographies (or "netnographies") and from studies that use the internet to conduct interviews (e.g., Beaulieu 2004; Deakin and Wakefield 2014; Hine 2000).

3. Lane 2018, 171.

4. During the COVID-19 pandemic, when social distancing measures prohibited much face-to-face qualitative data collection, scholars considered whether and how digital methods can supplement or replace ethnographic research (Howlett 2021; Kim et al. 2021; Kobakhidze et al. 2021).

5. As Lane (2018, 176) noted, "Checking my feed kept a foot in the field regardless of my geographic location."

6. One December, for instance, I saw on Snapchat that Florence was back in NC for break. I liked a selfie she posted on Instagram, and, in turn, she liked four of my recent photos. But when I texted Florence, she did not reply. I knew, however, since she had liked my photos, that she was not avoiding me. So I messaged Florence on Instagram, where she shared her new cell number and we scheduled a time to meet.

7. In such cases, it was interesting to ask which was the performance, the sobriety claim or the drinking?

8. The task of discerning meaning is not confined to digital ethnography. Interpretive challenges have long troubled field workers, especially the tension between what respondents say and what they do (e.g., Jerolmack and Khan 2014; Lamont and Swidler 2014). But the lack of cues and signifiers online—context, tone of voice, body language, and more—can make digital statements even harder to parse.

9. Colloquial abbreviation for "in real life," meaning in person, as opposed to online.

10. I found, as did Lane (2018, 174), that, "for the teenagers, the online connection wasn't any more unusual than the fact of my presence offline."

11. Lane 2018; Stuart 2020.

12. The sociologist Lorena Garcia (2012) suggests that researchers' self-disclosure can help mitigate power imbalances during fieldwork. Relatedly, bidirectional information flows online can potentially minimize or subvert field workers' power (on visibility and power, see Foucault 1975).

13. Even when such comments seemed humorous, I honored them.

14. Duneier 2000, 338.

15. Gans 1962, 405.

16. In an extensive "insider/outsider" debate, sociologists and anthropologists have considered whether studying people who share their identity characteristics *helps* knowledge construction—by, for example, building rapport and mutual understanding—or *hampers* it, when, say, participants feel more comfortable opening up to strangers, or more explicitly explain their thoughts and actions when there is no assumption of shared knowledge (Clifford and Marcus 1986; Headland, Pike, and Harris 1990; Jones 2009; Ladson-Billings 2003; Lamont 2004; Young 2004).

Yet notions of similarity and difference should not be reified. As the sociologist Nancy Naples (2013, 49) explains, "The bipolar construction of insider /outsider . . . sets up a false separation that neglects the interactive processes through which 'insiderness' and 'outsiderness' is constructed." Rather than fixed categories, "they are ever-shifting and permeable social locations that are differentially experienced and expressed by community members" (49). As such, researchers can be, and often are, simultaneously insiders and outsiders in various, nuanced ways. As Bettie (2003, 25–26) notes, "The logic of an identity politics in which identity is conceptualized as static and clearly bounded doesn't easily acknowledge the continuum of experience, relative sameness and difference."

17. Recognizing one's structural location neither dissolves power differences nor necessarily interrupts researchers' deeply held assumptions about themselves, their projects, or their participants (Smith 1990).

18. Reflexivity should burrow beyond researchers' individual identity characteristics and seek to unearth the impact of social and disciplinary assumptions (Emirbayer and Desmond 2012; Ladson-Billings 2000).

19. MacLeod 1987, 467.

20. Geertz 1979.

21. Duneier 2000; Jerolmack and Murphy 2017.

22. See Small 2014, 2015. For the same reason, I avoided the term "inner city," both because it was, in this case, inaccurate—Cambridge was not "inner" Boston; North Cambridge was not "inner" Cambridge—and because it leans on racist associations. As the anthropologist Elizabeth Chin (2001, 60) notes, "Dense, evocative terms like *inner city* now operate as quick descriptors behind which lurk a host of meanings and assumptions that are loaded like a semiautomatic: poor, black, drugs, gangs, violence, Latino, welfare, joblessness." Relatedly, I have not used terms like "at risk" or "disadvantaged"—which can elide systemic violence—or described people as "marginalized" without specifying by which inequitable social systems. Still biases doubtless remain in what I have written.

23. Tropes and labels do not just *describe* but also *construct* categories of people. Moreover, these constructions have political implications. Stanton-Salazar and Spina (2000, 230) caution against "the conventional emphasis on groups of words like success, against-the-odds, and failure," which can "romanticiz[e] adversity" and normalize individualistic definitions of resiliency.

24. This book contrasts the young women's stories with the negative academic and cultural narratives from which they depart more than it compares the NC girls to other teens. Except at a few explicit points, I do not compare the NC girls with other young people—either with peers they knew or with an imagined reference group of "average" teenagers. Social scientists have long tried to measure, quantify, and explain the deviance of groups labeled "other" from the "norm"—presumed to be white, male, middle class, and heterosexual (Ladner 1973, xxiii; Zuberi and Bonilla Silva 2008, 330–31). For critiques of the use of whiteness as a reference category in research, see, e.g., McKee 1993; Rios 2015; Winant 2007; Zuberi 2003).

25. Rather than consider how peer support was "caused by" or somehow representative of the NC girls' racial and socioeconomic identities, I focus instead on how racism and stigmatization shaped their experiences and formed the context of their friendships.

26. Boo 2012, 251.

27. While the IRB did not require assent forms, I chose to use them in the hope that they conveyed my trust in the young women's capacity to understand and participate in the research. And since I believe that consent is ongoing, I told the girls they were welcome to stop participating at any time, though none did.

28. I ultimately met up with eight of the nine girls, but I was unable to schedule a meeting with Seeta.

29. "Stories" are photos that, once posted, are visible only for twenty-four hours. Following friends' stories, which offer daily updates, implies more contact and closeness than noting photos posted "on main" or "to the grid," where they remain permanently accessible.

30. Geertz 1973, 30.

Final Reflections

1. Marciano et al. 2021; Orben, Tomove, and Blakemore 2020.

2. Byron 2020.

3. Marciano et al. 2021; Orben, Tomova, and Blakemore 2020; Charmaraman et al. 2022.

4. Okabe-Miyamoto and Lyubomirsky 2021. This suggests that researchers should consider not only *whether* people use social media but also *how* they do so. It also suggests that the positive effects of social media do not automatically cancel out possible harms, and vice versa.

References

Aboud, Frances, and Morton Mendelson. 1998. "Determinants of Friendship Selection and Quality: Developmental Perspectives." In *The Company They Keep: Friendships in Childhood and Adolescence*, edited by William M. Bukowski, Andrew F. Newcomb, and Willard W. Hartup, 87–112. Cambridge: Cambridge University Press.

Abu-Lughod, Lila. 1986. *Veiled Sentiments: Honor and Poetry in a Bedouin Society.* Oakland: University of California Press.

———. 1990. "The Romance of Resistance: Tracing Transformations of Power through Bedouin Women." *American Ethnologist* 17 (1): 41–55.

Adams, Rebecca G., and Graham Allan, eds. 1998. *Placing Friendship in Context.* Cambridge: Cambridge University Press.

Adler, Patricia A., and Peter Adler. 1998. *Peer Power: Preadolescent Culture and Identity.* New Brunswick, NJ: Rutgers University Press.

Ainsworth-Darnell, James W., and Douglas B. Downey. 1998. "Assessing the Oppositional Culture Explanation for Racial/Ethnic Differences in School Performance." *American Sociological Review* 63 (4): 536–53.

Akers, Ronald L., Marvin D. Krohn, Lonn Lanza-Kaduce, and Marcia Radosevich. 1979. "Social Learning and Deviant Behavior: A Specific Test of a General Theory." *American Sociological Review* 44 (4): 636–55.

Alba, Richard, Philip Kasinitz, and Mary C. Waters. 2011. "The Kids Are (Mostly) Alright: Second-Generation Assimilation: Comments on Haller, Portes and Lynch." *Social Forces* 89 (3): 763–73.

Alexander, Karl, Robert Bozick, and Doris Entwisle. 2008. "Warming Up, Cooling Out, or Holding Steady? Persistence and Change in Educational Expectations after High School." *Sociology of Education* 81 (4): 371–96.

Alon, Sigal, and Marta Tienda. 2005. "Assessing the 'Mismatch' Hypothesis: Differences in College Graduation Rates by Institutional Selectivity." *Sociology of Education* 78 (4): 294–315.

American Community Survey. 2016. "Poverty Status in the Past 12 Months." Table S1701

An, Weihua. 2011. "Models and Methods to Identify Peer Effects." In *The Sage Handbook of Social Network Analysis*, 515–32. London: Sage.

———. 2016. "On the Directionality Test of Peer Effects in Social Networks." *Sociological Methods & Research* 45 (4): 635–50.

Anderson, Elijah. 1990. *Streetwise: Race, Class, and Change in an Urban Community.* Chicago: University of Chicago Press.

———. 2000. *Code of the Street: Decency, Violence, and the Moral Life of the Inner City.* New York: Norton.

———. 2015. "The White Space." *Sociology of Race and Ethnicity* 1 (1): 10–21.

Armstrong, Elizabeth A., and Laura T. Hamilton. 2013. *Paying for the Party: How College Maintains Inequality.* Cambridge, MA: Harvard University Press.

Armstrong, Elizabeth, Laura Hamilton, and Paula England. 2010. "Is Hooking Up Bad for Young Women?" *Contexts* 9 (3): 22–27.

Auyero, Javier. 2012. *Patients of the State: The Politics of Waiting in Argentina.* Durham, NC: Duke University Press.

Ballou, Brian. 2012. "After Killing of Teen, a Vigil, Grief in Cambridge." *Boston Globe,* June 5. https://www.bostonglobe.com/metro/2012/06/05/outpouring-grief-over-slain-cambridge-teen/2VGAJgCxJC9ZkPBFd7Q7XJ/story.html.

Ballou, Brian, and John Ellement. 2012. "Teenage Slay Victim in Cambridge Remembered as Role Model, 'Good at Heart.'" Boston.com, April 6. https://www.boston.com/uncategorized/noprimarytagmatch/20-12/06/04/teenage-slay-victim-in-cambridge-remembered-as-role-model-good-at-heart.

Bankhead, Ursuline. 2015. "Barriers to Mental Health Services and African American Girls." In *Black Girls and Adolescents,* edited by C. F. Collins, 169–82. Santa Barbara, CA: Praeger.

Barcelos, Christie, and Aline Gubrium. 2014. "Reproducing Stories: Strategic Narratives of Teen Pregnancy and Motherhood." *Social Problems* 61: 466–81.

Baumgartner, M. P. 1989. *The Moral Order of a Suburb.* New York: Oxford University Press.

Baym, Nancy K. 2015. *Personal Connections in the Digital Age.* 2nd ed. Cambridge: Polity Press.

Beaulieu. Anne. 2004. "Mediating Ethnography: Objectivity and the Making of Ethnographies of the Internet." *Social Epistemology* 18 (2–3): 139–63.

Becker, Howard S. 1963. *Outsiders: Studies in the Sociology of Deviance.* Glencoe, IL: Free Press.

Berger, Peter L., and Thomas Luckmann. 1967. *The Social Construction of Reality: A Treatise in the Sociology of Knowledge.* Anchor.

Best, Amy. 2000. *Prom Night: Youths, Schools, and Popular Culture.* New York: Routledge.

———. 2006. *Fast Cars, Cool Rides: The Accelerating World of Youth and Their Cars.* New York: New York University Press.

———. 2017. *Fast-Food Kids: French Fries, Lunch Lines, and Social Ties.* New York: New York University Press.

Bettie, Julie. 2003. *Women without Class: Girls, Race, and Identity.* Berkeley: University of California Press.

Black, Steven P. 2018. "The Ethics and Aesthetics of Care." *Annual Review of Anthropology* 47 (1): 79–95.

Bogle, Kathleen A. 2008. *Hooking Up: Sex, Dating, and Relationships on Campus.* New York: New York University Press.

Boo, Katherine. 2012. *Behind the Beautiful Forevers.* New York: Random House.

Borsari, Brian, and Kate B. Carey. 2001. "Peer Influences on College Drinking: A Review of the Research." *Journal of Substance Abuse* 13 (4): 391–424.

Bourdieu, Pierre. 1977. *Outline of a Theory of Practice.* Translated by Richard Nice. Cambridge: Cambridge University Press.

———. 1984. *Distinction: A Social Critique of the Judgement of Taste.* Translated by Richard Nice. Cambridge, MA: Harvard University Press.

———. 1986. "The Forms of Capital." In *Handbook of Theory and Research for the Sociology of Education,* edited by John G. Richardson, 241–58. New York: Greenwood Press.

———. 1993. *The Field of Cultural Production: Essays on Art and Literature.* New York: Columbia University Press.

———. 2000. *Pascalian Meditations.* Stanford, CA: Stanford University Press.

Bourgois, Philippe. 1996. *In Search of Respect: Selling Crack in El Barrio.* New York: Cambridge University Press.

Bowen, William G., Matthew M. Chingos, and Michael S. McPherson. 2009. *Crossing the Finish Line: Completing College at America's Public Universities.* Princeton, NJ: Princeton University Press.

boyd, danah. 2014. *It's Complicated: The Social Lives of Networked Teens.* New Haven, CT: Yale University Press.

Bozic, Sasa. 2020. "Interaction Ritual Chains and Sustainability of Lockdowns, Quarantines, 'Social Distancing' and Isolation during the COVID-19 Pandemic." *Sociologija i proctor* 59 (219): 13-34.

Briggs, Xavier de Souza. 1998. "Brown Kids in White Suburbs: Housing Mobility and the Many Faces of Social Capital." *Housing Policy Debate* 9 (1): 177-221.

Brooks-Gunn, Jeanne, Greg J. Duncan, Pamela Kato Klebanov, and Naomi Sealand. 1993. "Do Neighborhoods Influence Child and Adolescent Development?" *American Journal of Sociology* 99 (2): 353-95.

Bryk, Anthony, and Mary Driscoll. 1988. "The High School as Community: Contextual Influences and Consequences for Students and Teachers." ERIC Document Reproduction Service No. ED 302 539. National Center on Effective Secondary Schools, University of Wisconsin-Madison.

Buch, Elana D. 2015. "Anthropology of Aging and Care." *Annual Review of Anthropology* 44: 277-93.

Bukowski, William M., Andrew F. Newcomb, and Willard W. Hartup, eds. 1998. *The Company They Keep: Friendships in Childhood and Adolescence.* Cambridge: Cambridge University Press.

Burton, Linda. 2007. "Childhood Adultification in Economically Disadvantaged Families: A Conceptual Model." *Family Relations* 56 (4): 329-45.

Burton, Linda M., and Robin L. Jarrett. 2000. "In the Mix, Yet on the Margins: The Place of Families in Urban Neighborhood and Child Development Research." *Journal of Marriage and Family* 62 (4): 1114-35.

Byron, Paul. 2020. *Digital Media, Friendship and Cultures of Care.* New York: Routledge.

Calarco, Jessica McCrory. 2011. "'I Need Help!': Social Class and Children's Help-Seeking in Elementary School." *American Sociological Review* 76 (6): 862-82.

Call, Kathleen Thiede, and Jeylan T. Mortimer. 2001. *Arenas of Comfort in Adolescence: A Study of Adjustment in Context.* Mahwah, NJ: Lawrence Erlbaum Associates.

Calogero, Rachel M., Stacey Tantleff-Dunn, and J. Kevin Thompson, eds. 2010. *Self-Objectification in Women: Causes, Consequences, and Counteractions.* Washington, DC: American Psychological Association.

Cambridge City Government. 2018. "Free or Reduced Price School Lunch." Cambridge, MA. http://www.cambridgema.gov/CDD/factsandmaps /educationdata/freereducedlunch.

Cambridge Public Schools. 2018. "Quick Facts." http://crls.cpsd.us/about_crls /quick_facts/.

Carnevale, Anthony P., Nicole Smith, and Jeff Strohl. 2013. "Recovery: Job Growth and Education Requirements through 2020." Georgetown Public Policy Institute, Center on Education and the Workforce.

Caron, Caroline. 2011. "Getting Girls and Teens into the Vocabularies of Citizenship." *Girlhood Studies* 4 (2): 70–91.

Carter, Prudence L. 2003. "Black Cultural Capital, Status Positioning, and Schooling Conflicts for Low-Income African American Youth." *Social Problems* 50 (1): 136–55.

———. 2005. *Keepin' It Real: School Success beyond Black and White.* Oxford: Oxford University Press.

Case, Anne C., and Lawrence F. Katz. 1991. "The Company You Keep: The Effects of Family and Neighborhood on Disadvantaged Youths." Working Paper 3705. National Bureau of Economic Research. http://www.nber.org /papers/w3705.

Charmaraman, Linda, Alicia Doyle Lynch, Amanda Richer, and Emily Zhai. 2022. "Examining Early Adolescent Positive and Negative Social Technology Behaviors and Well-Being during the COVID-19 Pandemic." *Technology, Mind, and Behavior* 3 (1).

Chen, Rong, and Stephen L DesJardins. 2010. "Investigating the Impact of Financial Aid on Student Dropout Risks: Racial and Ethnic Differences." *Journal of Higher Education* 81 (2): 179–208.

Chen, Xianglei. 2005. "First-Generation Students in Postsecondary Education: A Look at Their College Transcripts." US Department of Education, National Center for Education Statistics, Washington, DC.

Cherng, Hua-Yu Sebastian, Jessica McCrory Calarco, and Grace Kao. 2013. "Along for the Ride: Best Friends' Resources and Adolescents' College Completion." *American Educational Research Journal* 50 (1): 76–106.

Chetty, Raj, Matthew Jackson, Theresa Kuchler, et al. 2022. "Social Capital I: Measurement and Associations with Economic Mobility." *Nature* 608: 108–21.

Chin, Elizabeth. 2001. *Purchasing Power: Black Kids and American Consumer Culture.* Minneapolis: University of Minnesota Press.

Choy, Susan P., Laura J. Horn, Anne-Marie Nuñez, and Xianglei Chen. 2000. "Transition to College: What Helps At-Risk Students and Students Whose Parents Did Not Attend College." *New Directions for Institutional Research* 107: 45–63.

Clark, Meredith. 2014. "To Tweet Our Own Cause: A Mixed-Methods Study of the Online Phenomenon 'Black Twitter.'" PhD diss., University of North Carolina at Chapel Hill.

Clifford, James, and George E. Marcus, eds. 1986. *Writing Culture: The Poetics and Politics of Ethnography.* Berkeley: University of California Press.

Cloward, Richard A., and Lloyd E. Ohlin. 1966. *Delinquency and Opportunity: A Theory of Delinquent Gangs.* New York: Free Press.

Cobbina, Jennifer E., Jody Miller, and Rod K. Brunson. 2008. "Gender, Neighborhood Danger, and Risk-Avoidance Strategies among Urban African-American Youths." *Criminology* 46 (3): 673–709.

Cohen, Stanley, and Laurie Taylor. 1972. *Psychological Survival: The Experience of Long-Term Imprisonment.* Baltimore: Penguin Books.

Coleman, James S. 1966. "Equality of Educational Opportunity." Inter-university Consortium for Political and Social Research. http://www.icpsr.umich.edu/ICPSR/studies/06389/version/3.

———. 1988. "Social Capital in the Creation of Human Capital." *American Journal of Sociology* 94: S95–S120.

Coleman, James S., and Thomas Hoffer. 1987. *Public and Private High Schools: The Impact of Communities.* New York: Basic Books.

Collier, Peter J., and David L. Morgan. 2008. "'Is That Paper Really Due Today?': Differences in First-Generation and Traditional College Students' Understandings of Faculty Expectations." *Higher Education: The International Journal of Higher Education and Educational Planning* 55 (4): 425–46.

Collins, Kathryn, Kay Connors, Sara Davis, April Donohue, et al. 2010. "Understanding the Impact of Trauma and Urban Poverty on Family Systems: Risks, Resilience, and Interventions." Family Informed Trauma Treatment Center, Baltimore, MD. http://fittcenter.umaryland.edu/WhitePaper.aspx.

Collins, Randall. 2004. *Interaction Ritual Chains.* Princeton, NJ: Princeton University Press.

———. 2020. "Social Distancing as a Critical Test of the Micro-Sociology of Solidarity." *American Journal of Cultural Sociology* 8: 477–97.

Conrad, Peter. 1997. "It's Boring: Notes on the Meanings of Boredom in Everyday Life." *Qualitative Sociology* 20: 465–75.

Contreras, Randol. 2013. *The Stickup Kids: Race, Drugs, Violence, and the American Dream.* Berkeley: University of California Press.

Cook, Philip J., and Jens Ludwig. 1997. "Weighing the 'Burden of "Acting White"': Are There Race Differences in Attitudes toward Education?" *Journal of Policy Analysis and Management* 16 (2): 256–78.

Cooper, Brittney. 2018. *Eloquent Rage: A Black Feminist Discovers Her Superpower.* New York: Picador.

Corsaro, William A. 1985. *Friendship and Peer Culture in the Early Years.* Norwood, NJ: Ablex.

Corsaro, William A., and Donna Eder. 1990. "Children's Peer Cultures." *Annual Review of Sociology* 16: 197-220.

Cox, Aimee Meredith. 2015. *Shapeshifters: Black Girls and the Choreography of Citizenship.* Durham, NC: Duke University Press.

Crane, Jonathan. 1991. "The Epidemic Theory of Ghettos and Neighborhood Effects on Dropping Out and Teenage Childbearing." *American Journal of Sociology* 96 (5): 1226-59.

Crenshaw, Kimberle. 1991. "Mapping the Margins: Intersectionality, Identity Politics, and Violence against Women of Color." *Stanford Law Review* 43 (6): 1241-99.

Crosnoe, Robert, and Chandra Muller. 2014. "Family Socioeconomic Status, Peers, and the Path to College." *Social Problems* 61 (4): 602-24.

Csikszentimihalyi, Mihaly. 1990. *Flow: The Psychology of Optimal Experience.* New York: Harper & Row.

Cunningham, Alisa, and Deborah Santiago. 2008. *Student Aversion to Borrowing: Who Borrows and Who Doesn't.* Washington, DC: Institute for Higher Education Policy.

Cunningham, Vinsent. 2015. "Why Do We Change Our Avatars after Tragedy?" *New Yorker,* December 11.

Dance, L. Janelle. 2002. *Tough Fronts: The Impact of Street Culture on Schooling.* New York: Routledge.

Davis, Angela. 1981. *Women, Race & Class.* New York: Vintage.

Deakin, Hannah, and Kelly Wakefield. 2014. "Skype Interviewing: Reflections of Two PhD Researchers." *Qualitative Research* 14 (5): 603-16.

DeLuca, Stefanie, Susan Clampet-Lundquist, and Kathryn Edin. 2016. *Coming of Age in the Other America.* New York: Russell Sage Foundation.

Desmond, Matthew. 2012. "Disposable Ties and the Urban Poor." *American Journal of Sociology* 117 (5): 1295-1335.

———. 2016. *Evicted: Poverty and Profit in the American City.* New York: Crown.

Deterding, Nicole 2015. "Instrumental and Expressive Education: College Planning in the Face of Poverty." *Sociology of Education* 88 (4): 284-301.

Dewey, John. 1938. *Experience and Education.* New York: Free Press.

DiMaggio, Paul, Clark Bernier, Charles Heckscher, and David Mimno. 2019. "Interaction Ritual Threads: Does IRC Theory Apply Online?" In *Ritual, Emotion, Violence: Studies on the Micro-Sociology of Randall Collins,* edited by

Eliot B. Weininger, Annette Lareau, and Omar Lizardo, 81–124. New York: Routledge.

Dodson, Lisa, Randy Albelda, Diana Coronado, and Marya Mtshali. 2012. "How Youth Are Put at Risk by Parents' Low-Wage Jobs." Center for Social Policy Publications, Boston, MA.

Dodson, Lisa, and Jillian Dickert. 2004. "Girls' Family Labor in Low-Income Households: A Decade of Qualitative Research." *Journal of Marriage and Family* 66 (2): 318–32.

Domínguez, Silvia, and Celeste Watkins. 2003. "Creating Networks for Survival and Mobility: Social Capital among African-American and Latin-American Low-Income Mothers." *Social Problems* 50 (1): 111–35.

Drake, St. Clair, and Horace R. Cayton. 1945. *Black Metropolis: A Study of Negro Life in a Northern City.* New York: Harbinger.

Duncan, Greg, Aletha Huston, and Thomas Weisner. 2007. *Higher Ground: New Hope for Working Families and Their Children.* New York: Russell Sage Foundation.

Duncan, Greg J., W. Jean Yeung, Jeanne Brooks-Gunn, and Judith R. Smith. 1998. "How Much Does Childhood Poverty Affect the Life Chances of Children?" *American Sociological Review* 63 (3): 406–23.

Duneier, Mitchell. 2000. *Sidewalk.* New York: Farrar, Straus and Giroux.

Dupéré, Veronique, Tama Leventhal, Eric Dion, and Michel Janosz. 2014. "Stressors and Turning Points in High School and Dropout: A Stress Process, Life Course Framework." *Review of Educational Research* 85 (4): 591–629.

DuRant, Robert H., Alan Getts, Chris Cadenhead, and Elizabeth R. Woods. 1995. "Exposure to Violence and Victimization and Depression, Hopelessness, and Purpose in Life among Adolescents Living in and around Public Housing." *Journal of Developmental & Behavioral Pediatrics* 16 (4): 233–37.

Durkheim, Émile. [1912] 1995. *The Elementary Forms of Religious Life.* New York: Free Press.

East, Patricia L. 2010. "Children's Provision of Family Caregiving: Benefit or Burden?" *Child Development Perspectives* 4 (1): 55–61.

Eckert, Penelope. 1989. *Jocks and Burnouts: Social Categories and Identity in the High School.* New York: Teachers College Press.

Edin, Kathryn, and Maria Kefalas. 2005. *Promises I Can Keep: Why Poor Women Put Motherhood before Marriage.* Berkeley: University of California Press.

Edin, Kathryn, and Laura Lein. 1997. *Making Ends Meet: How Single Mothers Survive Welfare and Low-Wage Work.* New York: Russell Sage Foundation.

Ehrenreich, Barbara. 2003. *A Step Back to the Workhouse?* New York: New York University Press.

Elder, Glen H., Jacquelynne S. Eccles, Monika Ardelt, and Sarah Lord. 1995. "Inner-City Parents under Economic Pressure: Perspectives on the Strategies of Parenting." *Journal of Marriage and Family* 57 (3): 771–84.

Elliott, Delbert S., David Huizinga, and Scott Menard. 1989. *Multiple Problem Youth: Delinquency, Substance Use, and Mental Health Problems.* New York: Springer Verlag.

Elliott, Delbert S., and Scott Menard. 1996. "Delinquent Friends and Delinquent Behavior: Temporal and Developmental Patterns." In *Delinquency and Crime: Current Theories,* edited by David Hawkins, 28–67. Cambridge Criminology Series. Cambridge: Cambridge University Press.

Elliott, Delbert S., Scott Menard, Bruce Rankin, Amanda Elliot, William Julius Wilson, and David Huizinga. 2006. *Good Kids from Bad Neighborhoods: Successful Development in Social Context.* Cambridge: Cambridge University Press.

Emerson, Richard. 1976. "Social Exchange Theory." *Annual Review of Sociology* 2 (1): 335–62.

Emirbayer, Mustafa, and Matthew Desmond. 2012. "Race and Reflexivity." *Ethnic and Racial Studies* 35: 574–99.

Emirbayer, Mustafa, and Jeff Goodwin. 1994. "Network Analysis, Culture, and the Problem of Agency." *American Journal of Sociology* 99 (6): 1411–54.

Emirbayer, Mustafa, and Douglas W. Maynard. 2011. "Pragmatism and Ethnomethodology." *Qualitative Sociology* 34 (1): 221–61.

Emirbayer, Mustafa, and Ann Mische. 1998. "What Is Agency?" *American Journal of Sociology* 103 (4): 962–1023.

Engle, Jennifer, and Vincent Tinto. 2008. *Moving beyond Access: College Success for Low-Income, First-Generation Students.* Washington, DC: Pell Institute for the Study of Opportunity in Higher Education.

Esch, Kevin, and Vicki Mayer. 2007. "How Unprofessional: The Profitable Partnership of Amateur Porn and Celebrity Culture." In *Pornification: Sex and Sexuality in Media Culture,* edited by Kaarina Nikunen, Susanna Paasonen, and Laura Saarenmaa, 99–111. Oxford: Bloomsbury Academic.

Evans, Gary W., and Michelle A. Schamberg. 2009. "Childhood Poverty, Chronic Stress, and Adult Working Memory." *Proceedings of the National Academy of Sciences* 106 (16): 6545–49.

Everhart, Robert B. 1983. *Reading, Writing, and Resistance: Adolescence and Labor in a Junior High School.* Boston: Routledge & Kegan Paul.

Fader, Jamie. 2013. *Falling Back: Incarceration and Transitions to Adulthood among Urban Youth.* New Brunswick, NJ: Rutgers University Press.

———. 2021. "'I don't have time for drama': Managing Risk and Uncertainty through Network Avoidance." *Criminology* 59: 291-317.

Featherston, Elena, ed. 1994. *Skin Deep: Women Writing on Color, Culture and Identity.* Freedom, CA: Crossing Press.

Feinberg, Matthew, Robb Willer, Jennifer Stellar, and Dacher Keltner. 2012. "The Virtues of Gossip: Reputational Information Sharing as Prosocial Behavior." *Journal of Personality and Social Psychology* 102 (5): 1015-30.

Fields, Jessica. 2008. *Risky Lessons: Sex Education and Social Inequality.* New Brunswick, NJ: Rutgers University Press.

Fine, Michelle. 1988. "Sexuality, Schooling, and Adolescent Females: The Missing Discourse of Desire." *Harvard Educational Review* 58 (1): 29-51.

Fine, Michelle, and Sara McClelland. 2006. "Sexuality Education and Desire: Still Missing after All These Years." *Harvard Educational Review* 76 (3): 297-338.

Fiske, Susan T. 2000. "Stereotyping, Prejudice, and Discrimination at the Seam between the Centuries: Evolution, Culture, Mind, and Brain." *European Journal of Social Psychology* 30 (3): 299-322.

Flaherty, Michael G. 1999. *A Watched Pot: How We Experience Time.* New York: New York University Press.

———. 2011. *The Textures of Time: Agency and Temporal Experience.* Philadelphia, PA: Temple University Press.

———. 2014. "Afterword." In *Ethnographies of Youth and Temporality: Time Objectified,* edited by Dalsgård Anne Line, Frederiksen Martin Demant, Højlund Susanne, and Meinert Lotte. Philadelphia, PA: Temple University Press.

Foner, Nancy. 2014. "Intergenerational Relations in Immigrant Families Comparisons across Time and Space." In *What's New about the "New" Immigration? Traditions and Transformations in the United States since 1965,* edited by Marilyn Halter, Marilynn S. Johnson, Katheryn P. Viens, and Conrad Edick Wright, 113-30. New York: Palgrave Macmillan.

Fordham, Signithia, and John U. Ogbu. 1986. "Black Students' School Success: Coping with the Burden of 'Acting White.'" *Urban Review* 18 (3): 176-206.

Foucault, Michel. 1975. *Discipline & Punish: The Birth of the Prison.* London: Penguin.

FOX25 News. 2014. "NE Unsolved Exclusive: New Photos in Brianna Holmes Murder Case." https://www.youtube.com/watch?v=T15-MfG7vzI.

Fraser, Nancy. 1990. "Rethinking the Public Sphere: A Contribution to the Critique of Actually Existing Democracy." *Social Text,* no. 25–26: 56–80.

———. 2000. "Rethinking Recognition." *New Left Review* 3 (3): 107–18.

Froyum, Carissa M. 2010. "Making 'Good Girls': Sexual Agency in the Sexuality Education of Low-Income Black Girls." *Culture, Health, and Sexuality* 12 (1): 59–72.

Furman, Wyndol, and Duane Buhrmester. 1992. "Age and Sex Differences in Perceptions of Networks of Personal Relationships." *Child Development* 63: 103–15.

Furstenberg, Frank F. 1993. "How Families Manage Risk and Opportunity in Dangerous Neighborhoods." In *Sociology and the Public Agenda,* edited by William J. Wilson, 231–58. Newbury Park, CA.: Sage.

Furstenberg, Frank F., Thomas D. Cook, Jacquelynne Eccles, Glen H. Elder Jr., and Arnold Sameroff. 1999. *Managing to Make It: Urban Families and Adolescent Success.* Chicago: University of Chicago Press.

Futch, Valerie A. 2016. "Utilizing the Theoretical Framework of Collective Identity to Understand Processes in Youth Programs." *Youth & Society* 48 (5): 673–94.

Gans, Herbert J. 1962. *Urban Villagers: Group and Class in the Life of Italian-Americans.* Updated and Expanded. New York: Free Press.

———. 1992. "Second-Generation Decline: Scenarios for the Economic and Ethnic Futures of the Post-1965 American Immigrants." *Ethnic and Racial Studies* 15 (2): 173–92.

Garcia, Lorena. 2009. "'Now Why Do You Want to Know about That?': Heteronormativity, Sexism, and Racism in the Sexual(Mis)education of Latina Youth." *Gender & Society* 23 (4): 520–41.

———. 2012. *Respect Yourself, Protect Yourself: Latina Girls and Sexual Identity.* New York: New York University Press.

Garfinkel, Harold. 1967. *Studies in Ethnomethodology.* Englewood Cliffs, NJ: Prentice-Hall.

Geertz, Clifford. 1973. *The Interpretation of Culture.* New York: Basic Books.

———. 1979. *Works and Lives: The Anthropologist as Author.* Palo Alto, CA: Stanford University Press.

Gershon, Ilana. 2010. *The Breakup 2.0: Disconnecting over New Media.* Ithaca, NY: Cornell University Press.

Gibson, James J. 1979. *The Ecological Approach to Visual Perception.* Boston: Houghton Mifflin.

Gieryn, Thomas F. 1999. *Cultural Boundaries of Science: Credibility on the Line.* Chicago: University of Chicago Press.

Giordano, Peggy C. 2003. "Relationships in Adolescence." *Annual Review of Sociology* 29 (1): 257–81.

Goffman, Alice. 2014. *On the Run: Fugitive Life in an American City*. Chicago: University of Chicago Press.

Goffman, Erving. 1959. *The Presentation of Self in Everyday Life*. New York: Penguin Books.

———. 1966. *Behavior in Public Places: Notes on the Social Organization of Gatherings*. New York: Free Press.

———. 1967. *Interaction Ritual: Essays on Face-to-Face Behavior*. New York: Pantheon.

———. 1971. *Relations in Public: Microstudies of the Public Order*. New York: Basic Books.

Golden, Marita. 2021. *The Strong Black Woman: How a Myth Endangers the Physical and Mental Health of Black Women*. Coral Gables, FL: Mango Publishing Group.

Goldrick-Rab, Sara, and J. Roksa. 2008. "A Federal Agenda for Promoting Student Success and Degree Completion." Center for American Progress, Washington, DC.

Goldrick-Rab, Sara, and Kathleen M. Shaw. 2005. "Racial and Ethnic Differences in the Impact of Work-First Policies on College Access." *Educational Evaluation and Policy Analysis* 27 (4): 291–307.

Gómez, Jennifer. 2015. "Microaggressions and the Enduring Mental Health Disparity: Black Americans at Risk for Institutional Betrayal." *Journal of Black Psychology* 41 (2): 121–43.

Goodwin, Jeff, James M. Jasper, and Francesca Polletta, eds. 2001. *Passionate Politics: Emotions and Social Movements*. Chicago: University of Chicago Press.

Goulet, Lauren Sessions. 2012. *Friends in All the Right Places: Social Resources and Geography in the Age of Social Network Sites*. Philadelphia: Annenberg School for Communication, University of Pennsylvania.

Goyette, Kimberly A. 2008. "College for Some to College for All: Social Background, Occupational Expectations, and Educational Expectations over Time." *Social Science Research* 37 (2): 461–84.

Graham, Roderick, and Shawn Smith. 2016. "Shawn. The Content of Our #Characters: Black Twitter as Counterpublic." *Sociology of Race and Ethnicity* 2 (4):433–49.

Granovetter, Mark. 1973. "The Strength of Weak Ties." *American Journal of Sociology* 78 (6): 1360–80.

Guessoum, Sélim Benjamin, Jonathan Lachal, Rahmeth Radjack, Emilie Carretier, Sevan Minassian, Laelia Benoit, and Marie Rose Moro. 2020. "Adolescent Psychiatric Disorders during the COVID-19 Pandemic and Lockdown." *Psychiatry Research* 291. https://doi.org/10.1016/j.psychres.2020.113264.

Habermas, Jürgen. 1989. *The Structural Transformation of the Public Sphere: An Inquiry Into a Category of Bourgeois Society.* Cambridge, MA: MIT Press.

Hall, Peter, and Michèle Lamont. 2013. *Social Resilience In The Neoliberal Era.* Cambridge: Cambridge University Press.

Haller, William, Alejandro Portes, and Scott M. Lynch. 2011. "Dreams Fulfilled and Shattered: Determinants of Segmented Assimilation in the Second Generation." *Social Forces* 89 (3): 733–62.

Hamilton, Laura, and Elizabeth A. Armstrong. 2009. "Gendered Sexuality in Young Adulthood: Double Binds and Flawed Options." *Gender & Society* 23 (5): 589–616.

Hampton, Keith. 2016. "Persistent and Pervasive Community: New Communication Technologies and the Future of Community." *American Behavioral Scientist* 60: 101–24.

Hampton, Keith, Lauren Sessions Goulet, and Lee Rainie. 2011. *Social Networking Sites and Our Lives: How People's Trust, Personal Relationships, and Civic and Political Involvement Are Connected to Their Use of Social Networking Sites and Other Technologies.* Washington, DC: Pew Research Center.

Han, Wen-Jui. 2005. "Maternal Nonstandard Work Schedules and Child Cognitive Outcomes." *Child Development* 76 (1): 137–54.

Hannerz, Ulf. 1969. *Soulside: Inquiries into Ghetto Culture and Community.* Chicago: University of Chicago Press.

Harding, David J. 2009. "Violence, Older Peers, and the Socialization of Adolescent Boys in Disadvantaged Neighborhoods." *American Sociological Review* 74 (3): 445–64.

———. 2010. *Living the Drama: Community, Conflict, and Culture among Inner-City Boys.* Chicago: University of Chicago Press.

Harding, Sandra. 1991. *Whose Science? Whose Knowledge?* Ithaca, NY: Cornell University Press.

Harper, Gary, M. Margaret Dolcini, Shira Benhorin, et al. 2014. "The Benefits of a Friendship-Based HIV/STI Prevention Intervention for African American Youth." *Youth & Society* 46 (5): 591–622.

Harris, Angel. 2011. *Kids Don't Want to Fail.* Cambridge, MA: Harvard University Press.

Harris, Anita, ed. 2004. *All about the Girl: Culture, Power, and Identity.* New York: Routledge.

Hatch, Stephani, and Michael Wadsworth. 2008. "Does Adolescent Affect Impact Adult Social Integration? Evidence from the British 1946 Birth Cohort." *Sociology* 42 (1): 155–77.

Haynie, Dana L. 2001. "Delinquent Peers Revisited: Does Network Structure Matter?" *American Journal of Sociology* 106 (4): 1013–57.

Headland, Thomas, Kenneth Pike, and Marvin Harris, eds. 1990. *Etics and emics: The Insider/Outsider Debate.* Thousand Oaks, CA: Sage.

Hill Collins, Patricia. 2000. *Black Feminist Thought: Knowledge, Consciousness, and the Politics of Empowerment.* New York: Routledge

Hine, Christine M. 2000. *Virtual Ethnography.* London: Sage.

Hirsch, Barton J., Jennifer G. Roffman, Nancy L. Deutsch, Cathy A. Flynn, Tondra L. Loder, and Maria E. Pagano. 2000. "Inner-City Youth Development Organizations: Strengthening Programs for Adolescent Girls." *Journal of Early Adolescence* 20 (2): 210–30.

Hirsch, Nicole Arlette. 2014. "When Black Jokes Cross the Line: An Intersectional Analysis of Everyday African-American Humor about Race." Paper presented at the Second Annual Black Doctoral Network Conference, Philadelphia, PA, October 23–25. http://citation.allacademic.com/meta/p_mla_apa_research_citation/7/2/5/2/6/p725265_index.html.

Hochschild, Arlie Russell. 1979. "Emotion Work, Feeling Rules, and Social Structure." *American Journal of Sociology* 85 (3): 551–75.

———. 1983. *The Managed Heart: Commercialization of Human Feeling.* Berkeley: University of California Press.

Hodson, Randy. 2001. *Dignity at Work.* Cambridge: Cambridge University Press.

Homans, George Caspar. 1961. *Social Behavior: Its Elementary Forms.* New York: Harcourt, Brace & World.

Honneth, Axel. 1995. *The Struggle for Recognition: The Moral Grammar of Social Conflicts.* Cambridge, MA: MIT Press.

———. 2014. *The I in We: Studies in the Theory of Recognition.* Cambridge: Polity.

hooks, bell. 2000. *All about Love: New Visions.* New York: William Morrow.

———. 2003. *Rock My Soul: Black People and Self-Esteem.* New York: Washington Square Press.

———. 2014a. *Ain't I a Woman: Black Women and Feminism.* New York: Routledge.

———. 2014b. *Sisters of the Yam: Black Women and Self-Recovery.* New York: Routledge.

Howlett, Marnie 2021. "Looking at the 'Field' through a Zoom Lens: Methodological Reflections on Conducting Online Research during a Global Pandemic." *Qualitative Research* 22 (3): 387–402.

Hoxby, Caroline. 2000. "Peer Effects in the Classroom: Learning from Gender and Race Variation." Working Paper 7867. National Bureau of Economic Research.

Hunter, Margaret. 1998. "Colorstruck: Skin Color Stratification in the Lives of African American Women." *Sociological Inquiry* 68: 517–35.

———. 2002. "'If You're Light You're Alright': Light Skin Color as Social Capital for Women of Color." *Gender & Society* 16 (2): 175–93.

Hutchby, Ian. 2001. "Technologies, Texts and Affordances." *Sociology* 35 (2): 441–56.

———. 2013. *Conversation and Technology: From the Telephone to the Internet.* New York: John Wiley & Sons.

ilovedahatersz. 2012. *RIP BREE TRIBUTE.* https://www.youtube.com /watch?v=IK3hwBVN48k&index-=11&list=PL1wA-OU-hqf4t1ziYOf_ VizxgHB9IpztW.

Institute for Higher Education Policy. 2005. "The Investment Payoff: A 50-State Analysis of the Public and Private Benefits of Higher Education." Washington, DC.

Irvine, Janice M. 2002. *Talk about Sex: The Battles over Sex Education in the United States.* Berkeley: University of California Press.

Ito, Mizuko, Sonja Baumer, Matteo Bittanti, danah boyd, Rachel Cody, et al. 2010. *Hanging Out, Messing Around, and Geeking Out: Kids Living and Learning with New Media.* Cambridge, MA: MIT Press.

Jacobs, Jane. [1961] 1992. *The Death and Life of Great American Cities.* New York: Vintage.

Jarrett, Robin L. 1995. "Growing up Poor: The Family Experiences of Socially Mobile Youth in Low-Income African American Neighborhoods." *Journal of Adolescent Research* 10 (1): 111–35.

———. 1997. "African American Family and Parenting Strategies in Impoverished Neighborhoods." *Qualitative Sociology* 20 (2): 275–88.

Jencks, Christopher. 1997. Foreword to *Making Ends Meet: How Single Mothers Survive Welfare and Low-Wage Work,* by Kathryn Edin and Laura Lein, ix–xxvii. New York: Russell Sage Foundation.

Jencks, Christopher, and Susan E. Mayer. 1990. "The Social Consequences of Growing Up in a Poor Neighborhood." In *Inner-City Poverty in the United*

States, edited by L. E. Lynn Jr. and M. G. H. McGeary. Washington, DC: National Academy Press.

Jenkins, Richard. 1996. *Social Identity.* New York: Routledge.

Jensen, Gary. 1972. "Parents, Peers, and Delinquent Action: A Test of the Differential Association Perspective." *American Journal of Sociology* 78: 562–75.

Jerolmack, Colin, and Shamus Khan. 2014. "Talk Is Cheap: Ethnography and the Attitudinal Fallacy." *Sociological Methods & Research* 43 (2): 178–209.

Jerolmack, Colin, and Alexandra Murphy. 2017. "The Ethical Dilemmas and Social Scientific Trade-Offs of Masking in Ethnography." *Sociological Methods & Research* 48 (4): 801–927.

Joas, Hans. 1996. *The Creativity of Action.* Chicago: University of Chicago Press.

Johnson, Odis. 2010. "Assessing Neighborhood Racial Segregation and Macroeconomic Effects in the Education of African Americans." *Review of Educational Research* 80 (4): 527–75.

Johnson, Rucker C., Ariel Kalil, Rachel E. Dunifon, and Barbara E. Ray. 2010. *Mothers' Work and Children's Lives: Low-Income Families after Welfare Reform.* Kalamazoo, MI: W. E. Upjohn Institute.

Jones, Nikki. 2009. *Between Good and Ghetto: African American Girls and Inner-City Violence.* New Brunswick, NJ: Rutgers University Press.

Joshi, Pamela, and Karen Bogen. 2007. "Nonstandard Schedules and Young Children's Behavioral Outcomes among Working Low-Income Families." *Journal of Marriage and Family* 69: 139–56.

Kalil, Ariel, and Rachel Dunifon. 2007. "Maternal Work and Welfare Use and Child Well-Being: Evidence from 6 Years of Data from the Women's Employment Study." *Children and Youth Services Review* 29: 742–61.

Kalmijn, Matthijs. 1998. "Intermarriage and Homogamy: Causes, Patterns, Trends." *Annual Review of Sociology* 24 (1): 395–421.

Kandel, Denisee B. 1978. "Homophily, Selection, and Socialization in Adolescent Friendships." *American Journal of Sociology* 84 (2): 427–36.

Kaplan, Elaine Bell. 1997. *Not Our Kind of Girl: Unraveling the Myths of Black Teenage Motherhood.* Berkeley: University of California Press

———. 2013. *We Live in the Shadow: Inner-City Kids Tell Their Stories through Photographs.* Philadelphia, PA: Temple University Press.

Kasinitz, Philip, John H. Mollenkopf, Mary C. Waters, and Jennifer Holdaway. 2008. *Inheriting the City: The Children of Immigrants Come of Age.* New York: Russell Sage Foundation.

Katz, Jack. 1988. *Seduction of Crime.* New York: Basic Books.

Kelly, Yvonne, Afshin Zilanawala, Cara Booker, and Amanda Sacker. 2018. "Social Media Use and Adolescent Mental Health: Findings from the UK Millennium Cohort Study." *EClinicalMedicine* 6: 59–68.

Kemper, Theodore D. 1978. *A Social Interactional Theory of Emotion.* New York: Wiley.

Kim, Dongbin 2007. "The Effect of Loans on Students' Degree Attainment: Differences by Student and Institutional Characteristics." *Harvard Educational Review* 77 (1): 64–100.

Kim, Jaymelee, Sierra Williams, Erin Eldridge, and Amanda Reinke. 2021. "Digitally Shaped Ethnographic Relationships during a Global Pandemic and Beyond." *Qualitative Research.* https://doi.org/10.1177/14687941211052275.

Kiser, Laurel, J. Heston, S. Hickerson, P. Millsap, W. Nunn, and D. Pruitt. 1993. "Anticipatory Stress in Children and Adolescents." *American Journal of Psychiatry* 150 (1): 87–92.

Klebanov, Pamela Kato, Jeanne Brooks-Gunn, and Greg J. Duncan. 1994. "Does Neighborhood and Family Poverty Affect Mothers' Parenting, Mental Health, and Social Support?" *Journal of Marriage and Family* 56(2): 441–55.

Kling, Jeffrey R., Jeffrey B. Liebman, and Lawrence F. Katz. 2007. "Experimental Analysis of Neighborhood Effects." *Econometrica* 75 (1): 83–119.

Kobakhidze, Magna Nutsa, Janisa Hui, Janice Chui, and Alejandra A. González. 2021. "Research Disruptions, New Opportunities: Re-Imagining Qualitative Interview Study during the COVID-19 Pandemic." *International Journal of Qualitative Methods* 20: 1–10.

Kotlowitz, Alex. 1991. *There Are No Children Here: The Story of Two Boys Growing up in the Other America.* New York: Knopf.

Krappman, Lothar. 1998. "Amicitia, Drujba, Shin-yu, Philia, Freundschaft, Friendship: On the Cultural Diversity of a Human Relationship." In *The Company They Keep: Friendships in Childhood and Adolescence,* edited by William M. Bukowski, Andrew F. Newcomb, and Willard W. Hartup, 18–40. Cambridge: Cambridge University Press.

Kreager, Derek A., and Jeremy Staff. 2009. "The Sexual Double Standard and Adolescent Peer Acceptance." *Social Psychology Quarterly* 72 (2): 143–64.

Kuper, Leo. 1953. *Living in Towns: Selected Research Papers in Urban Sociology of the Faculty of Commerce and Social Science.* Birmingham: Cresset Press.

Ladner, Joyce A. 1971. *Tomorrow's Tomorrow: The Black Woman.* New York: Anchor.

———. 1973. *The Death of White Sociology: Essays on Race and Culture.* New York: Random House.

Ladson-Billings, Gloria 2000. "Fighting for Our Lives: Preparing Teachers to Teach African American Students." *Journal of Teacher Education* 51 (3): 206-14.

———. 2002. "I ain't writin' nuttin': Permissions to Fail and Demands to Succeed in Urban Classrooms." In *The Skin That We Speak,* edited by L. Delpit and K. Dowdy, 107-20. New York: New Press.

———. 2003. "Racialized Discourses and Ethnic Epistemologies." In *The Landscape of Qualitative Research,* edited by N.K. Denzin and Y.S. Lincoln, 398-432. London: Sage.

Lamont, Michèle. 1992. *Money, Morals, and Manners: The Culture of the French and the American Upper-Middle Class.* Chicago: University of Chicago Press.

———. 2000. *The Dignity of Working Men: Morality and the Boundaries of Race, Class, and Immigration.* Cambridge, MA: Harvard University Press.

———. 2004. "A Life of Sad, But Justified, Choices: Interviewing across (Too) Many Divides." In *Researching Race and Racism,* edited by M. Bulmer and J. Solomos, 162-71. London: Routledge.

———. 2018. "Addressing Recognition Gaps: Destigmatization and the Reduction of Inequality." *American Sociological Review* 83 (3): 419-44.

———. 2019. "From 'Having' to 'Being': Self-Worth and the Current Crisis of American Society." *British Journal of Sociology* 70: 660-707.

Lamont, Michèle, and Virag Molnar. 2001. "How Blacks Use Consumption to Shape Their Collective Identity." *Journal of Consumer Culture* 1 (1): 31-45.

———. 2002. "The Study of Boundaries in the Social Sciences." *Annual Review of Sociology* 28 (1): 167-95.

Lamont, Michèle, Graziella Moraes Silva, Jessica Welburn, Joshua Guetzkow, Nissim Mizrachi, Hanna Herzog, and Elisa Reis. 2016. *Getting Respect: Responding to Stigma and Discrimination in the United States, Brazil, and Israel.* Princeton, NJ: Princeton University Press.

Lamont, Michèle, and Ann Swidler. 2014. "Methodological Pluralism and the Possibilities and Limits of Interviewing." *Qualitative Sociology* 37 (2): 153-71.

Lane, Jeffrey. 2018. *The Digital Street.* Oxford: Oxford University Press.

Lareau, Annette. 2003. *Unequal Childhoods: Class, Race, and Family Life.* Berkeley: University of California Press.

Laub, John H., and Robert J. Sampson. 1988. "Unraveling Families and Delinquency: A Reanalysis of the Gluecks' Data." *Criminology* 26 (3): 355-80.

Laursen, Brett. 1998. "Closeness and Conflict in Adolescent Peer Relationships: Interdependence with Friends and Romantic Partners." In *The Company They Keep: Friendships in Childhood and Adolescence,* edited by William M.

Bukowski, Andrew F. Newcomb, and Willard W. Hartup, 186–210. Cambridge: Cambridge University Press.

LeBlanc, Adrian Nicole. 2004. *Random Family: Love, Drugs, Trouble, and Coming of Age in the Bronx*. New York: Scribner.

Leventhal, Tama, and Jeanne Brooks-Gunn. 2000. "The Neighborhoods They Live In: The Effects of Neighborhood Residence on Child and Adolescent Outcomes." *Psychological Bulletin* 126 (2): 309–37.

Leventhal, Tama, Véronique Dupéré, and Jeanne Brooks-Gunn. 2009. "Neighborhood Influences on Adolescent Development." In *Handbook of Adolescent Psychology*, vol. 2, edited by R. M. Lerner and L. Steinberg, 411–33. New York: Wiley.

Levy, Marc. 2012. "Two Girls Shot, One Dead on Willow Street." *Cambridge Day*, June 3.

Lewis, David Levering. 2009. *W. E. B. Du Bois: A Biography*. New York: Henry Holt.

Liebow, Elliot. 1967. *Tally's Corner: A Study of Negro Streetcorner Men*. Boston, MA: Little, Brown.

Light, Audrey, and Wayne Strayer. 2000. "Determinants of College Completion: School Quality or Student Ability?" *Journal of Human Resources* 35 (2): 299–332.

Linds, Warren, Linda Goulet, and Alison Sammel, eds. 2010. *Emancipatory Practices: Adult/Youth Engagement for Social and Environmental Justice*. Boston: Sense.

Ling, Richard. 2008. *New Tech, New Ties: How Mobile Communication Is Reshaping Social Cohesion*. Cambridge, MA: MIT Press.

Link, Bruce G., and Jo C. Phelan. 2001. "Conceptualizing Stigma." *Annual Review of Sociology* 27 (1): 363–85.

Loebach, Janet, Sarah Little, Adina Cox, and Patsy Eubanks Owens, eds. 2020. *The Routledge Handbook of Designing Public Spaces for Young People: Processes, Practices and Policies for Youth Inclusion*. New York: Routledge.

Lohfink, Mandy Martin, and Michael Paulsen. 2005. "Comparing the Determinants of Persistence for First-Generation and Continuing-Generation Students." *Journal of College Student Development* 46 (4): 409–28.

Lorde, Audre. 1982. *Zami: A New Spelling of My Name*. New York: Crossing Press.
———. 1984. *Sister Outsider: Essays and Speeches*. New York: Crossing Press.

Lotan, Gilad, Erhardt Graeff, Mike Ananny, Devin Gaffney, Ian Pearce, and Danah Boyd. 2011. "The Arab Spring| The Revolutions Were Tweeted: Information Flows during the 2011 Tunisian and Egyptian Revolutions." *International Journal of Communication* 5: 31.

Lotkowski, Veronica A., Steven B. Robbins, and Richard J. Noeth. 2004. "The Role of Academic and Non-Academic Factors in Improving College Retention." ACT Policy Report. https://eric.ed.gov/?id=ED485476.

Lovejoy, Meg. 2001. "Disturbances in the Social Body: Differences in Body Image and Eating Problems among African American and White Women." *Gender and Society* 15 (2): 239–61.

Lu, Weixu, and Keith N. Hampton. 2017. "Beyond the Power of Networks: Differentiating Network Structure from Social Media Affordances for Perceived Social Support." *New Media & Society* 19 (6): 861–79.

Luker, Kristin. 2006. *When Sex Goes to School: Warring Views on sex—and Sex Education—since the Sixties.* New York: Norton.

MacLeod, Jay. 1987. *Ain't No Makin' It: Aspirations and Attainment in a Low-Income Neighborhood.* Boulder, CO: Westview.

Magson, Natasha R., Justin Freeman, Ronald Rapee, Cele Richardson, Ella Oar, and Jasmine Fardouly. 2021. "Risk and Protective Factors for Prospective Changes in Adolescent Mental Health during the COVID-19 Pandemic." *Journal of Youth and Adolescence* 50: 44–57.

Mahoney, Joseph L., Reed W. Larson, and Jacquelynne S. Eccles, eds. 2005. *Organized Activities As Contexts of Development: Extracurricular Activities, After School and Community Programs.* Mahwah, NJ: Psychology Press.

Maimon, David, and Christopher R. Browning. 2010. "Unstructured Socializing, Collective Efficacy, and Violent Behavior among Urban Youth." *Criminology* 48 (2): 443–74.

Makice, Kevin. 2009. "Phatics and the Design of Community." In *CHI '09 Extended Abstracts on Human Factors in Computing Systems,* 3133–36. CHI EA '09. New York: ACM.

Malinowski, Bronislaw. 1923. "The Problem of Meaning in Primitive Languages." In *The Meaning of Meaning,* edited by Charles K. Ogden and Ian A. Richards, 146–52. London: Routledge.

Manago, Adriana, Tamara Taylor, and Patricia Greenfield. 2012. "Me and My 400 friends: The Anatomy of college Students' Facebook Networks, Their Communication Patterns, and Wellbeing." *Developmental Psychology* 48: 369–80.

Marciano, Laura, Michelle Ostroumova, Peter Johannes Schulz, and Anne-Linda Camerini. 2021. "Digital Media Use and Adolescents' Mental Health during the Covid-19 Pandemic: A Systematic Review and Meta-Analysis." *Frontiers in Public Health* 9. doi: 10.3389/fpubh.2021.793868.

Marwick, Alice, and danah boyd. 2011. "To See and Be Seen: Celebrity Practice on Twitter." *Convergence: The International Journal of Research into New Media Technologies* 17 (2): 139–58.

———. 2014a. "'It's Just Drama': Teen Perspectives on Conflict and Aggression in a Networked Era." *Journal of Youth Studies* 17 (9): 1187–1204.

———. 2014b. "Networked Privacy: How Teenagers Negotiate Context in Social Media." *New Media and Society* 16 (7): 1051–67.

Marx, Karl. [1867] 2010. *Capital: A Critique of Political Economy, Vol. 1.* n.p.: CreateSpace Independent Publishing Platform.

Massachusetts Department of Elementary and Secondary Education. 2018. "School and District Profiles." http://profiles.doe.mass.edu/general/general.aspx?topNavID=1&leftNavId=100&orgcode=00490506&orgtypecode=6.

Masten, Ann S., and J. Douglas Coatsworth. 1998. "The Development of Competence in Favorable and Unfavorable Environments: Lessons from Research on Successful Children." *American Psychologist* 53 (2): 205–20.

Matsueda, Ross L., and Kathleen Anderson. 1998. "The Dynamics of Delinquent Peers and Delinquent Behavior." *Criminology* 36 (2): 269–308.

Mauss, Marcel. 1967. *The Gift: Forms and Functions of Exchange in Archaic Societies.* New York: Norton.

Mayer, Susan. 1991. "How Much Does a High School's Racial and Socioeconomic Mix Affect Graduation and Teenage Fertility Rates." In *The Urban Underclass,* edited by Christopher Jencks and Paul E. Peterson, 321–41. Washington, DC: Brookings Institution.

Mazelis, Joan Maya. 2017. *Surviving Poverty: Creating Sustainable Ties among the Poor.* New York: New York University Press.

McBride Murry, Velma. 1996. "Inner City Girls of Color: Unmarried, Sexually Active Nonmothers." In *Urban Girls: Resisting Stereotypes, Creating Identities,* edited by Bonnie Leadbeater and Niobe Way, 272–90. New York: New York University Press.

McKee, James. 1993. *Sociology and the Race Problem.* Urbana: University of Illinois Press.

McLoyd, Vonnie C. 1990. "The Impact of Economic Hardship on Black Families and Children: Psychological Distress, Parenting, and Socioemotional Development." *Child Development* 61 (2): 311–46.

McMillan Cottom, Tressie. 2017. *Lower Ed: The Troubling Rise of For-Profit Colleges in the New Economy.* New York: New Press.

———. 2019. *Thick: And Other Essays.* New York: New Press.

McPherson, Miller, Lynn Smith-Lovin, and James M. Cook. 2001. "Birds of a Feather: Homophily in Social Networks." *Annual Review of Sociology* 27 (1): 415–44.

McRobbie, Angela. [1991] 2000. *Feminism and Youth Culture.* 2nd ed. New York: Macmillan.

———.2008. "Pornographic Permutations." *Communication Review* 11 (3): 225–36.

Mead, George Herbert. 1934. *Mind, Self and Society from the Standpoint of a Social Behaviorist.* Chicago: University of Chicago Press.

Merry, Sally Engle. 1981. *Urban Danger: Life in a Neighborhood of Strangers.* Philadelphia, PA: Temple University Press.

Metzler, Carol, John Noell, Anthony A. Biglan, et al. 1994. "The Social Context for Risky Sexual Behavior among Adolescents." *Journal of Behavioral Medicine* 17 (4): 419–38.

Milkie, Melissa A. 1999. "Social Comparisons, Reflected Appraisals, and Mass Media: The Impact of Pervasive Beauty Images on Black and White Girls' Self-Concepts." *Social Psychology Quarterly* 62 (2): 190–210.

Miller, Brent, and Brad Benson. 1999. "Romantic and Sexual Relationship Development during Adolescence." In *The Development of Romantic Relationships in Adolescence,* edited by W. Furman, B. B. Brown, and C. Feiring, 99–121. New York: Cambridge University Press.

Miller, Jody. 2008. *Getting Played: African American Girls, Urban Inequality, and Gendered Violence.* New York: New York University Press.

Milner, Murray. 2015. *Freaks, Geeks, and Cool Kids: Teenagers in an Era of Consumerism, Standardized Tests, and Social Media.* London: Routledge.

Mische, Ann, 2009. "Projects and Possibilities: Researching Futures in Action." *Sociological Forum* 24: 694–704.

Mohanty, Chandra. 1991. "Under Western Eyes: Feminist Scholarship and Colonial Discourses." In *Third World Women and the Politics of Feminism,* edited by Chandra Talpade Mohanty, Ann Russo, and Lourdes Torres, 51–80. Bloomington: Indiana University Press.

Morris, Monique. 2015. *Pushout: The Criminalization of Black Girls in Schools.* New York: New Press.

Nadal, Kevin, Katie E. Griffin, Yinglee Wong, Kristin C. Davidoff, and Lindsey S. Davis. 2017. "The Injurious Relationship between Racial Microaggressions and Physical Health: Implications for Social Work." *Journal of Ethnic & Cultural Diversity in Social Work* 26: 1–2, 6–17.

Naples, Nancy A. 2013. *Feminism and Method: Ethnography, Discourse Analysis, and Activist Research.* New York: Routledge.

Nelson, Margaret. 2000. "Single Mothers and Social Support: The Commitment to, and Retreat from, Reciprocity." *Qualitative Sociology* 23 (3): 291–317.

Ness, Cindy D. 2004. "Why Girls Fight: Female Youth Violence in the Inner City." *Annals of the American Academy of Political and Social Science* 595 (1): 32–48.

——. 2010. *Why Girls Fight: Female Youth Violence in the Inner City.* New York: New York University Press.

Newman, Katherine S. 1999. *No Shame In My Game: The Working Poor in the Inner City.* New York: Vintage.

Nielsen, Kelly. 2015. "'Fake It 'til You Make It': Why Community College Students' Aspirations 'Hold Steady.'" *Sociology of Education* 88 (4): 265–83.

Nightingale, Carl Husemoller. 1993. *On the Edge: a History of Poor Black Children and Their American Dreams.* New York: Basic Books.

Nunez, Anne-Marie, and Stephanie Cuccaro-Alamin. 1998. "First-Generation Students: Undergraduates Whose Parents Never Enrolled in Postsecondary Education." US Department of Education, National Center for Education Statistics, Washington, DC.

Oakley, Ann. 1981. "Interviewing Women: A Contradiction in Terms." In *Doing Feminist Research,* edited by Helen Roberts, 30–62. London: Routledge.

O'Connor, Pat. 1992. *Friendships between Women: A Critical Review.* Hertfordshire: Harvester Wheatsheaf.

Okabe-Miyamoto, Karynna, and Sonja S. Lyubomirsky. 2021. "Social Connection and Well-Being during COVID-19." *World Happiness Report* 2021, 131.

Orben, Amy, Livia Tomova, and Sarah-Jayne Blakemore. 2020. "The Effects of Social Deprivation on Adolescent Development and Mental Health." *Lancet Child & Adolescent Health* 4: 634–40.

Osgood, D. Wayne, and Amy L. Anderson. 2004. "Unstructured Socializing and Rates of Delinquency." *Criminology* 42 (3): 519–50.

Overstreet, Stacy, and Shawnee Braun. 2000. "Exposure to Community Violence and Post-Traumatic Stress Symptoms: Mediating Factors." *American Journal of Orthopsychiatry* 70 (2): 263–71.

Palladino, Grace. 1996. *Teenagers: An American History.* New York: Basic Books.

Park, Robert E., Ernest W. Burgess, and R. D. McKenzie. 1925. *The City: Suggestions for Investigation of Human Behavior in the Urban Environment.* Chicago: University of Chicago Press.

Park, Toby J. 2013. "Stopout and Time for Work: An Analysis of Degree Trajectories for Community College Students." Paper presented at the

Annual Meeting of the Association for the Study of Higher Education, November, St. Louis, MO.

Parker, Brock. 2012. "Cambridge Shooting Victim Addresses High School Graduation by Video." Boston.com, June. http://archive.boston.com/yourtown /news/cambridge/2012/06/cambridge_shooting_victim_a-ddr.html.

Pascarella, Ernest T., and Patrick T. Terenzini. 2005. *How College Affects Students: A Third Decade of Research.* San Francisco: Jossey-Bass.

Pascoe, C. J. 2007. *Dude, You're a Fag.* Berkeley: University of California Press.

———. 2011. "Resource and Risk: Youth Sexuality and New Media Use." *Sexuality Research and Social Policy* 8: 5–17.

Pattillo, Mary E. 2007. *Black on the Block: The Politics of Race and Class in the City.* Chicago: University of Chicago Press.

Pattillo-McCoy, Mary. 1999. *Black Picket Fences: Privilege and Peril among the Black Middle Class.* Chicago: University of Chicago Press.

Patton, Desmond, Jeffrey Lane, Patrick Leonard, Jamie Macbeth, and Jocelyn R. Smith-Lee. 2016. "Gang Violence on the Digital Street: Case Study of a South Side Chicago Gang Member's Twitter Communication." *New Media & Society* 19 (7): 1000–1018.

Paulle, Bowen. 2013. *Toxic Schools: High-Poverty Education In New York and Amsterdam.* Chicago: University of Chicago Press.

Petersen, Anne C., Pamela A. Sarigiani, and Robert E. Kennedy. 1991. "Adolescent Depression: Why More Girls?" *Journal of Youth and Adolescence* 20 (2): 247–71.

Pew Research Center. 2018a. "Teens, Social Media and Technology." Report. Washington, DC.

———. 2018b. "Teens' Social Media Habits and Experiences." Report. Washington, DC.

Pike, Gary R., and George D. Kuh. 2005. "First- and Second-Generation College Students: A Comparison of Their Engagement and Intellectual Development." *Journal of Higher Education* 76 (3): 276.

Polanyi, Karl. 1944. *The Great Transformation.* New York: Farrar & Rinehart.

Polletta, Francesca. 1998. "'It Was Like a Fever . . .': Narrative and Identity in Social Protest." *Social Problems* 45 (2): 137–59.

Polly, Lisa, Stephen Vodanovich, J. D. Watt, and M. J. Blanchard. 1993. "The Effects of Attributional Processes on Boredom Proneness." *Journal of Social Behavior and Personality* 8 (1): 123–32.

Popkin, Susan J., Tama Leventhal, and Gretchen Weismann. 2010. "Girls in the 'Hood: How Safety Affects the Life Chances of Low-Income Girls." *Urban Affairs Review* 45 (6): 715–44.

Portes, Alejandro. 2000. "The Two Meanings of Social Capital." *Sociological Forum* 15 (1): 1–12.

Portes, Alejandro, and Julia Sensenbrenner. 1993. "Embeddedness and Immigration: Notes on the Social Determinants of Economic Action." *American Journal of Sociology* 98 (6): 1320–50.

Portes, Alejandro, and Min Zhou. 1993. "The New Second Generation: Segmented Assimilation and Its Variants." *Annals of the American Academy of Political and Social Science* 530 (1): 74–96.

Posse Foundation. 2018. "About Posse." https://www.possefoundation.org/about-posse.

Pugh, Allison. 2009. *Longing and Belonging: Parents, Children, and Consumer Culture.* Berkeley: University of California Press.

———. 2011. "Distinction, Boundaries or Bridges? Children, Inequality, and the Uses of Consumer Culture." *Poetics* 39: 1–18.

Rainwater, Lee. 1970. *Behind Ghetto Walls: Black Family Life in a Federal Slum.* Chicago: Aldine.

Ray, Ranita. 2018a. "Identity of Distance: How Economically Marginalized Black and Latina Women Navigate Risk Discourse and Employ Feminist Ideals." *Social Problems* 65 (4): 456–72.

———. 2018b. *The Making of a Teenage Service Class: Poverty and Mobility in an American City.* Oakland: University of California Press.

Ray, Ranita, and Korey Tillman. 2019. "Envisioning a Feminist Urban Ethnography: Structure, Culture, and New Directions in Poverty Studies." *Sociology Compass* 1–10.

Rich, Adrienne. 1980. *Compulsory Heterosexuality and Lesbian Existence.* Chicago: University of Chicago Press.

Richardson, Joseph B., and Christopher St. Vil. 2016. "'Rolling Dolo': Desistance from Delinquency and Negative Peer Relationships over the Early Adolescent Life-Course." *Ethnography* 17 (1): 47–71.

Richardson, Richard C., and Elizabeth Fisk Skinner. 1992. "Helping First-Generation Minority Students Achieve Degrees." *New Directions for Community Colleges* 80: 29–43.

Rios, Victor M. 2011. *Punished: Policing the Lives of Black and Latino Boys.* New York: New York University Press.

———. 2015. "Decolonizing the White Space In Urban Ethnography." *City & Community* 14: 258–61.

Rivera, Lauren A. 2015. *Pedigree: How Elite Students Get Elite Jobs.* Princeton, NJ: Princeton University Press.

Robbins, Joel 2013. "Beyond the Suffering Subject: Toward an Anthropology of the Good." *Journal of the Royal Anthropological Institute* 19: 447–62.

Rosenbaum, James E. 2004. *Beyond College for All: Career Paths for the Forgotten Half.* New York: Russell Sage Foundation.

Rosenbaum, James, Caitlin Ahearn, Kelly Becker, and Janet Rosenbaum. 2015. "The New Forgotten Half and Research Directions to Support Them." William T. Grant Foundation Inequality Paper. New York: William T. Grant Foundation.

Rosenberg, Morris. 1990. "Reflexivity and Emotions." *Social Psychology Quarterly* 53 (1): 3–12.

Roseneil, Sasha. 2004. "Why We Should Care about Friends: An Argument for Queering the Care Imaginary in Social Policy." *Social Policy and Society* 3 (4): 409–20.

Roseneil, Sasha, and Shelley Budgeon. 2004. "Cultures of Intimacy and Care beyond 'the Family': Personal Life and Social Change in the Early 21st Century." *Current Sociology* 52: 135–59.

Rosich, Katherine. 2007. "Race, Ethnicity, and the Criminal Justice System." American Sociological Association, Washington, DC.

Roska, Josipa, Eric Grodsky, Richard Arum, and Adam Gamoran. 2007. "Changes in Higher Education and Social Stratification in the United States." In *Stratification in Higher Education,* edited by Yossi Shavit, Richard Arum, and Adam Gamoran, 165–91. Palo Alto, CA: Stanford University Press.

Roth, Julius A. 1963 *Timetables: Structuring the Passage of Time in Hospital Treatment and Other Careers.* Indianapolis, IN: Bobbs-Merrill.

Roy, Donald D. 1959 "Banana Time: Job Satisfaction and Informal Interaction." *Human Organization* 18: 158–68.

Rumbaut, Rubén G. 1997. "Ties That Bind: Immigration and Immigrant Families." SSRN Scholarly Paper ID 1888727. Rochester, NY: Social Science Research Network.

Russell, Stephen T. 2005. "Conceptualizing Positive Adolescent Sexuality Development." *Sexuality Research and Social Policy* 2 (3): 4.

Rutter, Michael. 1979. *Fifteen Thousand Hours: Secondary Schools and Their Effects on Children.* Cambridge, MA: Harvard University Press.

Sacks, Harvey, Emanuel A. Schegloff, and Gail Jefferson. 1974. "A Simplest Systematics for the Organization of Turn-Taking for Conversation." *Language* 50 (4): 696–735.

Sahi, Razia, Miriam Schwyck, Carolyn C. Parkinson, et al. 2021. "Having More Virtual Interaction Partners during COVID-19 Physical Distancing Measures May Benefit Mental Health." *Scientific Reports* 11: 18273.

Sahlins, Marshall. 1972. *Stone Age Economics.* New Brunswick, NJ: Routledge.

Sales, Nancy Jo. 2016. *American Girls: Social Media and the Secret Lives of Teenagers.* New York: Knopf.

Sampson, Robert. 2012. *Great American City: Chicago and the Enduring Neighborhood Effect.* Chicago: University of Chicago Press.

Sampson, Robert J., and W. Byron Groves. 1989. "Community Structure and Crime: Testing Social-Disorganization Theory." *American Journal of Sociology* 94 (4): 774–802.

Sampson, Robert J., Jeffrey D. Morenoff, and Felton Earls. 1999. "Beyond Social Capital: Spatial Dynamics of Collective Efficacy for Children." *American Sociological Review* 64 (5): 633. doi:10.2307/2657367.

Sampson, Robert, Jeffrey Morenoff, and Thomas Gannon-Rowley. 2002. "Assessing 'Neighborhood Effects': Social Processes and New Directions in Research." *Annual Review of Sociology* 28 (1): 443–78.

Schalet, Amy. 2000. "Raging Hormones, Regulated Love: Adolescent Sexuality and the Constitution of the Modern Individual in the United States and the Netherlands." *Body & Society* 6 (1): 75–105.

———. 2004. "Must We Fear Adolescent Sexuality?" *Medscape General Medicine* 6 (4): 44.

Scheff, Thomas. 1990. *Microsociology: Discourse, Emotion, and Social Structure.* Chicago: University of Chicago Press.

———. 1994. *Bloody Revenge: Emotions, Nationalism, and War.* Boulder, CO: Westview Press.

Scheff, Thomas J., and Suzanne M. Retzinger. 1991. *Emotions and Violence: Shame and Rage in Destructive Conflicts.* Lexington, MA: Lexington Books.

Schooler, Deborah, and Elizabeth A. Daniels. 2014. "'I Am Not a Skinny Toothpick and Proud of It': Latina Adolescents' Ethnic Identity and Responses to Mainstream Media Images." *Body Image* 11 (1): 11–18.

Schwab-Stone, Mary, Tim Ayers, Wesley Kasprow, et al. 1995. "No Safe Haven: A Study of Violence Exposure in an Urban Community." *Journal of the American Academy of Child and Adolescent Psychiatry* 34 (10): 1343–52.

Schwab-Stone, Mary, Chuansheng Chen, Ellen Greenberger, et al. 1999. "No Safe Haven. II: The Effects of Violence Exposure on Urban Youth."

Journal of the American Academy of Child and Adolescent Psychiatry 38 (4): 359–67.

Sennett, Richard, and Jonathan Cobb. 1972. *The Hidden Injuries of Class.* New York: Norton.

Sharkey, Patrick. 2013. *Stuck in Place: Urban Neighborhoods and the End of Progress toward Racial Equality.* Chicago: University of Chicago Press.

Sharpe, Christina. 2016. *In the Wake: On Blackness and Being.* Durham, NC: Duke University Press.

Shaw, Clifford R. 1931. *The Jack-Roller: A Delinquent Boy's Own Story.* Chicago: University of Chicago Press.

Shaw, Clifford R., and Henry D. McKay. 1942. *Juvenile Delinquency and Urban Areas: A Study of Rates of Delinquents in Relation to Differential Characteristics of Local Communities in American Cities.* Behavioral Research Fund Monographs. Chicago: University of Chicago Press.

Shedd, Carla. 2015. *Unequal City: Race, Schools, and Perceptions of Injustice.* New York: Russell Sage Foundation.

Shisslak, C. M., M. Crago, and L. S. Estes. 1995. "The Spectrum of Eating Disturbances." *International Journal of Eating Disorders* 18 (3): 209–19.

Silva, Jennifer M. 2013. *Coming Up Short: Working-Class Adulthood in an Age of Uncertainty.* New York: Oxford University Press.

Singer, Mark I., Trina Menden Anglin, Li yu Song, and Lisa Lunghofer. 1995. "Adolescents' Exposure to Violence and Associated Symptoms of Psychological Trauma." *JAMA* 273 (6): 477–82.

Small, Mario Luis. 2004. *Villa Victoria: The Transformation of Social Capital in a Boston Barrio.* Chicago: University of Chicago Press.

———. 2009. *Unanticipated Gains: Origins of Network Inequality in Everyday Life.* Oxford: Oxford University Press.

———. 2014. "No Two Ghettos Are Alike." *Chronicle Review,* March 17.

———. 2015. "De-Exoticizing Ghetto Poverty: On the Ethics of Representation in Urban Ethnography." *City and Community* 14 (4): 352–58.

Small, Mario, and Leah Gose. 2020. "How Do Low-Income People Form Survival Networks? Routine Organizations as Brokers." *Annals of the American Academy of Political and Social Science* 689 (1): 89–109.

Smith, Dorothy. 1987. *The Everyday World as Problematic: A Feminist Sociology.* Boston, MA: Northeastern University Press.

———. 1990. *The Conceptual Practices of Power.* Boston, MA: Northeastern University Press.

Smith, Sandra Susan. 2007. *Lone Pursuit: Distrust and Defensive Individualism among the Black Poor.* New York: Russell Sage Foundation.

Snellman, Kaisa, M. Jennifer Silva, B. Carl Frederick, and Robert Putnam. 2015. "The Engagement Gap." *Annals of the American Academy of Political and Social Science* 657 (1): 194–207.

Snow, David, and Leon Anderson. 1987. "Identity Work among The Homeless: The Verbal Construction and Avowal of Personal Identities." *American Journal of Sociology* 92 (6): 1336–71.

Snow, Kim, and Varda Mann-Feder. 2013. "Peer-Centered Practice: A Theoretical Framework for Intervention with Young People in and from Care." *Child Welfare* (92) 4: 75–83.

Snyder, Thomas D., Cristobal de Brey, and Sally Dillow. 2019. "Digest of Education Statistics 2017." National Center for Education Statistics, Washington, DC.

Snyder, Thomas D., and Sally A. Dillow. 2013. "Digest of Education Statistics 2013." US Department of Education, Washington, DC.

Sorokin, Pitirim, and Robert K. Merton. 1937. "Social Time: A Methodological and Functional Analysis." *American Journal of Sociology* 42: 615–29.

South, Scott J., and Eric P. Baumer. 2000. "Deciphering Community and Race Effects on Adolescent Premarital Childbearing." *Social Forces* 78 (4): 1379–1407.

Spencer, Margaret, and Sanford Dornbusch. 1990. "Challenges in Studying Minority Youth." In *At the Threshold: The Developing Adolescent,* edited by S. Feldman and G. Elliot, 123–46. Cambridge, MA: Harvard University Press.

Stack, Carol B. 1974. *All Our Kin.* New York: Basic Books.

Stanton-Salazar, Ricardo D., and Stephanie Urso Spina. 2000. "The Network Orientations of Highly Resilient Urban Minority Youth: A Network-Analytic Account of Minority Socialization and Its Educational Implications." *Urban Review* 32 (3): 227–36.

———. 2005. "Adolescent Peer Networks as a Context for Social and Emotional Support." *Youth & Society* 36 (4): 379–417.

Steinberg, Laurence 2004. "Risk Taking in Adolescence: What Changes, and Why?" *Annals of the New York Academy of Sciences* 1021: 51–58.

Stepick, Alex. 1998. *Pride against Prejudice: Haitians in the United States.* Boston, MA: Allyn & Bacon.

Stepick, Alex, Carol Dutton Stepick, Emmanuel Eugene, Deborah Teed, and Yves Labissiere. 2001. "Shifting Identities and Intergenerational Conflict:

Growing up Haitian in Miami." In *Ethnicities: Children of Immigrants in America,* edited by Rubén Rumbaut and Alejandro Portes, 229–66. Berkeley: University of California Press.

Stevenson, Howard C. 1998. "Raising Safe Villages: Cultural-Ecological Factors That Influence the Emotional Adjustment of Adolescents." *Journal of Black Psychology* 24 (1): 44–59.

Stuart, Forrest. 2020. *Ballad of the Bullet: Gangs, Drill Music, and the Power of Online Infamy.* Princeton, NJ: Princeton University Press.

Stuber, Jenny. 2011. *Inside the College Gates: How Class and Culture Matter in Higher Education.* Lanham, MD: Lexington Books.

Subrahmanyam, Kaveri, and Patricia Greenfield. 2008. "Online Communication and Adolescent Relationships." *Future of Children* 18 (1): 119–46.

Sue, Derald Wing, and Lisa Spanierman. 2010. *Microaggressions in Everyday Life: Race, Gender, and Sexual Orientation.* New York: Wiley.

Sullivan, Mercer L. 1989. *"Getting Paid": Youth Crime and Work in the Inner City.* Ithaca, NY: Cornell University Press.

Sutton, Jeannette N., Leysia Palen, and Irina Shklovski. 2008. "Backchannels on the Front Lines: Emergency Uses of Social Media in the 2007 Southern California Wildfires." In *Proceedings of the 5th International ISCRAM Conference,* edited by F. Fiedrich and B. Van de Walle, 624–31. Washington, DC: ISCRAM.

Tajfel, Henri. 1974. "Social Identity and Intergroup Behaviour." *Information (International Social Science Council)* 13 (2): 65–93.

Terenzini, Patrick T., Leonard Springer, Patricia M. Yaeger, Ernest T. Pascarella, and Amaury Nora. 1996. "First-Generation College Students: Characteristics, Experiences, and Cognitive Development." *Research in Higher Education* 37 (1): 1–22.

Tharps, Lori L. 2014. "The Case for Black with a Capital B." *New York Times,* November 18.

Third, Amanda, Philippa Collin, Lucas Walsh, and Rosalyn Black. 2019. *Young People in Digital Society: Control Shift.* London: Palgrave Macmillan.

Thoits, Peggy A. 1991. "Gender Differences in Coping with Emotional Distress." In *The Social Context of Coping,* edited by John Eckenrode, 107–38. Springer Series on Stress and Coping. New York: Springer.

Thomas, William I. 1923. *The Unadjusted Girl.* Boston: Little, Brown.

Thorne, Barrie. 1993. *Gender Play: Girls and Boys in School.* New Brunswick, NJ: Rutgers University Press.

Thrasher, Frederic Milton. 1927. *The Gang: A Study of 1,313 Gangs in Chicago.* Abridged ed. Chicago: University of Chicago Press.

Tolman, Deborah L. 1994. "Doing Desire: Adolescent Girls' Struggles for/with Sexuality." *Gender & Society* 8 (3): 324–42.

———. 2005. *Dilemmas of Desire: Teenage Girls Talk about Sexuality.* Cambridge, MA: Harvard University Press.

Tolman, Deborah, and Sara McClelland. 2011. "Normative Sexuality Development in Adolescence: A Decade in Review, 2000–2009." *Journal of Research on Adolescence* 21 (1): 232–55.

Turkle, Sherry. 2011. *Alone Together: Why We Expect More from Technology and Less from Each Other.* New York: Basic Books.

Turner, Jonathan H., and Jan E. Stets. 2006. "Sociological Theories of Human Emotions." *Annual Review of Sociology* 32 (1): 25–52.

Tyson, Karolyn. 2011. *Integration Interrupted: Tracking, Black Students, and Acting White after Brown.* New York: Oxford University Press.

Upcraft, M. Lee, John N. Gardner, and Betsy O. Barefoot, eds. 2004. *Challenging and Supporting the First-Year Student: A Handbook for Improving the First Year of College.* San Francisco: Jossey-Bass.

Urbanik, Marta-Marika, and Robert Roks. 2020. "GangstaLife: Fusing Urban Ethnography with Netnography in Gang Studies." *Qualitative Sociology* 43: 213–33.

US Census. 2013. "Selected Characteristics of the Native and Foreign-Born Populations." Table ID: S0501. American Community Survey.

US Department of Education. 2014. "Digest of Education Statistics." National Center for Education Statistics, Washington, DC. https://nces.ed.gov /programs/digest/d14/tables/dt14_502.30.asp.

US Department of Health and Human Services. 2001. "Women and Smoking: A Report of the Surgeon General." Washington, DC.

———. 2016. "Youth Risk Behavior Surveillance—United States, 2015." Centers for Disease Control and Prevention, Washington, DC.

US Department of Housing and Urban Development. 2012. "Moving to Work Annual Plan, Cambridge Housing Authority." Washington, DC.

Vaidyanathan, Brandon, Simranjit Khalsa, and Elaine Howard Ecklund. 2016. "Gossip as Social Control: Informal Sanctions on Ethical Violations in Scientific Workplaces." *Social Problems* 63 (4): 554–72.

Vaisey, Stephen. 2008. "Socrates, Skinner, and Aristotle: Three Ways of Thinking about Culture in Action1." *Sociological Forum* 23 (3): 603–13.

Vaisey, Stephen, and Omar Lizardo. 2010. "Can Cultural Worldviews Influence Network Composition?" *Social Forces* 88 (4): 1595–1618.

Van Der Kolk, Bessel. 2015. *The Body Keeps the Score: Brain, Mind, and Body in the Healing of Trauma.* New York: Penguin.

Veblen, Thorstein. [1899] 1994. *The Theory of the Leisure Class.* New York: Dover.

Venkatesh, Sudhir. 2000. *American Project: The Rise and Fall of a Modern Ghetto.* Cambridge, MA: Harvard University Press.

———. 2006. *Off The Books: The Underground Economy of the Urban Poor.* Cambridge, MA: Harvard University Press.

———. 2008. *Gang Leader for a Day: A Rogue Sociologist Takes to the Streets.* New York Penguin.

Vygotsky, Lev. 1978. *Mind in Society: The Development of Higher Psychological Processes.* Edited by Michael Cole, Vera John-Steiner, Sylvia Scribner, and Ellen Souberman. Cambridge, MA: Harvard University Press.

Wacquant, Loïc. 2005. *Body & Soul: Notebooks of an Apprentice Boxer.* Oxford: Oxford University Press.

Wade, Lisa, and Caroline Heldman. 2012. "Hooking Up and Opting Out: What Students Learn about Sex in Their First Year of College." In *Ex for Life: From Virginity to Viagra, How Sexuality Changes throughout Our Lives,* edited by John DeLamater and John Carpenter, 128–45. New York: New York University Press.

Warburton, Edward C., Rosio Bugarin, and Anne-Marie Nuñez. 2001. "Bridging the Gap: Academic Preparation and Postsecondary Success of First-Generation Students." US Department of Education, National Center for Education Statistics, Washington, DC.

Ward, Janie Victoria, and Beth Cooper Benjamin. 2004. "Women, Girls, and the Unfinished Work of Connection: A Critical Review of American Girls' Studies." In *All about the Girl: Culture, Power, and Identity,* edited by Anita Harris, 15–28. New York: Routledge.

Waters, Mary C. 1999. *Black Identities: West Indian Immigrant Dreams and American Realities.* Cambridge, MA: Harvard University Press.

Wellman, Barry, and S. Wortley. 1990. "Different Strokes from Different Folks." *American Journal of Sociology* 96: 558–88.

Werner, Emmy E., and Ruth S. Smith. 1992. *Overcoming the Odds: High Risk Children from Birth to Adulthood.* Ithaca, NY: Cornell University Press.

West, Candace, and Don H. Zimmerman. 1987. "Doing Gender." *Gender and Society* 1 (2): 125–51.

Weston, Kath. 1991. *Families We Choose: Lesbians, Gay Men and Kinship.* New York: Columbia University Press.

Whyte, William Foote. 1943. *Street Corner Society: The Social Structure of an Italian Slum*. Chicago: University of Chicago Press.

Wiggins, Tanya G. 2018. "Critical Friendship: Helping Youth Lift as They Climb Together." *Afterschool Matters* 27: 1–9.

Wilkins, Amy C. 2008. *Wannabes, Goths, and Christians: The Boundaries of Sex, Style, and Status*. Chicago: University of Chicago Press.

Williams, Terry, and William Kornblum. 1988. *Growing Up Poor*. Lexington, MA: Lexington Books.

Willis, Paul. 1977. *Learning to Labour: How Working Class Kids Get Working Class Jobs*. Farnborough: Saxon House.

Wilson, Timothy, David Reinhard, Erin Westgate, et al. 2014. "Just Think: The Challenges of the Disengaged Mind." *Science* 345: 75–77.

Wilson, William Julius. 1987. *The Truly Disadvantaged: The Inner City, the Underclass, and Public Policy*. Chicago: University of Chicago Press.

Winant, Howard. 2007. "The Dark Side of the Force: One Hundred Years of the Sociology of Race." In *Sociology in America: A History*, edited by C. Calhoun, 535–71. Chicago: University of Chicago Press.

Winiarski-Jones, Teresa T. 1988. "Adolescent Peer Groups: Their Formation and Effects on Attitudes towards Education and Academic Performance." *Research in Education* 40: 50–58.

Woods, Tyler, and Devlin Hanson. 2016. "Demographic Trends of Children of Immigrants." Washington, DC: Urban Institute.

Yates, Dave, and Scott Paquette. 2011. "Emergency Knowledge Management and Social Media Technologies: A Case Study of the 2010 Haitian Earthquake." *International Journal of Information Management* 31 (1): 6–13.

Yosso, Tara. 2005. "Whose Culture Has Capital? A Critical Race Theory Discussion of Community Cultural Wealth." *Race Ethnicity and Education* 8 (1): 69–91.

Young, Alford A. 2004. "Experiences in Ethnographic Interviewing about Race: The Inside and Outside of it." *Researching Race and Racism*, edited by Martin Bulmer and John Solomos, 187–202. London: Routledge.

———. 2008. "White Ethnographers on the Experience of African American Men." In *White Logic, White Methods: Racism and Methodology*, edited by Tukufu Zuberi and Eduardo Bonilla-Silva, 179–200. Lanham, MD: Rowman & Littlefield.

Zelizer, Viviana. 1997. *The Social Meaning of Money*. Princeton, NJ: Princeton University Press.

———. 2005. *The Purchase of Intimacy.* Princeton, NJ: Princeton University Press.

———. 2011. *Economic Lives: How Culture Shapes the Economy.* Princeton, NJ: Princeton University Press.

Zephir, Flore. 2001. *Trends in Ethnic Identification among Second-Generation Haitian Immigrants in New York City.* Westport, CT: Praeger.

Zerubavel, Eviatar. 1981. *Hidden Rhythms, Schedules, and Calendars in Social Life.* Berkeley: University of California Press.

Zuberi, Tukufu. 2003. *Thicker Than Blood: How Racial Statistics Lie.* Minneapolis: University of Minnesota Press.

Zuberi, Tukufu, and Eduardo Bonilla-Silva. 2008. *White Logic, White Methods: Racism and Methodology.* Lanham: Rowman & Littlefield.

Index

narratives, harmful, 227*n*21, 227*n*22, 257*n*23, 258*n*26, 262*n*22, 262*n*23, 262*n*24. *See also* low expectations, harm of
Natasha, 58–59
nationality, 12–14
Natty, 122, 125, 129, 156–57
needs: basic, 14–15, 24–25; changing, 216–17; emotional, 79, 80, 104, 184–85. *See also* care; friendships; money
"neighborhood disadvantage," 64
"neighborhood effects," 190–91, 226*n*3
nighttime, 112
noise, 46
nonreciprocity, 75–76
nonrecognition, 75, 77
North Cambridge, MA, 1, 9, 192–93, 262*n*22
nostalgia, 203, 220

objectivity, 12, 230*n*49
obstacles, structural, 187–88, 192, 228*n*22, 240*n*41. *See also* racism
Officer Jacks, 62, 237*n*1
online data, 198–99
"oppositional culture," 240*n*37, 251*n*3
oppression, 188, 258*n*26

pain, sharing, 208–9
Pandora, 115
parenting, 64, 65–66, 215, 237*n*7, 238*n*9, 259*n*43
parties, 53–54, 132–33, 167
patriarchy, 242*n*15
Pattillo-McCoy, Mary, 48
peer effects, 3–5, 134–35, 146, 186, 226*n*6, 227*n*7, 248*n*5
peer support: academic achievement and, 252*n*6; for boys, 191; in

different socioeconomic contexts, 192; economic connectedness and, 255*n*1; institutional support and, 186–87; research findings on, 227*n*10, 260*n*47; on social media, 230*n*41, 246*n*28
persistence, 180
personal qualities vs structural inequities, 188–89
Phelan, Jo, 249*n*11
photos on social media, 2, 49–50, 53–55, 57, 80–81, 194, 199. *See also* Instagram; social media
Pia, 144–45
pluralism, practicing, 138–42
poetry, 3, 37–38, 77–78, 87, 91–92, 108–9, 182
police interactions, 62, 237*n*1
policy, social, 186
poor neighborhoods: care in, 15, 185; "deviance" in, 5–6, 61; diversity in, 248*n*8; parenting in, 66; peer effects in, 4–5, 257*n*23; safety strategies in, 112–113, 243*n*30; social capital and, 256*n*6; social media in, 190–91; social mobility and, 255*n*1; students from, 251*n*3, 252*n*6; violence and trauma in, 111–12. *See also* poverty
positionality, 199–201
Posse Foundation, 187
post-traumatic stress disorder (PTSD), 111, 123
poverty: boredom and time in, 45–49, 60–61, 234*n*8; care in relationships, 185, 226*n*2; friendship approaches in, 238*n*15; friendships alleviating harm of, 24, 41–42, 187–88, 227*n*10; friendships as a threat in, 4–5; geographic clustering of, 190; harms of, 41, 80, 184–85; impacts on parenting, 64–66; peer support

decisions on, 155–56; self-expression and portrayals on, 135–36, 238*n*13; to stay in touch with friends, 174; teenagers' perspectives on, 188–89, 258*n*28; teenagers using, 6–7; trauma and, 114–16, 245*n*21, 247*n*38. *See also* Instagram; Snapchat; Twitter

social mobility: consumption and, 232*n*7; "economic connectedness" and, 255*n*1; "identity projects" and, 256*n*16; immigrants and, 259*n*45; peer effects and, 252*n*6; poverty and, 188; "risk behavior" framing and, 228*n*22, 257*n*23; social status, 24; social support compared to, 256*n*5

social ownership, 118–20

social work, 210

socioemotional education, 187

sororities, 179

Sparks, 94, 122, 123, 208

specificity, 202

Spina, Stephanie, 187

Stack, Carol, 226*n*2

Stanton-Salazer, Ricardo, 187

Stephanie: in adulthood, 209–10, 216, 217; background of, 34–35; on Bryan's death, 114, 122; college enrollment of, 158; friendship with Florence, 9, 29–30, 90, 139, 159; friendship with Rosie, 123, 124, 127; memories of violence of, 111; mother's schedule, 64; opinion on Junior, 94–95; orienting facts about, 10*t*; reviewing writing about her, 203; subway strategies of, 36–37

stereotypes, 72, 189, 202, 239*n*22, 240*n*36, 243*n*22, 253*n*15

Stevenson, 139–40, 141

stigma, 72, 74, 80, 135, 240*n*38, 243*n*20, 249*n*11

storytelling, 236*n*33

stress, 162, 168, 176–77, 188–89, 219, 243*n*30, 248*n*42, 254*n*22

structural inequalities, 192, 240*n*41, 250*n*22, 255*n*26, 257*n*25

Stuart, Forrest, 198

student debt, 156. *See also* financial aid; money

subliminal messages. *See* "sub" messages

"sub" messages, 85, 242*n*9, 242*n*11

subway, 36, 56, 57, 73–74, 112. *See also* transportation

summertime, 8, 11–12, 26, 44–45, 58

support. *See* care; friendships

surveillance: in poor neighborhoods, 4

teachers, 70–71, 116, 129. *See also* Ms. Flores

teenagers: communication between, 235*n*18; deviance and, 227*n*19; lack of freedom of, 24; mental health of, 258*n*29; perspectives on social media of, 258*n*28; role of friendship in lives of, 3–5; socializing as preparation for adulthood, 237*n*38

Thanksgiving, 88–89

therapy, 72–73, 213

time: boredom and, 45–49, 179, 234*n*2, 234*n*3, 234*n*7; clock time vs social time, 45–46, 234*n*3; management skills, 61; social media and, 50–53; stretching with social media, 55–60; taking photos to pass, 53–55; "time work," 49

tobacco, 144

train noise, 2, 9, 47. *See also* poor neighborhoods; subway

transactional support, 76

transactions on social media, 49

transportation, 36–38, 56, 58–59, 236*n*32

trauma: adults processing, 128–29; coping with through digital rituals, 125–26; coping with through grieving, 123–25; coping with through safety, 120–23; disseminating, 114–16; impact on NC girls of, 16; making sense of, 117–18; moving on from, 126–29; safety strategies to manage, 112–14; of shootings, 111–12, 245*n*11, 245*n*20; technologies of, 130–31; those closest to, 118–20

Truly Disadvantaged, The (Wilson), 190

trust, 68

Tsarnaev, Dzhokhar, 117, 125, 128–29

twatching, 236*n*24

Twitter: Aisha's updates on, 170, 172; Black Twitter, 258*n*33; Brittani's views on, 117; condolences on, 115, 124–25; grieving on, 114–15, 126; hashtags, 49–50; learning to use, 197; performing care on, 74–75, 113; posting about graduation, 152; processing racism on, 73–74; reciprocity on, 51, 75–76; social norms for, 235*n*20, 236*n*21, 246*n*25; venting about conflict on, 66–67; Zora's bio on, 135. *See also* social media

Ty, 28–29, 53–54

Uber, 203

Uganda, 1, 9, 39, 67, 205, 214, 215

UMass Amherst, 166, 179

UMass Boston, 159, 209, 210

urban ethnographies, 6

urban marginality, 7, 190

Val, 113, 239*n*18

validation, 79

van der Kolk, Bessel, 120–21, 248*n*42

Vato, 109, 121

Venkatesh, Sudhir, 233*n*21

vigilance, 112–14

Vincent: getting a new girlfriend, 88, 162; Joanne's older brother, 28, 165, 167; in the National Guard, 119; orienting facts about, 9; on racial profiling, 72; relationship with Florence, 87–90, 100–101

Vine, 52, 197. *See also* social media

violence: city-wide impact of, 246*n*27; dislocating, 120–23; impact in poor neighborhoods, 109–12, 245*n*11; impact on girls of, 6, 16, 208; in Jefferson Park neighborhood, 11; repeated, 126–27. *See also* safety strategies; trauma

visibility, 199

walking, 36–38. *See also* transportation

weed, 132, 136, 138–39, 141–44, 160, 175–76

welfare reform act, 64, 65, 237*n*7

white supremacy, 79

Wi-Fi, 6–7

Wiggins, Tanya, 187

Willow Street shooting, 109–11, 116, 121, 246*n*23

Wilson, William Julius, 190

winter, 12

wisdom, 216

witnessing life, 206

Worcester State University, 209

Workforce program, 48, 156, 186

writing, of book, 3, 202–3, 220

Yosso, Tara, 185

Young, Alford, 240*n*41

Founded in 1893,
UNIVERSITY OF CALIFORNIA PRESS
publishes bold, progressive books and journals
on topics in the arts, humanities, social sciences,
and natural sciences—with a focus on social
justice issues—that inspire thought and action
among readers worldwide.

The UC PRESS FOUNDATION
raises funds to uphold the press's vital role
as an independent, nonprofit publisher, and
receives philanthropic support from a wide
range of individuals and institutions—and from
committed readers like you. To learn more, visit
ucpress.edu/supportus.